Shamanism is a complex and confusing subject. There are many different ideas about what shamanism is, who is a shaman, and what a shaman does. *Explore Shamanism* provides a much-needed up-to-date guide to the study of shamanism.

Focusing mainly on the shamans of Siberia and Central Asia, *Explore Shamanism* includes a historical survey of academic approaches to shamanism, an overview of the various theories about shamanism, and a discussion of the origins of shamanism based on the latest ideas. There are also more detailed explorations of the initiation of shamans; the costumes, drums and other tools of the shaman's trade; journeys to the spirit world; and the place of trance, spirit possession and ecstasy in shamanic performance.

Explore Shamanism also surveys revived and reconstructed shamanisms in the world today.

Alby Stone has been studying and writing about shamanism for twenty years. This is his sixth work published by Heart of Albion Press.

The aim of the Explore Books series is to provide accessible introductions to folklore and mythology. Some books will provide overviews of quite broad topics, drawing together current academic research with popular beliefs. Other books in the series will deal with more specific topics, but still with the aim of providing a wide-ranging introduction to the topic.

Series editor: Bob Trubshaw

Other titles in the 'Explore' series include:

Explore Folklore Bob Trubshaw

Explore Mythology Bob Trubshaw

Explore Green Men Mercia MacDermott

Forthcoming titles include:

Explore Fairy Traditions Jeremy Harte

Explore Phantom Black Dogs edited by Bob Trubshaw

EXPLORE SHAMANISM

Alby Stone

Also by Alby Stone and published by Heart of Albion Press

Ymir's Flesh: North European creation mythologies

Straight Track, Crooked Road: Leys, spirit paths and shamanism

The Questing Beast and Other Cosmic Dismemberments

The Bleeding Lance: Myth, ritual and the Grail legend

The Splendid Pillar: Images of the axis mundi in the Grail Romances

EXPLORE SHAMANISM

Alby Stone

Heart of Albion Press

EXPLORE SHAMANISM

Alby Stone

Cover illustration by Bob Trubshaw

ISBN 1 872883 68 0

© Copyright Alby Stone 2003

The moral rights of the author have been asserted.
All rights reserved. No part of this book may be reproduced in any form or by any means without prior written permission from Heart of Albion Press, except for brief passages quoted in reviews.

Explore Books
An imprint of Heart of Albion Press
2 Cross Hill Close, Wymeswold
Loughborough, LE12 6UJ

albion@indigogroup.co.uk

Visit our Web site: www.hoap.co.uk

Printed in the UK by Booksprint

CONTENTS

List of illustrations	viii
Preface	ix
1: Introduction: What is shamanism?	1
2: Shamanism in literature and theory	18
3: Being a shaman	46
4: The shaman's costume and other tools of the shaman's trade	66
5: Journeying to other worlds	89
6: The prehistory of shamanism	124
7: A new age of shamanism	143
Suggested further reading	159
Bibliography	162
Index	177

LIST OF ILLUSTRATIONS

Lamut shaman, 1922.	x
Tungus (Evenk) shaman.	21
Saami noaide drumming, and lying supine covered with his drum.	23
A seventeenth century missionary's view of the Saami *noaide* falling into the hands of the Devil.	25
Female shaman of Krasnoyarsk District.	55
Front view of Nganasan shaman's coat donated to ethnographer A.A. Popov in the 1930s.	70
Tungus (Evenk) shaman.	72
Sakha shaman, early twentieth century.	75
Saami shaman drum of c. 1700.	77
Teleut shaman drum now in the Museum of Anthropology and Ethnology, St Petersburg.	79
Khakas shaman drum, nineteenth century.	79
Goldi shaman coat now in the American Museum of Natural History.	85
A seventeenth century depiction of the Saami *noaide* in action.	93
Therianthropic figure, Le Gabillou.	127
Abbé Breul's drawing of the therianthropic figure of Les Trois Frères.	129
Therianthropic figure with bison, Les Trois Frères.	130
'Entranced' human figure with bison and bird, Lascaux.	131
Rain animal with winged or feathered beings. Southern African San rock painting.	133
'Solar headed' petroglyph of second millennium BCE from Tamgaly Valley, Kazakhstan.	141

PREFACE

Shamanism is an incredibly difficult thing to summarise adequately, even when the writer has the luxury of a book-sized stack of blank paper – or the electronic equivalent – to play with. The sheer volume of published material to find, read and digest is daunting enough. Moreover, within the span of a century the scope of the subject has shifted from examination of a specific relatively localised ritual activity to a consideration of diverse spiritual and neurological processes on a global scale and throughout human history. That means there are many different places where ideas and information may be found.

The remit of the present book is to 'explore' shamanism. It is written as part of a series designed to both introduce a subject and provide signposts for its further study. As a consequence I feel that I have an obligation to point out potential pitfalls not only in the wider context of studying shamanism but also within the text of this book.

To begin with, I should point out that I am neither a practitioner of either shamanism or neo-shamanism, nor am I a field researcher. For some people that admission would be enough immediately to disqualify me from having anything of value to say about shamanism. Some anthropologists look askance at 'armchair scholars' and some practitioners are suspicious of outsiders. However, we are dealing with a field of human knowledge and experience, not some private territory to be defended. You don't need to be a field anthropologist to read and understand what a field anthropologist has written, nor do you need to be a shaman to be able to make some sort of sense of what shamanism is about. What you do need is background information, a sense of context and an idea of where to look to find out what you don't know. That is what I have tried to provide here.

Secondly, I should make it clear that this book does not address every single aspect of shamanism or all issues relating to it. Space has been a primary consideration and although I have tried to discuss all the major issues, especially the more contentious issues, there are inevitably some that a reader might find interesting but which I have either omitted or only mentioned in passing. The bibliography and my suggestions for further reading include material that ought to fill most of the gaps. I do understand that my focus on shamanism in the northern circumpolar regions might be frustrating for people who want to know more about shamanism elsewhere in the world, but I believe to be good reasons for narrowing the scope as I have done. Those reasons are given in chapter 1.

I think it would probably be helpful to say something about the terminology used here. I use the word 'shamanology' to signify the whole range of studies of shamanism, which otherwise generally occurs within several distinct but overlapping dsiciplines: ethnology, anthropology, archaeology, folklore, the history of religion, comparative religion, neuroscience, psychology, and so on. The terms 'shamanic' and 'shamanistic' are often used interchangeably, but here I will use 'shamanic' where something is integral to the shaman or shamanism but 'shamanistic' in contexts which refer to the general beliefs or culture of peoples among whom shamanism is practised. Similarly, 'shamanhood' and 'shamanship' are words that mean subtly different things – in general the former signifies the state of being a shaman while the latter refers more of what a shaman does.

As far as possible all quotations from other authors are given with spelling and punctuation unchanged. Where I have omitted parts of a text (for reasons of clarity, length or relevance) this is clearly shown by three dots followed by a space. Authors' names can be tricky when rendering them into Roman characters from Cyrillic and other scripts. Here for reference purposes I have given such names as they are in the sources rather than attempt to standardise them. Where such a source is discussed in the text I have chosen one form of the name and tried to stick to it. This may cause some slight confusion but it is simpler in the long run. Some accents and unusual characters have been rationalised due to typographical constraints.

Although writing is generally a solitary business, no book is written in complete isolation. I would therefore like to thank Helen Ward and Bob Trubshaw for their excellent production work on this book. Bob is also due some thanks, as is Jim Kimmis, for reading various parts of this book in draft and making useful criticisms and encouraging noises at times when I really needed to hear them. More thanks to Jim for many inspiring conversations that over a period of years have helped me formulate my thinking on various aspects of shamanism. And more thanks to Bob for giving me some useful ideas about neo-shamanism and related matters. Thanks too to Del, for vital assistance in guiding me through the dangerous and spooky world of MS-DOS to rescue a near-final draft from electronic oblivion – in the spirit of the enterprise, a true act of technological shamanism!

Translation of the extract from *Historia Norwegiae* in chapter 2 is by myself.

Lamut shaman, 1922. Ethnographical Museum of Sweden.

1: INTRODUCTION

WHAT IS SHAMANISM?

Shaman at work
Shamanism has come a long way since it first came to the attention of Europeans and became a focus of study for Western anthropologists. The first reports of shamanism in Siberia, and similar practices in the Americas, characterised shamans as devil-worshippers and idolaters. Later, shamans were thought to be mentally ill, elevated to a special status by superstitious fear. Some witnesses have opined that shamans are charlatans and rogues who pretend to supernatural power for their own advantage. Shamanism has been considered a survival of the earliest religious ritual techniques. Some authorities consider shamanism to be nothing more than performance. Others believe it to be a genuine method of making contact with spirits and other worlds.

Anyone who knows anything about shamanism will have some idea of what a shaman is and does. Their picture of a shaman at work will probably be something like this:

> *It is dark. The shaman is dressed in a coat embroidered with magical symbols or adorned with prophylactic trinkets, or is perhaps wearing animal skins, and a mask or head-dress with a fringe, horns or feathers. His eyes are wild, seeing nothing in this world but intent upon some other reality. Chanting and beating rhythmically upon a large decorated drum, the shaman dances frenziedly around a blazing fire as clients and others look on. Eventually, the shaman collapses exhausted and entranced. Before the eyes of the awed onlookers, the ecstatic shaman's spirit leaves his body, transformed perhaps, into the form of an animal, to ascend to the heavens to consult the gods or descend to the underworld in search of lost souls.*

Alternatively, the shaman might climb a pole or ladder, or might enter a trance while sitting on a high platform. The performance might take place indoors, or in daylight. The shaman might be a man, or a woman. The shaman might be possessed by spirits, or there might not be any trance or ecstasy at all. They might give a running commentary on their spirit journey as it happens – then again, they might not. The shaman might drum while seated. Perhaps no drum is used in the ceremony. A special costume might be worn, or it might not. Sometimes there might be more than one shaman working at a ritual. Shamans may perform for one of a number of reasons – to retrieve the absent souls of sick members of their community, neutralise spirits that cause disease, intercede with gods and spirits on behalf of their people, or influence spirits that govern the fertility of herds and game animals. Shamans are also known to travel to the spirit worlds to do battle with hostile shamans from rival tribes or clans.

There are many possible permutations. One of the first things to be learned about shamanism is that it comes in a wide range of shapes, sizes and colours.

What's in a name?

> Since the beginning of the century, ethnologists have fallen into the habit if using the terms 'shaman', 'medicine man', 'sorcerer', and 'magician' interchangeably to designate certain individuals possessing magico-religious powers and found in all 'primitive' societies. (Eliade 1964: 3)

If he was still alive today, Mircea Eliade, author of what is one of the best known and most influential books on shamanism, would no doubt be highly tempted to add a few more terms to his list of scholarly synonyms for *shaman*. The title has been bestowed on all kinds of people involved in professions or practices that flourish in those strange regions on the boundaries of ordinariness. Since Eliade's milestone book, *Shamanism: Archaic Techniques of Ecstasy*, was published (the French edition first appeared in 1951, the English translation in 1964) the terminology of shamanism has become ever more loosely used. All manner of magicians, seers, witches, fortune-tellers, priests or healers from all cultures, tribes and times are graced with the title 'shaman'; and just about everything they do, along with their attendant beliefs, myths, rituals and folklore, is called 'shamanism'. Claude Lèvi-Strauss writes of the 'modern version of shamanistic technique called psychoanalysis' (Lèvi-Strauss 1963: 204). I.M. Lewis notes that the word *shaman* 'is widely employed by American anthropologists, but rarely by their British colleagues, to denote a variety of social roles, the lowest common denominator of which is that of inspired priest' (Lewis 1971: 49).

Things have changed quite a bit in the thirty years or so that have passed since Lewis first made that assessment, even though it has been retained in two further editions of his *Ecstatic Religion* (in 1989 and 2002). British anthropologists in general now appear quite happy to follow the lead of their American colleagues. Piers Vitebsky writes that 'shamanic motifs, themes and characters appear throughout human history, religion and psychology' (Vitebsky 2001: 6). Graham Harvey, discussing the wide currency of the word *shaman* today, writes that it

> ... is now used to refer to communal leaders and religious practitioners who might otherwise be called by very different, more local names... At the same time, some words that *might* otherwise be translated as shaman are instead rendered as 'witch doctors', 'medicine men', 'magicians', 'conjurors' or even 'jugglers'... shaman also refers to practitioners within various therapeutic, spiritual and cultural movements in 'the West'. (Harvey 2003: 1)

Originally the word *shaman* denoted a person with a particular magico-religious and social function among the Evenk people of Siberia – formerly known as the Tungus – from whom anthropologists adopted the word. Over time, the word was applied to similar individuals among neighbouring peoples, tribal groups who were either linguistically related to the Evenk, or whose culture was very similar. *Shamanism* signified the activities of the shaman: ritual, performance and social function. But even before the First World War the terminology of shamanism had begun to be used as a multipurpose item in the lexical toolkit of Western anthropology. The words *shaman* and *shamanism* had become attached to peoples in Central Asia and Siberia who did not know them, and to their counterparts in North America. As time went by they were also applied to people and practices further afield that often bore only the faintest resemblance to the originals. This was especially true of American scholars but it was also the case in Europe. In her detailed 1914 study of Siberian ethnography Marie Antoinette Czaplicka summarised the views prevalent in her own day, beginning with what she clearly perceived to be the predominant one, held by a number of prominent Russian ethnologists:

> Shamanism is understood by some people to be a primitive form of religion or religio-magic practised by the aborigines of northern Asia as well as by all other aborigines in other parts of the world. (Czaplicka 1914: 166)

Nowadays the word *shamanism* is loosely employed to describe a broad spectrum of magical activities, and its original sense has been dissipated. This is as true of specialists as it is for popular writers and 'New Age' theoreticians. For instance, in their introduction to a collection of essays on shamanism anthropologists Nicholas Thomas and Caroline Humphrey criticise Mircea Eliade for divorcing shamanism from its political and social context and for using rigorous definition to produce a generalised shamanism. For them, Eliade's idea of the shaman is a romantic figure, who in reality 'has long floated free from the central Asian societies in which it was originally documented'. They 'find it more challenging now to loosen the classificatory paradigms that have slumbered through the decades since the publication of Eliade's book' (Thomas and Humphrey 1994: 2, 11).

Interestingly, Thomas and Humphrey do not give any restrictive definition of shamanism. Anthropologists nowadays tend to play fast and loose with the word. In fact this kind of usage was driven by American artists and French intellectuals from the 1960s onward, and given particular impetus by the likes of Roland Barthes, Jacques Derrida and Lévi-Strauss. Structuralist interpretation allowed almost any kind of inspirational, ritual or healing activity to be labelled shamanism. As Gloria Flaherty (1992: 6) remarks, 'the word "shaman" has come to mean many things to many people' – a phrase that puts the present status of the term into a nutshell. Ronald Hutton concurs that 'there is now absolutely no agreed definition of what the... term actually means' (Hutton 1993: 14–15).

One reason for the cavalier use of the word *shaman* is the fact that no genuinely satisfactory definition of shamanism has ever been made. Eliade's forceful work on the subject attempts to do so, but its value is dissipated by the author's extensive forays into cultures whose magical techniques bear only the vaguest resemblance to the 'classical' Siberian shamanism that Eliade used as his focal model. However, in this Eliade was really only following a trail blazed by earlier scholars. Willard Z. Park, for instance, writes:

... the shaman is one who acquires supernatural power through direct personal experience. This power is generally manipulated in such a way as to be a matter of concern to others in the society. Accordingly, the practice of witchcraft may be as important a part of shamanism as the curing of disease or the charming of game in a communal hunt. We will designate by the term shamanism, then, all the practices by which supernatural power may be acquired, by mortals, the exercise of that power either for good or evil, and all the concepts and beliefs associated with those practices. (Park 1938: 10)

Park is concerned with defining shamanism as it occurs in a particular context, among the indigenous tribes of Western North America, so his definition is really a statement of what he includes as elements of shamanism in that context. Even so, the parameters he allows shamanism are so wide that he effectively deters us from nailing it down.

Arguably, we might just as well use a word that has already been invested with meaning in a plurality of contexts. The words *wizard* and *wizardry*, for example, which have been extended from the specifically magical to denote thrilling or inspirational prowess in many fields, including science, art and sport, could be as easily and meaningfully employed as *shaman* and *shamanism* are in so many contexts. The reason that has not happened is a matter of semantics and context. Wizardry carries with it etymological connotations of learning and wisdom, whereas shamanism has a more exotic ring to it and has associations of mantic frenzy and primitive physicality. One is part of the European intellectual tradition, the other belongs to the illiterate, the instinctual. In other words, it is a thinly disguised case of the civilised *versus* the primitive. Unsurprisingly, the latter has greater appeal for those who see modern Western values as a barrier to their artistic and spiritual goals, or who are looking for a convenient catch-all term for those things that contrast so greatly with the civilised spirituality. (The rise of 'shamanism' as a favoured mode of modern spirituality has similar roots. Urban culture is rejected in favour of the idea of the wilderness, modernity in favour of archaism, and industrialisation in favour of ecological harmony.) Other potentially useful terms, such as 'medicine man', 'sorcerer' and 'witch' are seen as pejorative but also come with cultural baggage that renders them largely useless as overarching anthropological terms.

Just as specialists have an increasingly lax definition of shamanism, so do lay writers. There is a particular tendency for non-anthropologists to associate shamanism with a particular brand of creativity. For instance, *The Shamanism of Intent*, a multi-media exhibition at Uppingham in Rutland in 1991, explicitly accorded shamanic status to participants including contemporary artists Gavin Jones, Steve Dilworth and Laurence Bicknell, and writers Iain Sinclair, Brian Catling and Peter Riley. Some participants did refer to shamanic themes, notably Tom Lowenstein, whose contribution was based on aspects of Inuit tradition. But for all their 'sickness-vocation' and 'strange, otherworldy, out-of-it' behaviour – as Sinclair (1991) puts it – the participants were artists, not shamans. The surrealists Leonora Carrington and Max Ernst made explicit references to shamanism in their work, even depicting each other as cloaked shamans (Choucha 1991: 119). But they were painters, writers and sculptors rather than healers, soothsayers and sorcerers. They did not do the things shamans do. Similarly, a feature on musician and poet Patti Smith by journalist Sean O'Hagan perpetuates the pairing of shamanism with instinctual, creative improvisation:

> It strikes me, while watching her perform, that Patti Smith is perhaps the last of a lineage that stretches back beyond Jimi Hendrix and Jim Morrison to the likes of Antonin Artaud and Charles Baudelaire – the artist-performer as both shaman and catalyst, someone whose whole *raison d'être* is to evoke and invoke the transformative power of the Word. (O'Hagan 2003)

Evidently the writer is not familiar with the lyrics of too many shamans' songs, which tend to be simple, formulaic and repetitive ditties aimed at controlling spirits or keeping the audience informed of progress, rather than inspired, improvised flights of fancy designed to liberate the mind.

Ironically, the shaman-artist of today is not an exclusively modern phenomenon. Gloria Flaherty has shown how the romantic image of the shaman has had a profound influence on the arts and philosophy since the eighteenth century, when the phenomenon of Siberian shamanism was brought to the West's attention, mainly by German and Russian ethnographers. Indeed, the mantle of shamanism was shared out in much the same way as it is now, among magicians, artists, musicians, and so on. The trend continues to this day. Flaherty notes that Barthes, Derrida and other French intellectuals of the late twentieth century regularly refer to the shaman as an embodiment of intellectual freedom – but never define what a shaman is or does. Their shaman is nothing but a vague metaphor (Flaherty 1992: 6).

The Golden Ages of shamanism?

As a critique of contemporary Western intellectualism, the shaman of Barthes and Derrida is part of a long literary tradition, a close relative of Rousseau's 'noble savage' and a descendant of the virtuous barbarians Julius Caesar contrasted with the supposedly soft, decadent Romans of his own day. The same notion lies at the heart of Eliade's work. Alice Beck Kehoe observes that he 'perpetuates the classical myth that out beyond civilization roam noble savages preserving a primordial religion more pure and true than any in the West' (Kehoe 2000: 2). This attitude is implicit in many anthropological studies of shamanism. It is made explicit in the DIY shamanism manuals of New Age self-improvement gurus. Michael Harner writes of shamanism as a 'remarkable body of ancient techniques' and a 'great mental and emotional adventure', and of the shaman's 'heroic journey and efforts' and 'self-sacrifice' (Harner 1990: xvii).

The message is that we have strayed a long way from our natural spirituality and are seriously out of balance – but there is always a way back. For instance, Harner offers a course of exercises through which a person can attain a 'Shamanic State of Consciousness' and 'experience of shamanic power' (Harner 1990: xviii–xix). Terence McKenna, an advocate of psychoactive drugs and an inspiration for many neo-shamans, argues for a return to a formerly widespread 'direct experience of the mind behind nature' that has been suppressed by European (and particularly Christian) culture:

> An interrupted psychophysical symbiosis between ourselves
> and the visionary plants is the unrecognised cause of the
> alienation of modernity and the cultural mind-set of planetary
> civilization. (McKenna1992: 245)

McKenna's argument is based on the idea that the evolution of human consciousness and the development of culture were partly stimulated by the ingestion of psychoactive plants. His 'archaic revival' harks back to a golden age of human creativity in harmony with nature. It is essentially the same state that the shaman attains – an entranced awareness of the natural world and of dimensions that lie beyond it. It is a return to conditions that existed *in illo tempore*, to use one of Eliade's favourite terms: 'in those days'. This is the Dreamtime of Aboriginal Australians, the 'once upon a time' of fairy tales – an indefinable moment, some time before living memory, before the mythical and the mundane went their separate ways. In this worldview the shaman represents a spiritual condition that is antithetical to the modern world in more than one way. It exists outside civilisation. Where civilisation exists now, shamanism existed long ago. Shamanism simultaneously offers a religious alternative in the present and a spiritual outlet in nostalgia.

If McKenna and Eliade are alike in characterising shamanism and shamanic states of consciousness as 'archaic', they are really only falling into the pattern of thought about shamanism that has been prevalent for most of the nineteenth and twentieth centuries and which looks set to continue well into the twenty-first. It has long been supposed that shamanism was the earliest form of human spirituality. The therianthropic (combining human and animal features) figures of south-western European Palaeolithic cave paintings from have been interpreted as shamans since the mid-1900s, and at present there is a burgeoning belief that shamanism was the crucial factor in the form and function of prehistoric rock art. Significantly, current rock art research stresses the relationship of rock art imagery to cognitive changes observed in subjects who have taken psychoactive drugs or used other methods to alter consciousness (for instance, Clottes and Lewis-Williams 1998; Lewis-Williams 2002; Pearson 2002). In other words, shamanism is the oldest form of magical or religious practise in the world, its components are hard-wired into the human brain, and it has survived more or less unchanged in its essentials since the Upper Palaeolithic, about 50-60,000 years ago. According to this belief, the simple societies and nomadic lifestyles of Altaic and Uralic tribal groups allowed their religious and cultic institutions to remain relatively pure for fifty millennia or more. The argument extends to cover Native Americans and Australians, Africans and other indigenous peoples.

Allied to this is an increasing identification of shamanism in historical sources throughout the ancient world, particularly in Europe and the Middle East. For instance, as long ago as 1911 J.A. MacCulloch compared aspects of Celtic myth and religion with themes from Native American shamanism (MacCulloch 1911), while Anne Ross sees the druids as more or less the same as Eurasian shamans (Ross 1992: 80). Dag Strömbäck identifies an influence from Saami or Finnish shamanism in the magical technique *seiðr* mentioned in medieval Norse texts (Strömbäck 1935), an idea reiterated a number of times, recently by Thomas A. DuBois (1999). Elements of shamanism have been discerned in Old English poetry (Isaacs 1975; Glosecki 1989). E.R. Dodds has argued that shamanism was a significant factor in the development of ancient Greek thought (Dodds 1951). János Makkay argues that shamanism is evident in the Sumerian *Epic of Gilgamesh* (Makkay 1999). Shamanism has even been identified in the Old Testament (Kapelrud 1967). These are just a few examples.

These claims extend the reach of shamanism from remote prehistory into the historical roots of Western civilisation. The persistence well into the modern era of isolated practices sometimes perceived as relics or survivals of shamanism – such as witchcraft, tales of werewolves or the *benandanti* of northern Italy (Ginzburg 1990) – strengthens the idea of continuity while at the same time sharpening the sense of 'otherness'. Recent shamanism is 'uncivilised', distant from the urban, apart from the modern, the spiritual expression of 'primitive' lifestyles and economies. For Europeans, it is a phenomenon that begins where civilisation ends – the wilderness of northern Scandinavia and Siberia, and sub-Saharan Africa. For Americans, it begins where European colonialism ends – the remnant Native Americans. Within the geographical boundaries of the West its end began with the triumph of Christianity, and was completed by the Age of Reason.

It is no wonder that in recent years shamanism has become a potent expression of spirituality in the West. It offers a spiritual dimension to ecologically driven politics, McKenna's 'direct experience of the mind behind nature'. It offers a personal experience of divinity that the Christian churches cannot provide – interestingly, the rise of neo-shamanism parallels that of 'charismatic' Christianity, to which it bears some resemblance. Shamanism legitimises the use of drugs as facilitators of spirit journey, or a means of making contact with spirits or gods. Importantly, it is also seen as a way of getting in touch with deep cultural roots and returning to the earth-centred religion of our ancestors. These are core motivations for the growing number of people practising reconstructed forms of *seiðr* (Blain 2002), 'Celtic' shamanism, and so on (Wallis 2003). Clearly, neo-shamanism is not just a symptom of disaffection, a rejection of modern Western beliefs and values by an alienated group who do not feel represented in mainstream political or religious discourse. It is equally an embracing of something seen as older, more traditional, better suited to the practitioners' culture, more in tune with 'alternative' politics and values and, significantly, more natural.

Shamans and neo-shamans

There is no consensus among neo-shamans as to what shamanism actually is. Jenny Blain's study of *seiðr* among contemporary practitioners makes it clear that there are many current practices that bear the name. These range from gentle meditative states that would not be out of place in an ashram, to full-on frenzied shamanising that would meet with the approval of any Siberian shaman (Blain 2002). Much the same is true of so-called Celtic shamanism. And both Celtic shamanism and *seiðr* might incorporate elements of Amerindian or Siberian shamanism. Michael J. Harner's 'Core Shamanism', popular in the USA, has been stripped down to the bare essentials – the trance and imagery associated with shamanic spirit travel (Harner 1990). This inevitably leads us to ask how authentically shamanistic some neo-shamanisms actually are. Discussing the question of authenticity in neo-shamanism, Robert J. Wallis suggests that

> ... the term 'shaman' can arguably be seen as self-defining: essentially, people calling themselves shamans *are* shamans since the term is invented and means different things to different people. (Wallis 2003: 30)

Wallis qualifies this by making a distinction between neo-shamans who are 'neo-colonialist' (those who take other cultures' shamanisms as their own) and those who are not. He observes that most neo-shamans are not 'the *same* as shamans', although the distinction might not always be useful – as, for instance, in the growing revival of indigenous shamanism in urban areas of South America and the former Soviet Union.

> Critics of neo-Shamanisms tend to fall into a methodological trap of comparing neo-Shamanisms with indigenous shamanisms, when… the plurality of both, and their engagements, indicate that they may or may not be commensurable. (Wallis 2003: 31)

In other words, a form of neo-shamanism should not be compared for authenticity with a form of indigenous shamanism except where for specific purposes it is allowable to do so. This is because each category encompasses different varieties that may be so different from one another that they should not even be internally compared. Furthermore, an example of neo-shamanism that is deliberately modelled to resemble an indigenous one is neo-colonialist and therefore not really shamanism at all.

Evidently the decision to classify someone as an authentic neo-shaman is therefore partly ideological rather than wholly empirical, and partly subjective, driven by the beliefs of the person doing the classification. Wallis' suggestions raise further questions. If for typological and political reasons the two cannot realistically be compared, why should we accept any form of neo-shamanism as shamanism in any sense of the word? And if the diversity of even indigenous shamanism is such that it makes comparison so difficult, then surely we are talking about not one thing but a multiplicity? In which case, why exclude any form of neo-shamanism? And why use one term to describe them all? Wallis acknowledges that the variety of neo-shamanisms makes it impossible to study them as a single entity – their diversity 'resists such a metanarrative' (Wallis 2003: 32). Yet by considering neo-shamanism and indigenous shamanism side by side he is implicitly allowing an equivalent metanarrative for the latter. Wallis goes on to suggest that neo-shamanism 'becomes valid when countless people practise the techniques and get results' (Wallis 2003: 31). Putting to one side the notion of 'results' – which would require a discussion of whether acceptance of the validity of a spiritual system is necessary for its study – this seems to me little more than a judgement of worth based on the quantity of believers or practitioners.

I should make it clear that I am not deliberately singling out Robert Wallis for special attention here. It just so happens that, as I write, his book *Shamans/Neo-Shamans* (from which I quote above) is the most recently published work to discuss this issue in depth and is more or less 'cutting-edge' stuff that reveals a lot about the growth and present state of neo-shamanism. However, while I acknowledge that Wallis is not making hard and fast rules on the authentication of shamanism, his thoughtful discussion of authenticity does not clarify the issue. Instead it highlights two crucial facts. Firstly, that there are now so many magico-religious techniques labelled shamanism that any attempt to include them all in a discussion of what shamanism 'is' (in any thematic context) becomes so generalised and confused that it ultimately tells us precious little about the phenomenon or its practitioners. Secondly, that the classification of a practice as shamanism is often wholly arbitrary.

That which is not
Contemporary use and misuse of the terminology of shamanism is not the only problem. It has become clear with the passage of time

that some older definitions of shamanism are either too narrow or too generalised for comfort. In the case of Eliade, a too-tight focus on ecstasy and trance has resulted, paradoxically, in a generalised image of the shaman that lacks depth and fails to adequately accommodate divergent behaviour or symbolism. Eliade's stringent approach has somewhat perversely led to the exclusion of things that perhaps ought to be allowed as authentically shamanic, and the inclusion of things that are not really shamanic at all.

The muddle continues to this day. It is rare to find a study of shamanism that does not identify as 'shamanic' motifs, cosmology and other themes that are in reality so widespread and occur so often in non-shamanic contexts that they clearly derive from something other than 'shamanic' states of consciousness. A good example of this is Julian Baldick's *Animal and Shaman* (2000) which focuses almost exclusively on the relationship of animals to religion and shamanism in Central Asia (and Siberia), particularly transformation into animals, a theme he sees as central to the 'Inner Eurasian heritage'. However, tales of transformation into animals are found all over the world in areas well beyond the influence of any Central Asian or Siberian belief – in Africa and Australia, for instance. It makes more sense to see such folktale transformations in terms of a common human heritage, one that may have its origins in cognition and the way we think, arising from the 'metaphors we live by' (Lakoff and Johnson 1980; Kehoe 2000: 49–50). The importance of a shaman's transformation into an animal lies not the transformation itself but in why it takes place and what the shaman does when it happens.

Perhaps the most frequently misused idea is that of the 'shamanic cosmos'. Eliade is the main person responsible for promoting this as an aspect of shamanism – it permeates his *Shamanism* and has percolated down to the present day. Briefly, Eurasian shamans imagine the cosmos as being divided into three main parts: sky, earth and underworld. There is often more than one celestial or infernal realm, but the basic tripartition is constant. The shaman, in ecstasy, can ascend to the heavenly worlds or descend to the underworlds. The three basic cosmic segments are connected by the *axis mundi* – a tree, pillar or mountain that stands at the centre of all things. Otherworldly features vary – there may be roads, mountains, rivers or seas to be traversed, for instance – as do the spirits and deities the shaman encounters. Similar patterns are found outside the *milieu* of Eurasian shamanism. For Eliade, this type of cosmic structure is intrinsically shamanic. It derives ultimately from the central shamanic experience, the ecstatic journey to other worlds.

But this is really the everyday cosmological continuum inhabited and experienced by everyone, the shaman included. True, the shaman experiences their supernatural aspects at first hand, but they are the supernatural aspects of a structure everyone recognises, not just the shaman. The mere fact that the layers of both upper and lower worlds vary from one ethnic group to another should be enough to indicate that the so-called shamanic cosmos does not necessarily derive from patterns innate in shamanic ecstasy or trance. Indeed, there is plenty of evidence that the number of heavenly or infernal layers varies because of influence from Buddhism or Islam. (Though of course there are those who would claim a shamanic origin for those cosmologies too.) Yet, thanks largely to Eliade, the idea persists that the cosmos of shamanist peoples is wholly a product of shamanic experience.

Similarly, it is clearly wrong to speak of shamanism as a religion. It is a type of ritual performance that is found in a number of religious contexts – mainly indigenous forms of animism and polytheism but also Buddhism and Islam, Confucianism and Shinto – but it is certainly not a religion in its own right. Åke Hultkrantz agrees that 'the term shamanism ought to be used in a limited sense, denoting those conceptions and rites which focus on the person and performance of the shaman, rather than being extended to mean an entire religious complex (Hultkrantz 1979: 85–86).

Back to the roots

The broad range of practitioners and practices included as shamans and shamanism is a major problem. Where do we start? Who do we include as a shaman? What kind of religious, ritual or psychic activities count as shamanism? What do we omit or set aside as irrelevant or superfluous? Is there any kind of shamanism-shaped template that can be used to tell whether a candidate is an impostor or the real thing?

Eliade gives some useful pointers. A shaman is a psychopomp, one who conducts the spirits of the dead into the next world. Shamans may be distinguished from other magicians by demonstrating 'mastery over fire' and magical flight. Their methods of healing are different from those of medicine men. Most importantly, the shaman's ecstasy is more specialised than those of other religious ecstatics: 'the shaman specializes in a trance during which his soul is believed to leave his body and ascend to the sky or descend to the underworld'. Indeed, Eliade declares baldly that shamanism is 'an archaic technique of ecstasy'. For him, no shamanism is shamanism unless it involves ecstasy, and that ecstasy has to be of a specific kind, one which involves a journey to another world (Eliade 1964: 4–5).

Eliade's treatment of shamanism has been disputed and criticised. There are good reasons for this, as we shall see in the course of this book. But at least Eliade makes some sort of case for shamanism and shamans being different enough from the activities of other priests, magicians and healers to merit a specialised terminology of their own. More recently, Margaret Stutley has identified three factors that are common to all varieties of shamanism. These are belief in a world inhabited by spirits, who can interact with humans; the use of trance to enable a shaman to enter the spirit world; and the shaman's function as a healer or adviser to his community (Stutley 2003: 2).

Critically, Eliade and Stutley both base their criteria mainly upon a consideration of shamanism in Siberia and Central Asia. However, like other students of shamanism they extend the geographical range of shamanism to cover most of the globe. This is the option now preferred by the majority of scholars. For instance, according to Anna-Leena Siikala

> Although in Siberia alone the status of the shamanic institution, its belief systems and ritual paraphernalia have taken a number of very different forms, the basic elements of the shaman's duties are surprisingly consistent around the world. (Siikala 2002: 43)

In one sense Siikala's statement is true. Siberian shamanism does indeed exist in several different forms, and the basic duties of non-Siberians labelled 'shamans' are fairly consistent. But they are rarely found all together at the same time, and often lack the pivotal feature of Siberian shamanism, the ecstatic journey. As a coherent set of ideas, practices and beliefs focused upon a particular type of person, shamanism only occurs among the peoples of Siberia and Central Asia, and members of related ethnic groups in the far north of Europe, Asia and North America.

Other scholars have gone further than Eliade and Stutley in seeing shamanism as a primarily Siberian phenomenon. Hultkrantz has argued that shamanism is strictly specific to one culture, the Evenk, at a particular place and time (Hultkrantz 1973: 25–37). However, his view is by no means fixed. Hultkrantz is flexible enough to permit discussion of shamanism not only in Siberia in

What is Shamanism?

general and among the Native Americans but also elsewhere in the world (for instance, Hultkrantz 1979: 84ff). Ronald Hutton narrows the parameters considerably. Hutton briefly considers the options before deciding on 'the apparent geographical limits of Siberia's style of shamanism by looking only for those features which are characteristic of that style and accorded the priority which they are given in Siberia'. Hutton allows that he is making 'a personal and subjective choice' (Hutton 1993: 15). His position is worth a closer look. He locates shamanism in the circumpolar regions of Eurasia, in Siberia generally, with isolated pockets in Eastern Europe and the north-west of Canada. This is, of course, shamanism in the Siberian mode. Other instances of shamanism that *resemble* that model are rejected on the grounds that there is no evidence to show whether these are survivals from a common heritage or instances of parallel evolution. Hutton puts his case succinctly:

> If shamanism is defined as what went on in Siberia, the public performance of a recognised tribal expert in a ritual setting, going into trance by frenetic movement and sending forth a spirit-self, then it was practised in relatively few areas of the world... If, on the other hand, shamans are any people who are expert in entering trance and dealing with the spirit world, then the Siberian examples are not typical of the whole but an extreme and unusually elaborate variety of it. (Hutton 1993: 16–17)

The central problem of the study of shamanism has rarely been voiced with such precision and clarity. At the very least, Siberian-style shamanism is a special case. This has been recognised by other scholars. For instance, Czaplicka cites a similar view (Czaplicka 1914: 166). In his article on shamanism for the *Encyclopaedia Britannica* Vilmos Diószegi accepts that shamanistic activity is found to a greater or lesser extent all over the world, but observes that 'there is no single definition of shamanism' that applies to them all. Moreover, he suggests that in northern Asia 'shamanism developed into a more definitely articulated and specialized form than among other peoples' (Diószegi 1974). This is close to what Hutton is saying, but where Diószegi is relatively circumspect Hutton is direct and forceful. The wisdom of Hutton's statement is absurdly simple, but the decision it forces upon the reader is actually rather momentous. It offers a straight choice: on one hand a shamanism that can be whatever anyone wants it to be; on the other hand, a shamanism that is precisely what that word can be expected to signify, nothing more and nothing less.

Putting the shamanism back in Siberia
Far from being precise, as we might expect from technical terms, in both popular and academic usage the words *shaman* and *shamanism* can mean just about anything, depending on who is discussing them and in what context. This chimerical quality makes discussion rather difficult, as it could easily be extended to encompass just about the entire range of myth, religion, magic and traditional cosmology, and still be justified by one or another of the world's anthropologists, past and present. As the present work is supposed to be an exploration of shamanism, this untidy state of affairs poses something of a problem.

The simplest way to work around this difficulty is to focus on something that everyone agrees really is shamanism. No one would argue that the shamanism of Siberia and Central Asia is the real thing. That is where the word *shaman* came from, after all. Far from being an invented technical term as Wallis (2003: 30) asserts, the word shaman – in its Evenk form *šaman* – is a real word that means something very specific to the people from whose language it was taken. Adaptation and subsequent misuse of the word as a technical term by (mainly Western) anthropologists and others should not obscure the reality of its existence in Siberian languages. Cognates associated with shamanism are attested throughout the Tungusic and Mongol languages, as well as in Kirghiz and Uighur, and have been recorded among the Khanty (formerly known as the Ostyak) and Gilyak (Laufer 1917). In other words, variants of *shaman* are spread across a range of related languages spoken by peoples in eastern Siberia who are or have been shamanist. Furthermore, the same vocabulary exists among Turkic-speaking shamanists in Central Asia – and also among the Uralic-speaking Khanty and the Gilyak (whose language does not belong in either of the two main indigenous language families spoken in Siberia), both of whom have borrowed their words for a shaman from Altaic-speakers.

The extent to which the word *šaman* and its cognates is distributed among the Altaic-speaking peoples and some of their neighbours – and we might well include Russian ethnographers in this category – to mean precisely a shaman or some aspect of shamanism should give Western anthropologists pause for thought. It is not simply an invented word, nor is it one that has been borrowed by anthropologists as a technical term from the only tribal group who used it. It is a word that means something specific to quite a large number of relatively diverse people who between them inhabit a significant chunk of Asia. True, those people also use other words to denote shamans and shamanism. And there are wide variations in the style and status of shamanism among Altaic-speaking peoples, and among the Uralic-speakers whom we can legitimately call shamanists. But while these are variations on a theme, similar techniques and practices among other, more distant peoples are not shamanism in the same way as the Siberian ones. They are techniques and motifs which might *resemble* shamanism or particular aspects of it, sometimes pretty closely, but that is all.

Consequently, this present exploration is mainly concerned with shamanism as it is known from the Uralic- and Altaic-speaking peoples who inhabit Central Asia, Siberia and the far north of Europe. To keep things simple I have chosen not to engage in comparison with the shamanisms or pseudo-shamanisms associated with other peoples except for a few instances where a wider range seems appropriate. Even then I have largely confined comparison to other Siberian peoples and the indigenous peoples of North America. The main exceptions are where the major theories of shamanism are summarised, where the nature of trance and ecstasy are discussed, and where the origins and deep history of shamanism are considered. I believe this selectivity is justified by both the problems inherent in the study of the phenomenon and the nature of the theories that have been developed to deal with it. To explore shamanism we need a reliable map of its form, function and peculiar traits. We must identify what shamanism authentically is in the context of its undisputed home range. Discussion of shamanic initiation, costume, performance and function is similarly limited to those peoples that are indubitably shamanist.

2: SHAMANISM IN LITERATURE AND THEORY

Enter the shaman

We now have a situation where just about anything can be shoehorned into the category 'shamanism' and where all manner of priests, prophets, pagans, poets, painters, performance artists, physicians, psychoanalysts and psychotics can find themselves called shamans. And of course they would be able to point to one learned text or another to justify calling themselves shamans if they wished to do so, because in the academic study of healers and magico-religious practitioners in indigenous cultures the situation is much the same. In the previous chapter I have suggested that for all practical purposes the terms 'shaman' and 'shamanism' as they are so often used are so generalised and misapplied that they have become virtually meaningless. To understand how this has come about we must consider the literary history of shamanism and the theories that have developed along with it.

Although some professional anthropologists have grave reservations about 'armchair scholars', the study of shamanism has always been a highly literary enterprise. As in any other discipline anthropological texts, field reports as well as theoretical works, invariably refer to other texts. Each generation refers back in one way or another to those who went before, to support, modify or refute the teachings of the past. And in each generation there is competition and difference of emphasis. The history and development of a discipline is reflected in the literature that has grown up around it. The study of shamanism is no exception. It sheds some interesting light on how and why the treatment of shamanism by anthropologists and others has developed as it has done over the last few hundred years.

The first written accounts by Europeans of Eurasian shamanism appeared around a thousand years ago. Finnish and Saami shamans – characterised as powerful witches, seers and sorcerers – had long been notorious in Northern Europe. They appear fairly frequently as characters in Old Norse literature, in *Vatnsdœla saga* and Snorri Sturluson's *Haralds saga ins Hárfagra*, for instance. In Old Norse texts they are often associated, as teachers or practitioners, with the magical technique known as *seiðr*, a type of magic often identified as a form of shamanism. A detailed, if somewhat embellished, account of a Saami shamanic performance aimed at reviving an apparently dead woman is given in the *Historia Norwegiae*, written in Latin in the late twelfth or early thirteenth century. In its essentials the performance is similar to later accounts of Saami shamans.

> ... a wizard spread a cloth under which he made himself ready for unholy magic incantations and with extended hands lifted up a small vessel like a sieve, covered with images of whales and reindeer with harness, little skis, and even a tiny boat with oars. The devilish spirit would use these to travel over snowy heights, across mountain slopes and through the depths of lakes. After dancing there for a very long time to give his equipment magic power, at last he fell to the ground, black as an Ethiopian and foaming at the mouth like madman...

This particular *noaide* (the Saami word for a shaman) ended badly – hostile spirits ripped his belly open and he died, so another *noaide* was summoned to finish the job.

The author of the *Historia Norwegiae* uses this story as an example of the 'intolerable ungodliness' and 'devilish superstition' of the Saami for the benefit of more God-fearing folk. This must be seen in the context of eleventh- and twelfth-century Scandinavian law codes prohibiting consultation of 'Finn' seers (DuBois 1999: 129). Saami shamans seem to have been feared and respected in equal measure by ordinary people but the authorities clearly disapproved of them.

Northern Asian shamans made their first appearance in European literature soon after their Finnish and Saami counterparts. Mongol shamans (termed 'magi') are mentioned in the thirteenth-century *Travels* of Marco Polo, and by two of his near contemporaries, the Franciscan missionaries John of Plano Carpini and William of Rubruck. An account of John's mission, which lasted from 1245 to 1247, forms the core of his *History of the Mongols*. John mentions the Mongol deity Itoga, but tells us the god is also called Kam, which just happens to be the same as the Mongol word for a shaman. William of Rubruck, who set out six years after John, has much to say about the Mongol soothsayers who, he tells us, are called *chan*, and that the same title is given to Mongol rulers. While John of Plano Carpini may have mistaken *kam* for the name of Itoga, whose rites the *kam* would have presided over, William has evidently confused the two words *kam* and *khan*.

John and William differ from the author of the *Historia Norwegiae* in that they generally report the customs of their Mongol hosts, including their religion and ritual, in a rather matter-of-fact and non-judgemental way. The rites performed by the *kam* are not dismissed as superstition, nor is the *kam* accused of intercourse with devils. Clearly, John and William were tolerant and broad-minded men for their time and calling. Later Christians in Asia were less charitable.

Devil-worshippers and charlatans
The earliest known first-hand written description of a Siberian shamanic performance was by an Englishman. In 1557 Richard Johnson observed the 'devilish rites' of what was probably a Nenets shaman (Hutton 2001: 30–31). Johnson's text was lifted wholesale by Samuel Purchas, whose popular book *Purchas His Pilgrimage*, in which he set out to prove the intrinsic truth and superiority of Anglican Christianity to other forms of religion, appeared in 1613. However, it was not until late in the seventeenth century that more reports began to reach Europe of a strange type of person to be found deep in the new Russian territories of Northern Asia. In 1672 Avvakum Petrovich, a Russian priest who had been exiled to Siberia eleven years previously, published an account of his exile in the vast wooded lands of Siberia. His autobiography, as one might expect of a Christian priest of that time, portrays shamans as sinister workers of magic and worshippers of devils. Avvakum's tale did not have much of an impact on the world outside Russia. But he was the precursor of a small army of travellers, missionaries and exiles who brought tales of shamans and their rites from the far reaches of Siberia. In 1692 the Dutch traveller Nicolas Witsen (later mayor of Amsterdam) published *Noord en Oost Tartaryen*, an account of his experiences in Russia's Asian territories in which he described the *schaman*, a 'priest of the Devil', and shamanic performances in several Siberian tribes. Soon after Witsen another traveller, Everard Ysbrant Ides mentioned the *schaman* in *Drejaarige Reize naar China* (Amsterdam 1698), an account of Ides' journey to China with a Russian diplomatic mission in 1692–95. Witsen's book was printed in such a small edition that it was about as effective as Avvakum's in drawing European attention to the Siberian shaman; and Ides' book was no more galvanising. But these books were known and read in their day and were important

Tungus (Evenk) shaman.
From Nicolas Witsen, Noord en Oost Tartaryen *(1692)*

precursors to an explosion of travellers' descriptions of Eurasian peoples and their customs in the eighteenth century.

During the eighteenth century travellers and missionaries published more accounts of Siberian shamanism. Johann Georg Gmelin, a German scientist whose *Reise durch Siberien von dem Jahr 1733 bis 1743* was published in four volumes between 1751 and 1752, betrays an intense dislike of shamans. Like Gmelin, the Russian botanist Stepan Petrovish Krasheninnikov (whose account of his travels in Kamchatka, *Opisaniye Zyemli Kamchatki*, was published in 1755 and translated into German and English in the

1760s) thought shamans were frauds and charlatans. 1763 saw the appearance of *Travels from St Petersburg in Russia, to Diverse Parts of Asia* by the Scottish surgeon John Bell, which was possibly the earliest work in English to use the word 'shaman'. Bell, however, also thought shamans to be frauds, a 'parcel of jugglers'. Similar conclusions were reached by Daniel Gottlieb Messerschmidt, a German doctor who travelled in Siberia in the 1720s and whose voluminous records were made available to other scholars at the Royal Academy of Sciences in Berlin, though not published until the 1960s as *Forschungsreise durch Sibirien, 1720–1721*. These unsympathetic views were taken up by Dennis Diderot, whose *Encyclopédie* of 1765 included an unflattering entry for 'shaman'. The sentiment was echoed in 1776 by Petrus Simon Pallas (*Reise durch verschiedene Provinzen des russischen Reiches*, St Petersburg) and in 1790 by Mathieu de Lesseps (*Journal historique du voyage de M. de Lesseps, Consul de France*, Paris).

Shamanism among the Saami was studied fairly intensively in the sixteenth and seventeenth centuries by Swedish, Danish and Norwegian missionaries with an eye to conversion. Inevitably their view of Saami shamanism tended to be that it was a form of witchcraft, devil worship. But Saami shamans also interested people with more scholarly ambitions. The Swedish chancellor Magnus Gabriel de la Gardie asked his compatriot missionaries to gather information on the Swedish Saami. The results, as Huktkrantz (1992) observes, were of uneven quality and could be little more than exercises in prejudice, but they preserve invaluable information about Saami customs and religion. A year after Avvakum's book appeared Johan Scheffer (also known as Schefferus) described Saami life and customs, including a detailed account of their shamanism, in a book published in Latin as *Lapponia* (1673) and in German as *Lappland* (1675). This was to be the last study of Saami shamanism for two hundred years. And sadly, it was not long before scholarly endeavour lost out to Christian fervour and intolerance.

> At the end of the 17th century, the conversion to Christianity took a more energetic turn. The Lapps were forced to attend church ceremonies and to surrender their drums, which were subsequently burnt. Those of the Lapps who showed resistance, stowed away their drums or made new ones, were sentenced to fines or flogging. In some rare cases... resisting Lapps were sentenced to be burnt at the stake together with their drums, to serve as a warning. (Manker 1996: 13)

Saami noaide *drumming, and lying supine covered with his drum. From Johann Schefferus,* Lapponia *(1673).*

European explorers and missionaries were describing medicine men (and women) of the Americas almost as soon as the continent was discovered. For instance, the Spaniard Gonzalo Fernández de Oviedo published an account of the use of tobacco for communion with 'the Devil' on Hispaniola in his *Historia General y Natural de las Indias* (1535). In 1557 a French priest named André Thévet described 'certain ceremonies and diabolical invocations' he had witnessed in Brazil, in his book *Les Singularités de la France Antarctique*. In the 1630s Paul Le Jeune, another French priest, visited the Montagnais of Labrador, and described their customs and religion in a *Relation of What Occurred in New France in the Year 1635*. Devilish rituals involving tobacco in Guyana were recounted by yet another French priest, Antoine Biet, in *Voyage de la France Equinoxiale en l'Isle de Cayenne* (1664). In 1699 Lionel Wafer, physician and buccaneer, published *A New Voyage and Description of the Isthmus of America*, which described Amerindian 'conjurors' at work.

The accounts of travellers from the sixteenth, seventeenth and early eighteenth centuries fall into two broad but overlapping camps. Shamans are seen as diabolical or as fraudulent, though they might be both at once. Before we start fulminating against the dogmas of a bygone age, it is as well to reflect that, in relative terms, both these views were correct. Since the early Middle Ages Christians of all persuasions have identified the kind of ecstatic activities practised by shamans as either delusions or consorting with devils – with an increasing tendency to the latter interpretation. In Catholic Europe, for instance, the *Canon Episcopi* of around 960 makes it clear that sorcery is inspired by the Devil. But it also asserted that those who claim to undertake nocturnal rides with Diana 'the goddess of the pagans' or undergo transformations into animals are simply deceived by the devil into thinking they have done so. By the fifteenth century theologians and Church intellectuals believed that these and other things actually happened (Russell 1972). From then to late in the seventeenth century the witch-crazes were in full swing, among Protestants as well as Catholics, and the Eastern Orthodox churches were also affected.

With the Enlightenment the witch panics died down and a more rationalistic (if still essentially Christian) worldview became prevalent. The Devil and his infernal minions were no longer so prominent in educated minds. We see shamans called 'jugglers' – which in those days generally meant 'conjuror' as much as a performer of tricks – and described as charlatans playing on the superstition of their peoples. Diderot's *Encyclopédie* of 1765 is pretty much representative of this view. The shaman does 'tricks that seem supernatural to an ignorant and superstitious people' (Diderot 1765). The *Encyclopédie* makes a distinction between the Siberian shaman and Amerindian 'jugglers', but they are equally considered frauds. Krasheninnikov described a Kamchatkan shaman pretended to pierce his abdomen with a knife and drink his own blood from the wound. The shaman performed this trick so crudely that the deception was obvious to Krasheninnikov, but it was enough to fool the audience (Krasheninnikov 1972).

In fact, most shamans practise trickery of some kind – sleight of hand, ventriloquism and suchlike – to enhance their performances. Ethnographers have documented many instances of such tricks and there are instances of shamans freely admitting to observers that they are designed to impress and make performance more believable.

The interesting thing about these two views of Siberian shamans is that, in the context of the observers' time and cultural background, they are wholly justified. They lived in an age where diabolical influence was accepted without question as part and parcel of the world in which they lived, where witches and sorcerers were *known* to deal with demons, and where the spirits and deities of non-Christian religions were *known* to be demons. This was as true for intellectuals as it was for rural clerics and the masses. How else would a priest or devout layman explain the shaman except as someone in league with devils? During the next hundred years, the

A seventeenth century missionary's view of the Saami noaide falling into the hands of the Devil.

intellectual climate was changing rapidly: the Devil was less of a factor in the lives of the learned and people who had seen a bit of the world. Where religion was a factor in their reasoning, it was to suppose shamanist peoples were just unenlightened savages who believed in false gods. Their shaman was still a sinister figure, but now one given to manipulating the ignorant and superstitious tribes they served. And the trickery was a fact that fitted the scenario.

Enlightenment
Asian shamanism was certainly known to some Europeans long before Russia came to rule Siberia and parts of Central Asia. Yet the early accounts did not fire the European imagination as the later ones did – the soothsayers and sorcerers of the barbarian peoples of Central Asia were just one more bizarre detail of those strange heathen lands, the idolaters demanded by the early Christian worldview. By the time the Siberian shaman was hoisted onto the world stage the European witch panics were in full swing, with the Enlightenment about to usher in a more sceptical age. This was a time when priests and missionaries might still have considered shamans to be vicars of the Devil, but the secular craving was for the Noble Savage, embodiment of the purest human state. In the eighteenth century intellectuals and sensation-seeking aristocrats ensured that the shaman received a certain amount of attention in

fashionable circles. The news began to spread – hence the entry in Diderot's acclaimed *Encyclopédie*.
Not all descriptions of Eurasian shamans were hostile. The sixteenth and seventeenth century accounts showed European thought at its depressing worst, hidebound first by religious dogmatism then by a perceived cultural superiority. But there were also the first stirrings of a new objectivism, in which things were studied and evaluated rather than judged and condemned. As early as 1730 a Swede named Philipp Johann Tabbert von Strahlenberg, at one time a travelling companion to Messerschmidt, broke the mould with arguably the first true anthropological study of indigenous Siberians. *Der Nordöstliche Theil von Europa und Asien* (translated into English in 1736) included a chapter detailing Siberian religion. Adopting a multidisciplinary approach – including linguistics and archaeology – Strahlenberg wrote only of what he had witnessed and discovered for himself. By present day standards his book is rather patronising, but in the context of its time it represents a major development, a work of objectivity and honest investigation untainted by religious prejudice or the kind of scorn expressed even by supposedly enlightened people such as Diderot. The German doctor Georg Wilhelm Steller, who was in Kamchatka with the explorer Bering in the early eighteenth century, showed a similar degree of respect. Steller's account *(Beschreibung von dem Landes Kamtschatka, dessen Einwohnern, dern Sitten, Nahmen, Lebensart und verschiedenen Gewohnheiten,* 1774) is largely concerned with native sexuality but includes both notes on the local *schamannery* and his own illustrations of fully costumed shamans in action.

In the eighteenth century the missionary view of Devil-worshipping Amerindian savages too began to be superseded by a more rational – if not exactly sympathetic – outlook. Joseph François Lafitau – in those days the Americas seem to have been crawling with French priests – described the ecstasy of Iroquois and Huron 'jugglers' in *Moeurs des Sauvages Amériquaines Comparées aux Moeurs des Premiers Temps* (1724).

Later in the eighteenth century, more academics of Strahlenberg's character – objective and liberal in contemporary terms, but still Eurocentric and paternalistic by modern standards – entered Siberia to study the natives. For instance, Johann Peter Falk's account of his travels in Russian territory during the 1760s combined ethnography with demographics to paint a sad picture of declining belief in shamanism and local heathenism. A major breakthrough came when Johann Gottleib Georgi published several volumes of findings from his fieldwork in Russia. In 1775 the two volumes of his *Bemerkungen einer Reise im Russischen Reiche in Jahr 1772* appeared, followed between 1776 and 1780 by four instalments of *Beschreibung aller Nationen des Russischen Reichs*. In the latter work Georgi included illustrations of shamans from different peoples in full costume. Importantly, Georgi seems to have been the first scholar to suggest that shamanism represented an archaic form of religion, the original source of all other faiths. However, like earlier travellers Georgi thought shamans were fanatical frauds whose activities encouraged the worship of evil. Continued contempt for shamans was not confined to travellers and scientists. Catherine the Great of Russia loathed shamans, which she saw as representing the irrational, Asiatic face of Russia holding back the benefits of Enlightenment Europe. In 1786 she published *Der sibirische Schaman, ein Lustspiegel*, an attack on the European passion for shamans. The eponymous shaman is, of course, a posturing fraud.

Siberia and Central Asia: before, during and after the Iron Curtain
In the nineteenth and early twentieth centuries the Asian shaman was scrutinised still more closely by people who by now thought of themselves as anthropologists, though their methods were much less stringent or intensive than their present day counterparts. A number of landmark ethnographic studies describing shamanism appeared. An important contribution came from Matthias Alexander Castren, who seems to have been the first to argue (in 1853) that shamanism is a ritual technique rather than a religion. S. Shashkov published the first general description of Siberian shamanism in 1864. At around this time it was generally accepted that there was a 'black' shamanism depending on evil spirits and a 'white' form dealing with benevolent ones, though some individual shamans could practise both types.

Later, V.M. Mikhailowski's *Shamanstvo* (Moscow 1892) drew together and summarised earlier Russian ethnographers' writings on shamanism. Other major works included *Yakuty*, an account of the Yakut (now known as the Sakha) by Wenceslas Sieroshevski (1896), *The Chukchee* by Waldemar Bogoras (1904), and Waldemar (or Vladimir) Ilich Jochelson's *The Koryak* (1908) and *The Yakut* (1933). These and other Russian scholars of the time produced the first true ethnographies of Siberian peoples among whom shamanism was practised. The information gathered by these and other pioneer ethnographers formed the basis of Marie Antoinette Czaplicka's *Aboriginal Siberia*, published in 1914, which included the first major survey of Siberian shamanism and religion in English and promoted the idea of shaman as an expression of mental illness. This idea was taken up with enthusiasm by Åke Ohlmarks in a number of studies, including *Studien zum Problem des Schamanismus* (Lund 1939), and was eagerly seized upon by Soviet researchers.

The studies by Bogoras (who was, confusingly, at various times also known as Vladimir Bogoraz and Vladimir Bogoraz-Tan) and Jochelson were based on their field research conducted on the Jesup North Pacific Expedition of 1897–1902. This ethnographic expedition to eastern Siberia was personally financed by – and named after – Morris K. Jesup, director of the American Museum of Natural History, and managed by the famous anthropologist Franz Boas. Bogoras was later instrumental in establishing ethnography as a discipline in Russia and the Soviet Union. After the revolution Jochelson moved to New York where he continued to publish his work on Siberian peoples.

After the Russian revolution of 1917, scholars of the new Soviet Union did little serious work on Siberian shamanism. The atheistic communist regime banned shamanism across the Soviet republics. Shamans were killed or re-educated as good Marxist-Leninists. Under Stalin it became all but impossible for researchers from non-communist countries to gain access to either Siberia or its peoples, especially after the Second World War. Some Soviet anthropologists studied shamanism only to disparage it – many published papers were little more than thinly disguised justification for stamping out a tradition that was regarded as a non-productive, primitive superstition. For instance, from 1936 onward Dimitri Zelenin expounded a typically materialistic explanation of shamanism as a response to disease based on totemism. Gradually, Siberian shamanism – and its close cousins in Soviet Central Asia and parts of communist China – began to die out, and the study of Siberian shamanism began to atrophy. In 1963 Henry N. Michael edited an important collection of essays on shamanism by Soviet anthropologists, including A.F. Anisimov, whose approach was strictly Marxist and similar in tone to that of Zelenin. Michael observes in his preface that most of the fieldwork was done in the 1920s and 1930s, before Soviet policies began to be felt 'to a decisive degree'. Similarly, before the Revolution Sergei M. Shirokogoroff carried out extensive fieldwork among the Tungus and neighbouring peoples, but published work based on his findings while a refugee in China. (Shirokogoroff was the first ethnographer to recognise that the shaman's assistant played a crucial part in shamanic performance, and in that function he participated in many performances. He was also convinced that shamanism originally derived from Buddhist, especially Lamaist, religion.) His major work on shamanism, *Psychomental Complex of the Tungus*, a richly detailed and comprehensive study of Evenk shamanism and belief, was published in 1935, long after his data had been collected. Russian anthropologists were reduced to living in the past.

Meanwhile, the spirit of the old European ethnographers was still very much alive. The Finnish scholar Uno Holmberg (later known as Uno Harva) travelled to Siberia to investigate shamanism. In 1922 he published an important book on shaman costume that remains a classic. In the 1950s the Hungarian scholar Vilmos Dioszégi travelled to Siberia seeking the roots of the pre-Christian beliefs of his native land. The result, a first-person narrative akin to the eighteenth-century ethnographies, was published in 1960 and translated into English in 1968 as *Tracing Shamans in Siberia*. Despite a lack of co-operation on the part of the Soviet authorities, and their refusal to allow him back into Siberia after 1964, Dioszégi continued to study Siberian shamanism and write prolifically on the subject until his death in 1972. Dioszégi is a pivotal figure in the study of shamanism in the latter half of the twentieth century. In addition to his writings, which include the *Encyclopaedia Britannica* entry on shamanism (unchanged since its first publication in 1974) he established the Archive of Siberian Shamanism in the Ethnographic Institute of the Hungarian Academy of Sciences. He was also an inspiration to other anthropologists behind the Iron Curtain. In 1963 he edited a collection of essays on Siberian folklore and shamanism by Soviet and other Eastern European scholars (recently reprinted as Dioszégi and Hoppál, ed. 1996b). Shortly before his death Dioszégi organised contributions to *Shamanism in Siberia*, a collection of papers by scholars from both sides of the Iron Curtain – this was not published until 1978, with Mihály Hoppál sharing the editorial credits.

The publication of *Shamanism in Siberia* led to an apparent thawing of Soviet attitudes to shamanism. From 1980 Soviet anthropologists were increasingly ready to participate in domestic and international debate on shamanism and forms of indigenous religion. But most were careful to stay well within the boundaries of Marxist methodology and to emphasise the appropriate ideological loyalty (for instance, Basilov 1980). Some even called for the destruction of shamanism, in terms reminiscent of the Stalinist era (Mikhailev 1987). This is not to say that such attitudes contradicted the spirit of Dioszégi, who had after all written approvingly of the inevitable disappearance of Siberian shamanism (Dioszégi 1968: 209). Even so, the Soviet climate became gradually more hospitable. In 1990 Marjorie Mandelstam Balzer edited a collection of Soviet scholars' papers on shamanism. As with previous collections of Soviet studies of shamanism, the contents were frankly Marxist-Leninist. A second edition of the book seven years later saw a new title and the omission of some of the more devoutly Marxist-Leninist contributions (Balzer ed. 1997). With the advent of Mikhail Gorbachev and the twin doctrines of *glasnost* and *perestroika* at the end of the 1980s, things really did get better for shamanism and its study in the Soviet Union and its subsequent incarnations.

(On the history of Russian and Soviet action in Siberia and the effects on shamanism and traditional belief, see Glavatskaya 2001, Hutton 2001, Reid 2002).

From Russia with love
As in Siberia, the nineteenth century saw the advent of the anthropologist in the study of Amerindian shamanism and practices that many anthropologists would now call shamanism. Everard F. Im Thurn studied medicine men of the Macusi of British Guiana (*Among the Indians of Guiana*, 1883). Toward the end of the century Franz Boas conducted extensive fieldwork on the Kwakiutl, and visited the Eskimo of Baffin Island. After Boas a growing number of anthropologists formally investigated Amerindian ritual and religion, with an increasing focus on ritual practitioners, with a growing tendency to take the subject further south into central and South America. Consequently, the literature of Amerindian shamanism is vast, a reflection of the greater intellectual and physical freedom of anthropologists in the West and a stark contrast with the privations of Soviet scholars.

By the beginning of the twentieth century the mantle of shamanism had already been thrust upon 'primitive' peoples elsewhere in the world. Anthropologists studying healers, diviners and magicians among peoples in the Americas, Africa, Australia and elsewhere began to use the word 'shaman' as a label for indigenous wonder-workers. Some resembled the Siberian shaman fairly closely – in Lappland and parts of North America, for example. Others resembled them a bit less than that. Some bore only a partial resemblance. But most were nothing like the Siberians whose title they were accorded. As early as 1903 Arnold van Gennep decried the inaccurate use of the word 'shamanism' as a generalised term that suggested a shared form of religion among practitioners of magic and healing in very different cultures. Van Gennep, however, agreed that the shamans of Siberia were more or less the same in form and function as the medicine men, witch doctors and sorcerers of other cultures in Africa, the Americas and Asia (van Gennep 1903).

In 1908 Roland B. Dixon's important paper 'Some aspects of the American shaman' was published in the *Journal of American Folk-Lore*. In this survey of Amerindian ritual practice Dixon roundly equated the North American medicine man with the Siberian shaman, although he noted some important differences, such as the comparative rarity of spirit journeys among the Native Americans. This seems to have been a turning point: after this it became acceptable to use the word *shaman* to describe medicine men and other people imbued with ritual power, and *shamanism* to signify the things they did. Alfred L. Kroeber suggested that the first settlers brought shamanism with them from Siberia across the Bering Strait (Kroeber 1923).

Academic interest in Amerindian shamanism and religious beliefs increased as the first half of the twentieth century wore on. Willard Z. Park's *Shamanism in Western North America* (1938) examined the relationships between the shamanism practised among different West Coast tribes, concluding that relationships did exist between the tribal varieties in shamanism. With shamanism specifically in mind Park cautioned against breaking cultures up into their component elements for separate study without first determining their history. 'Isolating segments of culture as cultural units without this historical knowledge is based on *a priori* ethnological conceptualizing and as such may lead to misleading and indefensible inference of the past' (Park 1938: 158).

Popular interest in Amerindian shamanism was boosted in 1932 when the poet John G. Neihardt published *Black Elk Speaks*. Black Elk, an Oglala Lakota Sioux medicine man who had fought at Wounded Knee and against Custer at the Little Big Horn, was credited as co-author. Black Elk's prayers, prophecies and stories have been hugely influential, but not greatly so in academic circles. Rather, Black Elk's utterances have found a receptive audience among successive generations of young people. Interest surged in the 1960s when hippies and fellow travellers found contemporary resonance in Black Elk's words. More recently Green activists, eco-warriors and anti-capitalist protesters have taken Black Elk to heart.

In the last few decades the torch of Amerindian shamanism has been carried with distinction by Åke Hultkrantz, a Swede well versed in Eurasian shamanism but specialising in Amerindian religion, has explored Native American shamanism in a number of studies. Of particular note here are his books on North American traditions concerning the soul (Hultkrantz 1953), Amerindian analogues to the Orpheus myth (Hultkrantz 1957), overviews of native religion, including shamanism (Hultkrantz 1979) and a study of Amerindian healing traditions (Hultkrantz 1992). Hultkrantz perceived greater differentiation in Amerindian shamanism than in Siberia and proposed three different types of shamanism based on its forms in the Americas: genuine ecstatic shamanism, imitative shamanism and demonstrative shamanism. The first is much like 'classical' Siberian shamanism. Imitative shamanism occurs where the shaman does not undergo a spirit journey but enacts a kind of ritual pantomime of an otherworld journey and soul-retrieval. Demonstrative shamanism is an 'intermediary form' in which 'the shaman proves his success in curing the sick by holding up for all to see the disease object that he has extracted or the soul he has restored' (Hultkrantz 1979: 91).

Weston La Barre, a supporter of the idea that shamanism is the oldest form of religious observance (La Barre 1970, 1972), is another major contributor to the study of Amerindian shamanism. His works on the Ghost Dance, a monumental book inspired by the nineteenth century Amerindian religious movement (La Barre 1970), and the peyote cult (La Barre 1989) are important studies that provide an interesting insight into the social dynamics of Amerindian shamanism and the nature of religion. Also worth noting is John A. Grim's examination of Ojibway ritual in comparison with Siberian shamanism (Grim 1983), though like many other studies it leans heavily on the idea that shamanism is mainly concerned with healing.

If Hultkrantz and La Barre are arguably the most eminent of recent scholars of Amerindian shamanism, then Michael J. Harner is without doubt the most prominent. Harner began his professional life as an anthropologist, earning a doctorate for work among the Shuar tribe (formerly known as the Jívaro) in Ecuador. Through his experiences with the drugs *ayahuasca* and datura in Ecuador, Harner came to believe that shamanic techniques really could open doorways to other realities. In 1973 Harner edited *Hallucinogens and Shamanism*, a collection of keynote texts that focused mainly on South America, including several papers by Harner, among them 'The Sound of Rushing Water' (first published in 1968) describing *ayahuasca* use among the Shuar. He later ran workshops on shamanism in tandem with his academic career, but resigned from the latter to concentrate on promoting his own vision of 'core shamanism', which he claims is shamanism stripped down to its most basic form, free from culturally specific elements. In 1980 Harner published *The Way of the Shaman*, a condensed version of his course on shamanism, a text which has inspired many imitations.

No survey of the literature of Amerindian shamanism would be complete without a mention of Carlos Castaneda. This controversial figure burst onto the scene in 1968 with *The Teachings of Don Juan*, supposedly an account of the author's encounters with a Yaqui shaman in New Mexico, which became an instant hit with the counter-culture. Castaneda wrote several more books about his experiences with Don Juan, and achieved cult status, not least because his training by Don Juan involved the use of hallucinogenic drugs. The message was that there are other realities beyond our mundane world that can be accessed by spiritual training and use of drugs. Castaneda's books were given some credibility by his claim that he was a student engaged in anthropological fieldwork when he met the Yaqui shaman Don Juan, and by his use of authentic terminology. Although the Don Juan books were later exposed as frauds (see chapter 7), they do seem to have been based on genuine anthropological research and consequently have been accorded a degree of grudging acceptance but not scholarly status. In spite of this it must be allowed that Castaneda's books enhanced the popularity of Amerindian shamanism among the young for two decades and were critical in shaping the nascent neo-shamanisms of recent years.

Hysterics and psychopaths
From as early as the mid-seventeenth century, there has been a body of opinion to the effect that shamans suffer from one form or another of mental illness. From Gmelin, Georgi and Krasheninnikov in the late eighteenth century almost to the present day it was widely accepted that the 'primitive' peoples of Northern Asia were prone to a nervous condition that came to be known as 'Arctic hysteria'. This condition was thought to result from the debilitating and depressing effects of their harsh environment. Shamans were thought to be exceptionally liable to the illness, which became identified with the initiatory sickness experienced by many nascent shamans. And, of course, with many of the ailments and behaviours, such as possession by spirits or 'soul loss', suffered by the people they treated. This notion was especially popular in the late decades of the nineteenth century and the first half of the twentieth. At that time it was held by many observers of Siberian shamanism, such as Jochelson, Czaplicka and Bogoras, for example. After Ohlmarks took

the reins as the theory's main proponent from the 1930s, the notion became entrenched in anthropological circles, not least in the Soviet Union. Shamans were diagnosed as epileptic, schizophrenic, psychopathic, or simply mentally unstable, even 'deranged' (Siikala and Hoppál 1998: 122).

In reality, while there are some shamanic traits, notably those associated with initiatory illness, that may be related to neurological conditions such as schizophrenia or epilepsy, there is a marked absence of neurosis. Eliade argued strongly that far from being neurotic or insane, shamans ought realistically to be healthy and intelligent people with excellent powers of concentration, drawn from the healthiest members of a community (Eliade 1964: 27–31) and recent research has borne this out (Siikala and Hoppál 1998: 122–123). Far from being twitchy neurotics, shamans are generally composed, creative and self-controlled individuals.

If shamans are so clearly in such good psychological shape, why were they so often characterised as neurotics or madmen by keen-eyed anthropologists? Once again, we must look to the prevailing intellectual winds. In the first place, by the end of the nineteenth century it was almost axiomatic that all 'primitive' peoples, not only those who inhabited the cold north, were prone to neurosis and other psychopathologies. 'Many writers have noticed the extreme liability of primitive peoples to hysterical diseases' wrote Czaplicka (1914: 308), who seems to have been the first to look at shamanism in terms of Arctic hysteria. Secondly, the nineteenth century saw the birth of psychiatry a wide range of deviant, unusual or socially unacceptable behaviours were interpreted in scientific language, in terms of mental illness and within the social mores of the time. The twentieth century consolidated this process, thanks mainly to the work and ideas of Sigmund Freud. Thomas Szasz has shown that people who would formerly have been accused of being witches were now classified as suffering from various forms of insanity (Szasz 1971). Ethnographers were clearly not averse to interpreting shamanism in the same way, and today there are still scholars who persist in discussing shamanism in terms of pathological mental conditions.

Ecstasy and trance

Anthropologists and scholars of religion have long been in general agreement that ecstasy is a central feature of shamanic performance. Shamans are supposed to enter a peculiar state in which their spirits somehow separate from their bodies and allow them to visit supernatural realms where they may communicate with gods and spirits. As we have seen, Eliade termed the varieties of shamanism collectively 'archaic techniques of ecstasy'. The idea that ecstasy is the most important part of shamanism was around long before Eliade set his sights on shamanism. But particularly since Eliade it has become axiomatic for most students of shamanism that ecstasy – temporarily quitting the body to commune directly with the supernatural – is *the* defining aspect of shamanism. Consequently any magical or religious practice that involves trance, possession or some other altered state of consciousness, even nominally or metaphorically, is generally classed as shamanism. Effectively, trance and ecstasy (through any means of induction or for any purpose) are now often seen as being identical to shamanism. However, in spite of various neurological researches there is still no general agreement as to what that ecstasy might actually entail. I shall explore this phenomenon more fully in chapter 5.

Eliade and the New Age

The popular appeal of shamanism received another major boost in 1951 when the Romanian scholar Mircea Eliade published *Le chamanisme et les techniques archaiques de l'exstase*, which was translated into English in 1964. This hugely influential book was a dense study correlating types of shamanism from around the globe and through the ages. Eliade saw evidence for a 'shamanic' cosmology, and a basic unity of imagination across the spectrum of shamanism. For Eliade the defining characteristic of shamanism was ecstasy in which the shaman travelled in spirit to other worlds. Although Eliade did not see shamanism as a religion in itself, it was the primal expression of the human religious impulse, an 'archaic technique' that harked back to the dawn of human spirituality. The importance of Eliade's book to the study of shamanism cannot be exaggerated. It was the first truly major work to pull together elements of shamanism and similar or equivalent practices from all over the world and attempt to establish commonality of function and origin. Other writers, such as John Lee Maddox (1929) had tried but none had matched Eliade for either range or attention to detail. Eliade's approach has been heavily criticised from the day it was published, and rightly so – as well as dragging its subject too far in the direction of Christian mysticism, the author was guilty of altering ethnographic texts to fit in with his own ideas. But for all its flaws the book has a distinct appeal. Like Eliade's other works it has a mystical flavour that found favour with lay readers from the 1960s onward. More importantly, with his book Eliade cemented the syncretic view of shamanism that had been growing slowly but steadily since the beginning of the twentieth century and appeared to confirm shamanism as a common form of human religious expression and the source of many aspects of later religion. The stress on shamanism as a 'primitive' religious technique also went some way toward popularising the shaman as a symbol of rebellion against modern constraints in religion, the arts and fundamental attitudes to life.

Eliade returned to shamanism in a number of books over the next couple of decades – usually in attempts to relate it to a broader religious experience within the major faiths (e.g. Eliade 1960), or to compare it with aspects of other systems, such as yoga (Eliade 1969). *Rites and Symbols of Initiation* (1958) set shamanic initiation in the context of other religious rites of passage. But *Shamanism* remains the most popular and frequently cited of his works. Eliade has had influential allies, none more so than Joseph Campbell, author of *The Hero with a Thousand Faces* (1949), a book reported to have been a strong influence on George Lucas' film *Star Wars*. In *The Hero with a Thousand Faces* the shaman's otherworld journey is one of a number of mythic or folkloric themes directly equated with the Self's journey toward individuation in accordance with C.G. Jung's system of analytical psychology. Campbell's next major work, the four-volume *The Masks of God*, the first volume of which, dealing with 'primitive' mythology, appeared in 1959 and was revised ten years later. Campbell followed up with *The Way of the Animal Powers* (1984), the lavishly illustrated first volume of his *Historical Atlas of World Mythology*. In these and other writings Campbell has reiterated Eliade's mystical interpretation of shamanism in tandem with Jung's analytical psychology, in his later years adding a drizzle of Californian self-improvement philosophy. Between them, with Jung as the third member of an impressively heavyweight triumvirate, Eliade and Campbell account for a large part of New Age mystical ideology. Thanks to them, shamanism is a significant element of the New Age movement. It is easy to see why: in their perception shamanism is above all a direct personal encounter with the numinous, conducted in a raw mystical state. The emphasis is squarely upon the individual shaman's own relationship with other worlds, the realms of the spirit.

The oldest religion

Since Johann Gottlieb Georgi proposed the idea in 1775 that shamanism was the oldest Asian religion it has often been claimed that shamanism is probably the earliest form of religious practice and the source of later forms of religion. I have already mentioned this idea, and will return to it later in this chapter and in chapter 6. However, it has many implications and has inspired a number of theories on the origins and development of shamanism to historical times. The opposite is also true – recent shamanism has increasingly been used as a model to explain the meaning and significance of prehistoric ritual and art. Indeed, it would be accurate to state that in recent years a number of archaeologists and anthropologists have substituted a kind of generic shamanism for the unknown quantity that is prehistoric religion, especially in connection with ancient rock art. The chief instigators of this have been J.D. Lewis-Williams and Thomas Dowson (1988), whose ideas are based on supposed shamanistic practices that are reflected in the rock art of southern Africa and California.

Lewis-Williams and Dowson have followed the long-standing twentieth century trend of interpreting certain figures in European cave paintings as shamans by relating the trance experiences of the present day San Bushmen and the Shoshonean Coso to ancient rock art in roughly the same areas of Africa and California that those people inhabit today. The types of imagery found in these African and Amerindian paintings has been related to a model of entoptic (perceived as being outside the eye) images that are supposed to develop during three stages of trance. This model was extended to rock art in other places and of different times, notably the Upper Palaeolithic in Europe. Although Lewis-Williams and Dowson, and others who have taken up their ideas have been subjected to strong criticism, notably from Alice Beck Kehoe (2000, 2002) and Paul Bahn (2001, 2002), the theory has been gaining support steadily since 1988.

Neo-shamanism and revivalist shamanism

In the 1980s there was an unprecedented upsurge of popular interest in shamanism. This was partly due to the activities of Michael J. Harner, who set up the Foundation for Shamanic Studies in 1985, and the writings of Carlos Castaneda. However, it occurred in the context of the establishment of a mesh of New Age and other spiritual counter-cultures growing out of the alternative movements of the 1960s and 1970s. The writings of Joseph Campbell and Mircea Eliade were important pillars of this phenomenon, along with the ideas of C.G. Jung. As more people in the West began to reject conventional, organised religion and explore their ancestral pre-Christian spiritual heritage, with an emphasis on individual experience and personal growth, shamanism became one of the more attractive avenues of exploration. In addition to these, the 1980s also saw a dramatic rise in environmentalism in response to escalation of the Cold War and the threat of nuclear war, intensive road building programmes in the UK and high profile pollution scares. Shamanism, linked popularly with a supposedly earth-centred Amerindian spirituality, became an obvious tool for those who believed in a magical form of direct action. The result has been a proliferation of neo-shamanisms that some anthropologists have since studied both separately and alongside traditional forms of shamanism. Among these are Jenny Blain's study of *seiðr* as a reinvented tradition of trance induction among present day Westerners (Blain 2002), and Robert J. Wallis' study of the nature of the relationship between neo-shamanism and traditional shamans, ancient and modern, real and imaginary (Wallis 2003). Graham Harvey has also made important contributions to this phenomenon (Harvey 1997) – see chapter 7. The consensus is that neo-shamanism is as worthy of anthropological study as any type of traditional shamanism or magico-religious system, and may be as valid for its adherents as any traditional belief system – though claims to their authenticity in the sense of historical continuity of belief and practice are unfounded.

Witchcraft as shamanism

The idea that the witches persecuted in medieval and early modern Europe were shamans of some sort has been growing since early in the twentieth century. The roots of this trend lie in the works of Margaret Murray, notably *The Witch-Cult in Western Europe* (1921) and *The God of the Witches* (1933). In these books Murray argued that witchcraft was a survival of the 'Old Religion' of Western Europe, with origins back to Palaeolithic fertility cults. The god of the witches was not the Devil but the ancient horned god. Murray did not actually identify witchcraft with shamanism – the latter is not mentioned at all in her work on witchcraft – but she did explicitly identify the 'sorcerers' of Palaeolithic cave art as depictions of the horned god and made the same connection with animal disguises of recent folk ceremony. Murray's tracing of the supposed witch-cult back to cave art has since dovetailed with the supposition that the cave paintings and engravings represented shamanic states, and also with the New Age adoption of shamanism.

Although Murray's 'Old Religion' and matters arising from it have been rigorously tested and found wanting (for instance, Rose 1962; Cohn 1975), the idea still has many adherents, especially among practising pagans and Wiccans. Most of these also accept that European pre-Christian religion and witchcraft had a significant shamanist element (Harvey 1997: 107–125). Anthropologists and historians are, on the whole, less impressed. A more realistic view has been offered by Carlo Ginzburg, who in an illuminating study has claimed that the sixteenth-century *benandanti* of the Friuli region of Italy were an ecstatic fertility cult, perhaps a relic of local shamanism. Unlike Murray's alleged witch-cult, Ginzburg's idea does at least have the advantage of unimpeachable textual evidence – there is no hint of the selectivity or omission that fatally undermine Murray's ideas – which shows how *benandanti* beliefs were distorted under pressure from the Inquisition. The *benandanti* began by protesting their innocence of wrong-doing or heresy, claiming that they were actually leaving their bodies at night to fight evil witches in Christ's name; by the end they were freely confessing to witchcraft in terms familiar from other examples of Inquisition workmanship (Ginzburg 1983). In a later work, Ginzburg traced the origins of the Witches' Sabbath, and much else about European witchcraft, magic and lycanthropy, to the magical flights and transformations of Eurasian shamanism (Ginzburg 1990).

In an appendix to *The Witch-Cult in Western Europe*, A.J. Clark points out that the ingredients of 'flying ointments' could well cause hallucinations and the sensation of flying or floating. Similarly, Michael Harrison and Michael J. Harner have attempted to show that witches in medieval and early modern Europe used hallucinogenic plants (Harrison 1973; Harner 1973). With Murray, these have been among the key texts in the recent 'shamanisation' of European witchcraft. They certainly press all the right buttons, linking witchcraft to the Palaeolithic cave paintings, emphasising magical flight, and making great play of the possible use of hallucinogenic plants. Harner argues, correctly, that there were quite a few Old World hallucinogens available to the witches. He then looks at the pharmacological implications of the flying ointment described in witch confessions. Many of the ingredients are from plants with hallucinogenic properties: hemlock, nightshade, henbane, mandrake, and so on. Harner also found such plants implicated in accounts of lycanthropy. He is not oblivious to the problem of maintaining ritual control while under the influence:

> ... the fact that traditional European witchcraft involves the separation of trance states from ritual operations may be largely due to the problems of coping with the particular hallucinogens

they used... and also raises the question of whether shamans have to be in a trance state at the same time that they are engaged in their manipulative activities. (Harner 1973: 114–7)

This of course rests on accepting that there really were witches as presented by accusations and trials, and that they really did use a flying ointment made up of the plants cited. Whatever the truth about witches and flying ointment, Harner has failed to take account of the context of their recipes. Witches' confessions were made under duress, either psychological or physical, and usually contained what prosecutors wanted to hear. And what the inquisitors wanted to hear was what they already knew. Norman Cohn (1975: 206–24) has shown how the 'night-flying witch' originated in widespread European folktales about flying female demons, lore that has parallels in other cultures today, which resonated with ecclesiastic misogyny. While we might fully accept that some imagery found in accounts of European witchcraft has features that might in another culture be thought 'shamanic,' these images might occur in dreams, in fever, or in various neuropsychological conditions. Furthermore, they were obtained under duress and so are automatically suspect.

Hans Peter Duerr (1985: 2–11) is in no doubt that flying ointments really existed and were manufactured to give sensations and visions of flying and wild nocturnal revelry. He is at a loss as to why Cohn 'can say that there are no eye-witness accounts' of witches using their magic salve. Duerr is right that there are many accounts of what witches confessed to doing while flying under the influence. But the eyewitnesses he cites are mostly accused witnesses testifying at their own trials or those of other accused witches. Duerr is basically saying that there are so many accounts of flying ointment that we should believe at least some of them. But as he acknowledges, officials and judges at witch trials 'simply assumed the existence of a salve; it was part of the stereotype they had formed of witches' (Duerr 1985: 143). The occurrence of the ointment was as inevitable as the appearance of the director in an Alfred Hitchcock film.

The plants listed in flying ointment recipes are hallucinogenic but also highly toxic and potentially fatal, whether ingested orally, absorbed through the skin as an ointment – or soaked up by the vaginal membranes when applied on a dildo, as Harrison (1973) speculates. Early modern witches were often also accused of being poisoners or plague-spreaders – for instance, witches in sixteenth-century Switzerland were sometimes called *engraisseurs*, 'greasers,' because they were believed to poison wells and food stocks with a toxic or plague-laden grease (Monter 1976). Bearing that in mind, we might expect to find the accused under duress and leading questioning admitting the use of toxic plants in their ointments. Common sense dictates that rural people would know which local plants were toxic – it requires no specialist pharmacological training, only experience and shared knowledge. Why should we believe that those accused did use flying ointments just because they confessed to doing so? We might as well believe the rest of the things they often confessed to doing – cannibalism, infanticide, sterilising cattle, blighting crops and kissing the Devil's arse.

This preoccupation with hallucinogens reflects a growing tendency to see drug effects as a synonym for shamanic ecstasy. That is true up to a point in Amerindian ritually altered states of consciousness – but drug use is rare in Eurasian shamanism (see chapter 6). While there is no objection to the idea of drug use for various purposes in medieval and early modern Europe, ther seems no point in looking to it as evidence for an indigenous European shamanism. However, there may be scope for considering shamanic elements as part of the general background of witchcraft beliefs in Europe. For instance, in a study of early medieval European belief in magic Richard Kieckhefer (1989: 52) notes that magicians in the Icelandic sagas often resemble shamans and suggests this may be due to the influence of Saami or Inuit shamanism on Germanic magic. As DuBois (1999) confirms, Saami shamans were certainly influential in medieval Scandinavia. However, the costumes and paraphernalia of Icelandic wizards and seeresses (völva) are markedly different from what is known of Inuit and Saami shamans. Maybe that represents a convergence of traditions, or perhaps an adaptation of a wholly different shamanic tradition. Or it could represent the survival of an old Germanic form of shamanism that had developed with no Inuit or Saami input. Further balanced research is needed in this area.

From primitive to modern, and beyond
This brief survey of important contributors and theories only scratches the surface of an enormous body of work. Many names, studies and theories have been left out, though some will be mentioned later in this book. However, it is sufficient to show a broad pattern that highlights the ways in which the study of shamanism has continually reflected the times. The study of shamanism in the Americas followed the same developmental pattern as in Eurasia. First came descriptions of local life and

customs, usually with a strong element of disapproval, by travellers and missionaries travellers who saw the shaman in terms of their own beliefs – shamans were worshippers of devils, agents of evil. With the beginnings of rationalism and the Enlightenment, shamans became frauds, charlatans who used trickery and the power of superstition to maintain their authority over their unsophisticated fellows. Then came studies of indigenous tribes by ethnographers, with shamanism treated in the context of the whole culture. In keeping with the time, shamans' behaviour was interpreted in terms of mental illness. Finally it became common to study the shamans and their practices as discrete phenomena embedded within their cultures, as well as to engage in comparative or syncretic studies of shamanism, such as that of Eliade.

One important issue arising from this is that accredited agents or informal representatives of colonial powers have conducted most of the major ethnological studies of shamanism in Eurasia or North America and similar practices elsewhere in the world. Siberian shamanism first came to the attention of Europeans as a result of Christian missionary activity in Asia. Later accounts by exiles, missionaries and travellers appeared while Russia was colonising Northern Asia. More recent Siberian ethnographies are effectively the study of conquered tribes by the victors. Much the same is true of the Americas, Africa and Australia. The impetus was initially twofold: the 'duty' of Europeans to take Christianity to the ignorant, superstitious savages; and the imperialist drive for territory and resources to exploit. Once colonies were established these drives were rationalised – civilisation, education and development.

The 'Noble Savage' notwithstanding, the nineteenth century saw a further, scientific rationalisation of colonialism. The publication of Charles Darwin's epochal *On the Origin of Species* in 1859 was embraced not only by biologists but by social scientists. The theory of evolution was even extended to the history of religion and merged with a view of human dveleopment as an analogue of geological processes. For example, the British anthropologist John Lubbock saw several progressive stages in the evolution of religion: atheism (the human condition before the development of religious ideas); fetishism; nature worship; totemism (the allocation of animals to clans); shamanism; anthropomorphism; monotheism; and lastly the pinnacle of the process, ethical monotheism (Lubbock 1870). At around the same time another Briton, Edward B. Tylor, wrote that animism 'characterizes tribes very low in the scale of humanity' (Tylor 1871). Kehoe, discussing nineteenth-century anthropologists' use of comparison to show that some peoples represented an earlier, less evolved stage of humanity, summarises the evolutionists' view of indigenous peoples:

> Anthropologists accepted the comparative method to flesh out pictures of ancient human societies. They discussed whether civilized children are the equivalents of ancient humans, stage by stage as they grow up, a discussion resolved by claiming that "primitive" living "races" are child-like. The ethnocentric premise that non-Westerners are less evolved compared to Europeans and Euro-Americans was combated as early as the late nineteenth century by a few anthropologists… but generally the notion prevailed that peoples overcome by European invaders were simple-minded. (Kehoe 2000: 21)

In other words, the colonised peoples were like children who through lack of moral guidance had remained wedded to bad habits that could be Christianised, clothed or worked out of them. Their major contribution to human knowledge was to provide models that could be projected back in time to tell us what early human societies were like. This idea has largely determined the course of anthropology, by drawing a firm line between European civilisation and the primitive 'other', a line that has stubbornly resisted attempts to erase it. Indeed, until fairly recently anthropology was implicitly – and often explicitly – the study of 'primitive' peoples by 'civilised' (culturally and intellectually more highly evolved) Europeans (Kuper 1988). In the Soviet Union and other communist states – or among Marxist scholars in the West – this attitude did not really die out. Rather, the Western idea of socio-cultural evolution as an adjunct to human biological evolution was paralleled by progressivism based on Marxist dialectic. In practical terms it amounted to much the same thing: primitive peoples, worthy of study but not of equality, must be led by the hand – or marched at gunpoint if necessary – toward a state of civilisation.

The implications for shamanism are clear enough. Shamanism has been extrapolated from Siberia to nearly all other indigenous cultures, expanded to encompass virtually all aspects of magic, religion and cosmology in that global context, then squeezed into a theoretical framework that is little more than an ideological straitjacket. It suited anthropologists and archaeologists to categorise indigenous magico-religious practices as shamanism – really only a convenient ready-made label – because the idea of progression demands a point to progress *from*. Shamanism is practised by primitive peoples, who are at an earlier stage of development than civilised humans. Therefore shamanism is a primitive practice representing an early stage of religion. This underpins Eliade's characterisation of shamanism as an 'archaic' technique, Harner's 'Core Shamanism', and other ideas that see shamanism as a relic of the earliest religious life. While Eliade and Harner – and others who see shamanism as a primal religion – might seem dissimilar, they effectively share an ideology.

This ideology has unfortunately cast shamanism as an obstacle to progress and modernisation. Rather than seeing shamanism as a contemporary practice, political authorities have identified it as a throwback, a regressive belief system that undermines efforts to progress, to modernise. It is also seen as a potential or actual rallying point for nationalists and dissident natives seeking to oust colonial structures and reinstate traditional ones. Hence the Soviet Union's systematic suppression or extermination of shamans, the nineteenth-century US Government's antipathy toward the Ghost Dance cult and the British suppression of tribal cults in Africa. (The idea goes back as far as the Roman suppression of the druids in Gaul and Britain.) Discussing the recent re-emergence of shamanism as a cultural force in Siberia, Mihály Hoppál observes that

> Modernity was always accompanied by destruction. In most cases, transformation meant the destruction of earlier structures. Parallel with the technical development, the social structures changed, especially in those cases when the transformation was urged or even directed by political and ideological forces. It was perhaps folk culture that was mosr affected by these changes. In the eyes of the militants of modernity, cultural traditions were the most hated enemy. This was particularly true in Siberia where the archaic beliefs and mythology, the heroic epic and narrative tradition preserved the identity of the ethnic minorities. This meant that shamanism was among the elements of traditional culture to be eradicated. (Hoppál 1996: 1)

The irony is that for much of the colonial era, and throughout the history of the Soviet Union, the idea of shamanism as a continuation of archaic magic and religion has been pushed hard by anthropologists with a vested interest in the survival of indigenous beliefs and practices. For instance, Michael Harner has laudably done a lot to support the revival of indigenous shamanic traditions, particularly in Siberia and South America, as a teacher and source of funding. Yet his notion of shamanism as an ancient way to ecstasy is in tune with the views of authoritarian ideologues that have sought to extirpate indigenous religions since colonialism began. I suspect most anthropologists, historians and archaeologists who have contributed to the idea of shamanism as a global prehistoric or archaic religious practice would be horrified at the very idea. But, as the saying goes, the road to Hell is paved with good intentions. In its time, in its place, it has been a useful theory – if not an entirely rational one – but unfortunately people with good intentions rarely have the last word.

Time will tell whether postmodernist anthropology will produce any lasting or worthwhile results, particularly with regard to shamanism – while many academics would claim it already has, there are just as many who suspect that it will be another ideological suitcase filled with the emperor's new clothes. But whatever happens, it will surely prove once again that the literature of shamanism is always a product of its time.

3: BEING A SHAMAN

The shaman in society
One of the most important things about being a shaman is belonging to a community. Isolated shamans do not exist: each and every shaman is an integral part of a community they live and work in. What shamans do is done for their people. That might mean they work for a family, a clan or an entire tribe – the degree of responsibility varies considerably across Eurasia. But on the whole shamans heal, foretell the future, perform the rites of death and intercede with the gods not on their own behalf but for a cluster of people with whom they have a special affiliation. This is usually a family or tribal relationship, though shamans will often act for people outside their immediate family or clan, sometimes even for a different ethnic group altogether.

However, much as any shaman might belong to a community, and as much as shamanism might be an important institution integral to a society's structure and cohesiveness, a shaman is often set apart from ordinary people in a several ways. This is because the things that make someone a shaman are also traits and qualities that may place them outside the ordinary. A shaman's nature is a person who can move between worlds, who is a master of things that threaten the community, and who acts as a bridge between the people and spirits and gods. In a sense, preparation for shamanhood destroys a person's humanity and makes them something else entirely. Shamans may belong to a community, marrying and living among people, joining in community activities like anyone else – but they are different.

In many ways the shaman is an outsider. According to Victor Turner, outsiderhood is

> ... the condition of being other permanently and by ascription set outside the structural arrangements of a given social system, or being situationally or temporarily set apart, or voluntarily setting oneself apart from the behaviour of status-occupying, role-playing members of the system. Such outsiders would include, in various cultures, shamans, diviners, mediums, priests, those in monastic seclusion, hippies, hoboes, and gypsies. They should be distinguished from 'marginals', who

are simultaneously members (by ascription, optation, self-definition, or achievement) of two or more groups whose social definitions and cultural norms are distinct from, and opposed to, one another. (Turner 1974: 233)

Turner's definition of the outsider certainly fits some aspects of shamanism. But most shamans are also what Turner calls 'marginals', people that belong to two groups or classes of person at the same time. Either way they are anomalous, people who do not fit easily into ordinary socio-cultural categories.

A shaman does what a shaman is

As we saw in chapter 1, Eliade (1964: 4–5) broadly summarised a shaman as a psychopomp, a practitioner of magical flight, a master of fire, a healer, and an ecstatic traveller to the sky or underworld. Stutley (2003: 2) identified three characteristics of shamanism: belief in a world inhabited by spirits, the use of trance to enable a shaman to enter the spirit world; and the role of shamans as healers or advisers to their community. These two views are a useful starting point but they are rather limited. Eliade, concerned with the magical and mystical elements of shamanism, has separated the ecstatic otherworld journey from being a psychopomp, one who conducts the spirits of the dead to the hereafter, and magical flight. But being a psychopomp involves travelling with the dead soul to the land of the dead. And in the shamanic traditions travel to the underworld and magical flight (to the sky) occur during shamanic ecstasy – they are part of the same thing. (We shall return to ecstasy and travel to other worlds in chapter 5.) Meanwhile, one of Stutley's main characteristics of shamanism is belief in a world inhabited by spirits. There is nothing really shamanic about that. Many non-shamanist peoples believe in a spirit world. By Stutley's definition many mediums in spiritualist groups in the West are fully-fledged shamans. There is much more to shamanism than that. Of course, both Eliade and Stutley expand upon these definitions and broaden their scope considerably – but the danger in trying to summarise shamanism in a few sentences is that it can result in a skewed and badly incomplete picture.

Hultkrantz (1996) has a more satisfying and expansive view. He suggests that shamanism is defined by four main constituents: 'the shaman establishes contact with the supernatural world,' 'the shaman is the intermediary between the human group and the supernaturals,' 'the shaman receives his inspiration from his guardian or helping spirits,' and 'the shaman has ecstatic experiences.' In a nutshell, the shaman is the person for dealing with the spirit world on behalf of a community and this is done indirectly, by communicating with spirits in this world, or by journeying as a spirit to the supernatural realms to contact the gods and spirits directly. Within these parameters a shaman has five main tasks: healing, obtaining knowledge of the future or of how to proceed in a particular course of action; acting as psychopomp, one who conducts the dead to the afterlife; locating and charming game animals; and sometimes acting as sacrificial priest.

This is a very brief summary of Hultkrantz' acknowledged simplification of the shaman's job description and general areas of competence. While it is a fair summary of what a shaman does, it is inevitably incomplete and it is a generalisation. In fact the shaman's duties depend on specific cultural context. For instance, Hultkrantz is right to say that the priestly aspect of shaman, particularly presiding over sacrifice, is exceptional. In certain cultures it is quite a significant part of what shamans do. The matter of what a shaman does is further complicated by the fact that some peoples recognise different types of shaman or different grades of shamanship within a particular type. But, by and large, Hultkrantz accurately delineates the major aspects of being a shaman.

To these we should perhaps add a fifth constituent, one that is often overlooked but might actually be the most important of all. The shaman is a particular kind of person who is fitted for the role of shaman by virtue of heredity or because they have been chosen and prepared by means of certain experiences to commune with and control spirits, and to journey at will beyond this world.

These factors are of great importance. A shaman does the job because that is what they are by nature. Shamans are people who have the ability, inborn or induced, to travel between worlds, see and communicate with spirits, and so on. Shamans are different from ordinary people. Not everyone can become a shaman, and not all people who have shamanic potential can fulfil it. Sometimes a person is marked from birth, either through heredity or by some physical sign that they are born to straddle the barriers between worlds. Sometimes the mark of shamanhood does not become apparent until they reach maturity. Some shamans are chosen by the spirits, seemingly at random. The traditional characteristics of a potential shaman vary from one culture to another, and within cultures, as do the ways in which someone crosses the line that divides the ordinary person from the shaman. And the experiences that make a shaman tend to prefigure what the shaman will be expected to do in the maturity of shamanhood.

Becoming a shaman

Shamans in Eurasia generally do not choose shamanism as a career option, though a person can apply for the job, by asking an ancestral shaman for spirits, for instance (Diószegi 1968: 54). And even though most shamans inherit the position, not all people who come from a line of shamans can or wish to become shamans themselves. For those who are chosen but wish to decline the invitation, some form of ritual might be required:

> ... the will of the ancestral shaman can be changed. If someone should become a shaman because of his origin, but he does not want to, he must 'go', accompanied by a shaman, to 'invite' the ancestral shaman for a feast. Then they can beg the ancestral shaman to call back the spirits. (Diószegi 1968: 54)

Among the Nganasan 'a *nga* or shaman must be a man whose ancestors were shamans and who has inherited the gift of the shamans' (Popov 1996: 61). The shamans of Tuva inherit shamanic ability if they are members of a clan or family whose ancestors included shamans (Diakanova 1994). Inheritance of shamanhood also occurs among the Evenk and other Tungusic peoples (Vasilevic 1996) and, less formally, among the Tofa (Diószegi 1996) and the Sagai (Diószegi 1962a).

Quite why shamanism should be hereditary in these peoples is unclear. Although it is obviously seen as a family trait there is no tradition that all descendants of a shaman will become shamans themselves. In most cases shamanic ancestry is merely a prerequisite – the nascent shaman must undergo an initiatory process and be accepted by the spirits before being able to shamanise. Popov (1996) seems to imply that shamanism is hereditary because of genetic predisposition to hysteria, a view shared by Shirokogoroff, for example. However, as we have seen there is no evidence that active shamans are prone to hysteria or mental health problems. On the contrary, according to recent studies shamans appear to be unusually psychologically robust. In any case, as we shall see in chapter 5, there are good reasons to suppose that shamans are not in any way predisposed to the kind of neurological or psychological factors that result in trance or ecstasy as they are defined medically.

Hereditary shamanism does not depend solely descent from a line of shamans. Saami shamans also inherit their shamanhood, though this generally seems less a case of inherited ability than of inheriting older relatives' collections of spirits, much as someone might be bequeathed any kind of family heirloom (Hultkrantz 1992a). According to the Sagai shaman Yegor Mikhaylovich Kyzlasov, in an interview with Vilmos Diószegi,

> The profession of the *kam* is hereditary, it descends from one generation to the other... It was not the talent I inherited, but the shaman spirits of my clan... Most of them become kams obeying the wish of the ancestral shaman and receive the spirits from him. The spirits are the ghosts of deceased shamans, they live on in clans. The new shaman may receive the spirits of his own family, but not as many as he wants, only the necessary number. (Diószegi 1968: 53–4)

Whatever their ancestry people do not become shamans without an initiation of some kind. Quite often this involves a severe sickness, sometimes protracted, or a series of dreams, in the course of which the person travels to an otherworld where spirits prepare them for shamanhood. Some Saami candidates for shamanhood underwent a period of insanity and self-imposed isolation, during which time they were approached by spirits (Hultkrantz 1992).

Dismemberment by spirits, after which the shaman is reassembled or given a new body forged by a spectral smith, is a common feature of shamanic initiation. For instance it is a major feature of shamanic initiation among the Sakha, and is also found in both North and South America. Sagai shamans undergo a typical dismemberment when the spirits search for the signs of shamanhood, as Diószegi was told in his interview with Kyzlasov, another shaman, and Kyzlasov's wife:

> The candidate loses consciousness while sick. During this time he presents himself to the shaman-ancestor of his clan. When he gets there, they seek his excess bone. They cut up his whole body into pieces, they separate the heart and the lungs and examine each piece by the light. Meanwhile he sees himself cut up, he sees as his whole body and his viscera are being measured, whilst they are looking for the excess bone...
> I have been sick and I have been dreaming. In my dreams I had been taken to the ancestor and cut into pieces on a black table.

They chopped me up and then threw me into the kettle and I was boiled... while the pieces of my body were boiled, they found a bone around the ribs, which had a hole in the middle. This was the excess-bone. This brought about my becoming a shaman. Because, only those men can become shamans in whose body such a bone can be found. One looks across the hole of this bone and begins to see all, to know all and, that is when one becomes a shaman. (Diószegi 1968: 61–2)

Hoppál suggests that initiatory ordeals of this sort are deliberate evocations of physical pain designed to facilitate the shaman's healing powers. The shaman becomes a living symbol of a community's pain and so is also an embodiment of the community itself.

Pain, according to the anthropological concept, features, in the shamanic initiation, as symbolic dismemberment; yet, it also denotes the endurance of physical pain. The individual, the shaman, suffers alone for the community, because the experience of pain is a pivotal element in the human formula for obtaining knowledge. Suffering is part of the healing process, since healing is invariably a collective action; thus symbolic pain, such as dismemberment is made subservient to the healing of collective fears (social pain). (Hoppál 1992: 156)

This is the 'wounded healer' motif popular among New Age shamans. Sick candidates for shamanhood must be able to exercise self-healing before they may tackle the ills of their people. This sounds logical, in the sense that the person's recovery from life-threatening illness demonstrates to the community that shamanic ability is indeed present, much as a medical diploma would reassure the patients of any GP. Yet it is not a universal prerequisite for shamanhood. Sickness, torture and blood-chilling ordeals are by no means universal features of shamanic initiation. For instance, the Nganasan shaman Sereptie Djaruoskin experienced dreams and visions in which a spirit asked him a number of questions to test his wisdom and in turn imparted a limited amount of knowledge to the shaman-to-be. Sereptie was introduced to other spirits, shown the things he needed for shamanising and told how to obtain them when he became a shaman (Popov 1996).

Why should some shamanic initiations require sickness and pain, real or hallucinatory, while others require only a gentle induction to shamanhood, sometimes little more than a handing over of family spirits? Initiatory sickness and visions involving dismemberment and being boiled or hammered out on a demonic smith's anvil are powerful statements of shamanhood. Yet it is apparent that they are not mandatory ordeals. Plenty of shamans manage quite well without them. But the many instances of non-painful initiations are frequently overlooked in favour of the potent image of suffering, the idea of the 'wounded healer' that has become an icon of shamanism. This is because shamanism has come to be seen mainly as a form of traditional healing, of the self and of others, both physically and psychically. So central is healing to some people's idea of shamanism that other shamanic tasks are often sidelined. Academics are as vulnerable as New Age devotees to this way of thinking. For instance, James McClenon sees the origins of religion in the types of 'wondrous healing' performed by shamans. Humans have a 'genetic propensity to benefit from ritual treatment' by which McClenon basically means hypnosis within a context of healing symbolism manipulated by the shaman. For McClenon healing is the shaman's primary activity, which he claims is supported by evidence for altered states of consciousness in Palaeolithic shamanistic activity (McClenon 2002: 171, 157–8). McClenon might well be right to assume altered states of consciousness in Palaeolithic shamans, if there were indeed such people – there is frankly not enough evidence to settle the matter one way or the other, so the odds are pretty much even. However, if the main evidence for Palaeolithic shamanism, the European cave art, is any guide then there is nothing at all to support his implication that shamanism always was primarily about healing. The main concern of supposedly 'shamanic' cave art is quite clearly hunting or relationships between humans and animals, particularly game animals. There is nothing whatever to suggest healing rites; although we can suppose that ritual healing probably existed, if what is depicted in cave art was shamanic activity then the primary concern of any hypothetical Palaeolithic shamans was evidently hunting magic.

Taken within the context of shamanism as an aggregation of themes and roles centred upon the individual practitioner, the dismemberment and other ordeals – where they occur – seem designed to mean something other than, or in addition to, an acquired fitness for healing. The dismemberment in particular has a distinctly mythic quality, echoing as it does the division of a primordial entity and the rearrangement of its parts to make the cosmos, a theme that occurs in creation myths across the globe, including those of the shamanist peoples of Eurasia (Stone 1998).

This hints at an identification of the shaman with the primordial being and therefore with the cosmos itself. The recurrent idea that the shaman inherits shamanic ability, either genetically or through a gift of spirits presided over by the ancestral shaman, means that in effect each shaman traces their shamanhood back to the fabulous ancestral shaman, the first to be dismembered and reassembled. A shaman is more likely an analogue, a living embodiment, of the cosmic creation, rather than merely a personification of sickness and healing.

Paradoxically, this idea is underlined by the initiatory visions of Sereptie Djaruoskin, a shaman who seems not to have undergone the dismemberment ordeal. Sereptie's visions include a series of questions posed by a mysterious spirit who also acts as an instructor. Most of the questions and proffered information are concerned with aspects of cosmology – the seasons, birth and death, protective spirits, the structure of the cosmos, and so on (Popov 1996). Sereptie's innate wisdom and understanding of the cosmos is brought out and augmented by his teacher, a process which confers shamanhood – instead of his being taken apart and put back together as *a shaman* in the same way as Kyzlasov. Furthermore, Sereptie's conversations with his guiding spirit were also concerned with the meaning of a shaman's possessions, the costume, drum and other items. As we shall see in the next chapter, the shaman's paraphernalia illustrates the shaman's nature. The costume is a diagram not only of the cosmos but often of the shaman, especially where it represents the shaman's own skeleton or that of an animal or bird that is also imagined as belonging to the shaman. The costume may include the shaman's weapons, spirits and means of travel. In short, it summarises everything the shaman is – it is a virtual image of the shaman. And that includes a symbolic acknowledgement of the essential unity between cosmos and shaman. The dismemberment and other ordeals are the ways in which a shaman may acquire knowledge of the nature of things, and that knowledge is embodied in the shaman.

This agrees with what is understood of the shaman's ecstatic journeys and functions within the community. The shaman is a healer, most certainly, but also a diviner, a psychopomp, an influencer of animals, an accomplice in sacrifice and a traveller between worlds. These things are done by means of the things a shaman obtains through initiation: knowledge and spirits. To put it simply, shamanhood is recognised not by the self-healing of the candidate but by their going away to an otherworldly location where they obtain the things necessary for shamanhood.

Gender, sex, sexuality – and shamanism

Female and male shamans coexist on more or less equal terms in some ethnic groups. But in others one sex will predominate, either being considered superior as shamans to the other sex or dominating to the exclusion of the other. For instance, Saami shamans are almost always male, though some women have been known to rise to prominence (Lundmark 1987), whereas in Uzbekistan, Korea and Japan, and among the Itelmen, shamans are usually women. For the Sakha and Koryak, male shamans are considered superior to men. Some tribal groups have a tradition that the first shamans were female. A Buryat story of the origins of shamanism tells how the first shaman sent to humans by the gods was an eagle – the bird could not make himself understood but he had sexual intercourse with a woman to whom shamanic abilities were thereby transferred. (See Eliade 1964: 69–71 for the association of eagles with shamanism among a number of Siberian peoples.)

Many shamans occupy an unusual position with regard to sexuality and gender-roles. Some male shamans dress as women, adopt traditional women's pastimes and may even marry a man or enter into an equivalent relationship with a male spirit. The best-documented example of this phenomenon is the 'soft man' of the Chukchi. Soft men are shamans who are ordered by their spirits to become women. They wear female garments and adopt women's hairstyles, and behave like women in almost every respect. Some soft men marry other men, though the common practice is for them to continue living with their own wives. Where a male shaman chooses a husband the relationship may be homosexual, but equally the relationship might be non-sexual, with the shaman (and his partner) taking a mistress. Each soft man enters into a liaison with a spirit husband – the spirit is regarded as the head of their family or household.

Importantly, Chukchi women shamans were also known to undergo equivalent transformations. Even widowed female shamans with children might marry a younger woman (Bogoras 1904). A similar custom regarding both men and women was remembered among the Koryak at the beginning of the twentieth century but apparently no longer adhered to, though one had died shortly before Jochelson's visit. Among the Koryak, women shamans are considered more powerful than male shamans – but a transformed male shaman was considered their equal (Jochelson 1905). Similar customs have been recorded among the Sakha and Itelmen; and also among the Yukaghir and, to a lesser extent, other Uralic or Altaic-speaking

Female shaman of Krasnoyarsk District. From Johann Gottlieb Georgi, Beschreibung aller Nationen des Russischen Reichs *(1776).*

peoples, although this is marked by their shamans' costumes sometimes including elements of dress or even full costume normally characteristic of the opposite sex. Basilov (1996) finds evidence for there having been full sexual inversion among Uralic and Altaic shamans in the past.

This phenomenon of sexual inversion has led to much speculation regarding shamanic gender reversal or blurring. One school of thought holds that shamanism is a way of ritually normalising homosexuality within the confines of social structures that rigidly define sex and gender roles. Instead of being seen as aberrant men, shamans are a 'third sex' that exists outside the normal social constraints (see for example Hollimon 2001). But while some of these transgender shamans are certainly homosexual, others are clearly not. Many are simply transvestite or playing the woman's role in an elaborate charade that may perhaps be considered a ritual in its own right. Furthermore, soft men were disapproved of among the Chukchi, though this was not usually expressed openly because people were wary of the shamans' powers. Another suggestion, made early on by Bogoras, is that cross-dressing and naming helped to conceal a shaman's identity by confusing hostile spirits. Some shamans adopted names of the opposite sex. However, as Bogoras also reports that transformed shamans usually retained their original names — which in the Chukchi language clearly label their owners as men or women — there is little reason to take this seriously with regard to the Chukchi. However, transsexual Sakha shamans did adopt female names. In 1902 V.F. Troshchanski suggested that the tendency of Yakut shamans to behave like women arose because shamanism was supposed to have originated among women (Czaplicka 1914: 246–7). Eliade's suggestion that such ritual sexual inversion 'is probably explained by an ideology derived from the archaic matriarchy' (1964: 258) doesn't really tell us anything at all, and would certainly not explain the female shamans who become men.

Balzer observes that 'gender ambiguity' in shamanic inversion 'is not the same as full transformation, and neither is congruent with ritual reversals.' She continues:

> Yet I argue that these are related phenomena, variations on themes that can help us understand more completely the full range of symbolic, socially constructed meanings for human sexual diversity... instead of seeing gender reversals as deviant,

we may see a mirror image: anomaly turned into sacred power. (Balzer 1996: 254)

She goes on to note that gender ambiguity – effeminate men, masculine women and homosexuality – is now being openly explored among the general population of post-Soviet Sakha (the Yakut home region), including direct reference to traditions of shamanic sexual inversion.

The shaman's transsexuality touches on three issues that are bundled together by post-feminist and 'queer' theory, and which in everyday usage are often casually used as synonyms – gender, sex and sexuality. Although these three concepts are, of course, closely intertwined, they are still different things. 'Sex' is a basic biological division based on a creature's genetic identity and its role in the reproductive process. Sex may be expressed metaphorically or by metonymy, often relating to dress or occupations considered appropriate to the each sex – for instance, in genealogy the spear and distaff represent the maternal and paternal lines respectively – and semantically merges with our linguistic representations of gender. 'Sexuality' is categorisation according to a particular social behaviour – attraction to a particular type of person, object or behaviour for purposes of sexual satisfaction – which in the absence of any single definitive explanation may be due to any one, or a combination of, biological predisposition, acculturation or personal preference.

Sex and sexuality are clear enough, but gender is less easy to grasp. Social scientists' use of the word 'gender' derives from the classification of things in language. In linguistics the term 'gender' strictly denotes the way things (nouns and sometimes verbs) are classified within a language according to how they affect or are affected by context – different genders affect grammatical construction in different ways. For instance, in Modern English, gender is mainly confined to pronouns relating to living things that are biologically male or female. French has two genders, masculine and feminine, and all nouns fall into one or the other category. German has three: masculine, feminine and neuter. Altaic and Uralic languages do not have gender at all, although some have masculine and feminine personal pronouns. In Bantu languages there are many genders, based solely on number – so, for instance, the gender of two men is different to the gender of five men, but the same as that of two women. Other languages too base gender on qualities other than the sex (actual or notional) of a thing. In language gender is not necessarily based on sex.

Social scientists have borrowed the term 'gender' to denote the roles played by members of the two sexes and the qualities that are associated with them. But because this has occurred within an exclusively European and American context it reflects the nature of gender in Indo-European languages – especially English and French, where gender is binary. Historical linguistics indicates that like its close cousins Altaic and Uralic, Proto-Indo-European had no genders. First an additional 'masculine-neuter' gender arose, and later a feminine form derived from that, so that late Proto-Indo-European had three genders, which are retained in modern German, for instance. This suggests a response to increasing social complexity – a growing need to categorise things in a certain way was reflected in the language. Just why this occurred in Indo-European but not in Altaic or Uralic – the main languages of Eurasian shamanism – is hard to say. But the upshot is that in two major languages (as far as the major scholars in social studies are concerned) we are left with a binary system of noun classification that has become closely identified with biological sex and the qualities or behaviours associated with its members. This means that in the West gender theory began with the assumption of gender as a specific opposition between masculine and feminine, male and female. It also means that in the West we have a built-in structural ideology with regard to gender difference, and this has coloured the ways in which we approach gender issues in ways that may not always be appropriate to various non-western peoples.

Do non-Western cultures classify people according to their sex or sexuality? To the best of my knowledge all languages have different words for 'man' and 'woman' and – genital deformities and anomalies aside – all cultures recognise that men are not put together in quite the same way as women and that the two have different reproductive roles. They may also have words or phrases that denote homosexuals, hermaphrodites or people who cross dress. Are transsexual shamans really representative of a 'third sex' that supports the postmodern challenge to traditional ideas of sex and gender? Czaplicka makes an interesting observation:

> Socially the shaman does not belong to either the class of males or to that of females, but to a third class, that of shamans. Sexually, he may be sexless, or ascetic, or have inclinations of

homosexualistic character, bur he may also be quite normal. (Czaplicka 1914: 253)

She goes on to note that shamans, whether biologically male or female, are surrounded by taboos that apply to shamans and no one else. These effectively mark the shaman as a person apart from ordinary society, not bound by the same rules as other people. But is Czaplicka saying that shamans are a third sex?

Czaplicka's remarks about the shaman's sexuality makes it clear that what she means is that shamans are not a 'third class' of sex *in addition to* male and female. Effectively that would mean a third sex more or less equivalent to androgyny or hermaphroditism, or asexuality. But it would be meaningless if the shaman was sexually 'quite normal' – unless the shaman is actually a separate class of person from everyone else irrespective of sex or sexuality. Czaplicka points out that normal taboos and ritual privileges and restrictions only apply when they do something that is explicitly and unambiguously masculine or feminine and cannot be done by a member of the opposite sex. For instance, when a female shaman is pregnant or menstruating, during those times she cannot shamanise but must endure the same taboos and other observances as any other woman. In other words, she becomes an ordinary woman for the duration.

The shaman's sexuality is incidental. Shamans who are clearly heterosexual may undergo gender inversion. Some happily continue normal sexual relations with a spouse of the opposite sex. Some who marry a person of the same sex continue to engage in heterosexual activity with no homosexual activity at all. And there are those who are sexually bivalent. Furthermore, homosexual men who were not shamans were known among the Chukchi and Koryak. The only rule seems to be that when instructed to do so transsexual shamans must *appear to become* members of the opposite sex. Men dress as women and take up sewing and other tasks considered the domain of women, while women wear men's clothing and abandon the needle and thread in favour of hunting with a rifle and other manly pursuits. Occasionally the spirits might exhort their shaman to fully take on the role of wife to another man or husband to another woman – but this can be resisted, even though it may incur the spirits' anger. Bogoras reports that some Chukchi shamans prefer suicide to becoming a soft man or a 'woman that is like a man' – evidence that this phenomenon is not a means of accommodating homosexuals within cultures with rigidly defined gender roles and tight rules governing sexual behaviour. It is a magical act, one dictated by supernatural forces rather than by the shaman's sexual orientation. And some shamans do not like it.

A shaman's seeming transformation, whole or partial, into someone of the opposite sex is not simply a matter of androgyny. The shaman's spirits tend to urge a full transformation rather than a partial one. The Chukchi terminology refers to men who are like women and women who are like men. But it is evident from shamans' adopted behaviour and appearance that the idea is only to *appear* to 'become' a member of the opposite sex. There is no unisex clothing or hairstyle, no ritualised sexual bivalency and no exclusive concentration on domestic activity that is the shared province of both men and women. Duality of the sexes is maintained. Inverted shamans obviously cross gender boundaries but only as the Western tradition understands gender – the categorisation of people, things and behaviour according to whether they are perceived as masculine or feminine in terms of Western values. Judith Butler, for example, argues that sex (the state of being male or female) underlies the concept of gender, and that in turn gender determines desire toward the opposite gender. But conceptualised gender is actually the model for the behaviours and qualities attributed to the sexes. 'There is no gender identity behind the expressions of gender... identity is performatively constituted by the very "expressions" that are said to be its results' (Butler 1990: 25). In other words, gender is a performance a person gives in a manner dictated by cultural expectations of how a person of whichever sex should behave. (Butler also argues for what she calls 'gender trouble' – the subversion of supposed gender identities by blurring gender boundaries and extending genders beyond the binary.)

Whether or not we agree whole-heartedly with Butler – and I for one would argue that hormones, pheromones and hard-wired reproductive instincts might be more potent than concepts as drivers of desire – she is certainly correct to identify expressions of gender as performances. The qualities and behaviours associated in the West with being masculine or feminine are essentially costumes we wear to announce ourselves as men or women. This is expressed in stereotypes. When we say a man is 'effeminate' what we mean is that he is a man who acts like a woman. And the act is accorded more importance than his biological sex – we assume that effeminate men are sexually attracted to other men, as we would 'normally' expect a woman to be. Similarly, we assume 'macho' men to be sexually attracted to women. Clearly, these stereotypes do not reflect actual behaviour – these days the more a man conforms to the old macho stereotype – moustache, muscles and sexually rampant – the more likely he is to be gay. And the 'lipstick lesbian' is a well-known phenomenon. The fact is that the stereotypes have always been acts. For instance, even in the recent past it was quite possible – and sometimes essential for personal safety – for a gay man to play the part of what was essentially a stereotyped heterosexual. Nowadays quite a few heterosexual men act in a way that would once have been thought effeminate. The question is, does acting a part actually blur gender boundaries? It seems to me that performing gender roles, whether as parody or as irony, may well 'queer' those roles in the West but not in cultures that do not share the West's visions of gender or its sexual morality

Balzer seems mistaken in believing that exploration of ritual sex change in Siberian shamanism may dissuade us from 'seeing gender reversals as deviant' – they were evidently seen as such by Chukchi at the beginning of the twentieth century. Nor is it necessarily 'anomaly turned into sacred power' – although shamanic power may be enhanced by sexual inversion, still the shamans had a fair amount of that power before they were transformed. Furthermore, not all homosexuals or 'soft men' in shamanist cultures are shamans and their sexuality or transvestism does not make those men any more powerful. And even if gender transformation increased the powers of male shamans among the Koryak, there is no reason why it should do the same for women, who were considered more powerful than men anyway.

Shamanic sexual transformation does not blur gender boundaries in the same way, nor does it add a third gender. Their gender – as post-feminist theory would understand the word – changes superficially but not in terms of biological functionality and not necessarily in terms of sexual desire. Soft men are still seen as men, even if they are men who are like women. The Chukchi terminology is explicit and precise: the soft man is not a true biological hermaphrodite, nor an androgyne. He is not necessarily homosexual or sexually bivalent. He embodies two sexes in parallel, a biological and probably heterosexual male; but his appearance and social behaviour are those of a woman. This is not a third sex as Western thinkers might interpret it – it is something quite different and outside the parameters of Western gender debate. It is not an expression of sexuality, nor of gender. Rather, it is a demonstration of the shamanic ability to inhabit two worlds at once, a display of power and a constant reminder that normal rules do not apply to the shaman. And the more powerful a shaman is, the less the rules that bind non-shamans apply.

This does not mean that the shaman is 'queered' as some Western theorists might claim. Shamans (whether 'soft men' or not) are integral parts of their communities, and the special rules that apply to them are an integral part of those communities' belief system and exist as part of the social and moral structure. Shamanism – and all that goes with it – is a permanent institution, and in that it is not at all like the seasonal ritual reversals that have developed in European tradition. Those are special rules for special occasions only. Shamans would only be 'queer' in Western society or some other where their role does not exist and where their exploitation of gender would be thought subversive.

Living between worlds

Initiation ordeals and sexual inversion are both implicated as major factors in the ability of shamans to perform their tasks, especially those involving travel to the spirit worlds. Shamanic initiation frequently involves a sickness of some kind, commonly with fevered visions of dismemberment which may involve the replacement of certain human body parts with stronger ones of iron or crystal from the spirit world. Sometimes these hallucinatory ordeals occur in dreams. Saami shamans become withdrawn and unsociable, or feel impelled to remove themselves from human company, sometimes running wild in the forest plagued by spirit voices (Hultkrantz 1992). Whatever their cause, these terrifying experiences are critical in preparing the shaman for the life they are to lead. They help define what nature of being a shaman is. A shaman is both healer and the healed, both whole and incomplete (or, where the spirits find an extra bone, more than complete), both living and dead. These ambiguities are paralleled or reinforced where sexual inversion occurs: without becoming androgynous or hermaphroditic the shaman is still effectively two sexes at the same time – a man who is like a woman or a woman who is like a man. These attributes confer a unique status upon the shaman – they place the shaman between states of being.

This state of being 'in-between' states is sometimes known as *liminality*, from the Latin word for a threshold. There are two basic types of liminality. One occurs where a person is at a point of transition. Typical liminal states occur when someone reaches puberty, when people pass from life to death, during birth, and so on.

Arnold van Gennep recognised long ago that these are moments when people switch from one social group and that they are times when loss of clear social definition invites danger: Consequently to control the danger they are subjected to ritual, what van Gennep called 'rites of passage':

> The life of an individual in any society is a series of passages from one ago to another and from one occupation to another. Wherever there are fine distinctions among age or occupational groups, progression from one group to the next is accompanied by special acts... every change in a person's life involves actions and reactions between sacred and profane – actions and reactions to be regulated and guarded so that society as a whole will suffer no discomfort or injury... For every one of these events there are ceremonies whose essential purpose is to enable the individual to pass from one defined position to another which is equally well defined. (Van Gennep 1960: 2–3)

For van Gennep, these passages are transitions between one state and one that logically or naturally comes next – such as the passage from being single to being married, or passing from childhood to adulthood. Other in-between states that are not explicable as natural or socially endorsed changes of this sort are less easily absorbed into van Gennep's thinking. In particular, when van Gennep cites Jochelson on Koryak shamanism he draws a parallel between transvestism within a shaman's (heterosexual) marriage and the transvestism of the priests of Hercules on Kos, claiming that the priests were seen as wives of the god. He offers no explanation but decides that these examples of transvestism are simply part of marriage ritual (van Gennep 1960: 172). Mary Douglas (1966: 51–7) makes things a little clearer. Discussing the dietary and other restrictions of Leviticus, she notes that the text is essentially taxonomic – it classifies creatures according to various criteria and forbids the consumption of animals that are ambiguous. Leviticus has very definite ideas of how an ordered cosmos – God's holy creation – should be arranged. Things that do not agree with that arrangement threaten the cosmic order. Douglas applies this insight to van Gennep's rites of passage. The passage from one state to another places a person in a state of ambiguity that threatens the established order of things, the structure of the cosmos and all that it contains.

The social states a person passes through – age sets, bachelorhood and marriage, childhood and adulthood – are ways of classifying people, of defining the way things are supposed to be ordered within a society. Douglas' examination of Leviticus shows that dangerous ambiguity is not limited to passages between social states. It occurs when something is anomalous – such as when it has mixed traits of two things that are conceptually very different from one another and are therefore classified as separate types of thing. Douglas and van Gennep both characterise passage and ambiguity as inherently dangerous.

> Danger lies in transitional states, simply because transition is neither one state nor the next, it is undefinable. The person who must pass from one to another is himself in danger and emanates danger to others. (Douglas 1966: 96)

But anomalies are not inherently dangerous. As Rodney Needham observes, '...there are no necessary anomalies. Certainly it cannot be alleged that an anomaly automatically gives rise to wariness or unease or a fear of danger. One proof of this is that everywhere people make up classificatory oddities: they are attracted by them, and it might even be said that they seem to need them' (Needham 1979: 46). Bruce Lincoln extends Needham's argument: 'there are only things that appear anomalous within the framework of a given taxonomic system... One can, in fact, define anomaly in rather neutral terms as any entity, the existence of which goes unrecognized under the terms of a given taxonomy' (Lincoln 1989: 165). In short, anomalies only come into being where taxonomy creates them – where there is a space between categories, or where categories are simply too few in number to cater for everything.

A shaman is a walking anomaly, stuck midway through the passage from life to death; and existing between categories, both healer and healed, both man and woman. The first is obvious enough: being permanently between life and death, this world and the spirit world, a shaman may inhabit both worlds. The last sharpens the discussion of gender as it relates to shamanism. The transsexual shaman is a person who is not accounted for within local taxonomies of sex. It seems to me that this is not a question of proliferating genders in the sense of Butler's 'gender trouble' nor of Balzer's 'socially constructed meanings for human sexual diversity' – gender is taxonomy, so by virtue of their anomalous status transsexual shamans have their own gender quite apart from the standard male and female. But it is not one that is based on a gradation or mixing between categories of sex or sexuality. This is in spite of their being both men and women at the same time. The primary function of ritual transvestism is to reflect that a shaman exists in a state that does not allow for categorisation under normal rules. The shaman's bilateral sex mirrors the shaman's position between worlds. It is both a metaphor for and an enhancement of the shaman's status as a person who lives between worlds, someone who occupies a position outside the normal cosmological structures. When existing on the threshold between two states, by analogy one has access to all other interfaces. By exploiting such loopholes in the perceived natural order a shaman ceases to be bound by the same laws that restrict others.

Although ritual sexual inversion is not historically a pan-Eurasian shamanic phenomenon, there are indications that might once have been (Basilov 1966). It is also known to have occurred among the Inuit and a number of Native American peoples. Óðinn's practise of the magic known in medieval Scandinavia as *seiðr* – which is seen by some scholars as a variety of shamanism (for instance, Strömback 1935) – was said to be accompanied by *ergi*, a word that in other contexts signified the passive role in anal intercourse (Ström 1974). Ritual transvestism and sexual inversion are features of certain religious cults and magical practices around the world, from ancient times up to the present day (Eliade 1964: 258, 351). Furthermore, there is a scattered but lengthy tradition of cross-dressing male priests in ancient Indo-European and Middle Eastern religions. In the ancient world the *galloi*, castrated priests of the goddess Kybele, dressed as women; and the Scythian diviners known as *enareis* were characteristically effeminate. (Interestingly, in Indo-European history the ritualisation of effeminacy seems to have been much more extreme and explicitly concerned with sexual identity than in Siberian shamanist societies.) Priests, like shamans, occupy an ambiguous position as bridges or channels of communication between their community and the gods. Catholicism has preserved this into the present day – priestly ceremonial attire is essentially female clothing of long ago, and the call to celibacy is a removal from sexual relationships. Priests are anomalous in other senses – for instance, they are 'fathers' who do not father children. As Needham and Lincoln suggest this does not result in priests being seen as dangerous – quite the reverse – but it does set them firmly apart from the community even though, like the shamans of Siberia, they live in its midst and are integral to its fabric.

4: THE SHAMAN'S COSTUME AND OTHER TOOLS OF THE SHAMAN'S TRADE

You are what you wear

The shaman's magical costume is one of the most appealing elements of shamanism. Everyone likes a good show and many shamans give full value for money, with impressive singing, drumming and dancing, conjuring tricks, and plenty of eye-rolling and melodramatic grimacing. However, it is the shaman's costume that really grabs the attention. Many Eurasian shamans' costumes are certainly interesting, both eye-catching and brimful of symbolic meaning, and they come in a variety of styles. Their designs have been studied and their meanings pondered by generations of anthropologists. Early anthropologists were largely content to record details of costume and beliefs surrounding them. They do not tell us much about the deeper significance of decoration or paraphernalia, nor do they really address the meaning of costume as a complete assemblage. Mikhailowski, for instance, thought that shamans' costumes and accessories were intended to awe onlookers with their bizarre appearance and noise; only shamans and their believers knew the meaning of their symbolism (cited in Czaplicka 1914: 204). Czaplicka is hardly more expansive:

> They are of great importance, for the spirits will not hear the voice of the shaman unless the right dress and implements are used, and the drum beaten; they are sacred because of their contact with a supernatural and often dangerous power. (Czaplicka 1913: 204)

Later scholars were prepared to be more probing and more forthcoming. Eliade states that

> The shaman's costume itself constitutes a religious hierophany and cosmography; it discloses not only a sacred presence but also cosmic symbols and metaphysical itineraries. Properly

studied it reveals the system of shamanism as clearly as do the shamanic myths and techniques. (Eliade 1964: 145)

In plainer language, the costume is a kind of diagram of how and where the shaman operates. Other scholars concur. 'The complete set of vestments was a symbolic representation of the shamanistic worldview' writes Diakanova (1994) of the Tuvan shaman costume. Caroline Humphrey and Urgunge Onon – the latter a practising Daur Mongol shaman – observe that Daur costume incorporates concepts of time, space travel and renewal, and establishes the shaman's position in society (Humphrey and Onon 1996: 208).

Like other aspects of a shaman's life, their costume is surrounded by ritual. For example, a Tuvan shaman is not allowed to try on the costume while it is being made. Items of Tofa costume must be made in the order prescribed by the spirits. Nganasan shaman costumes must be stitched together using only thread made from the hair of a wild deer. Often a costume needs to be 'enlivened' or ritually activated before it can be worn for shamanising. In most cultures the shaman's costume must be stored in a special way. The costume is a powerful magical tool – it can be the shaman's protection, a means of transformation, a weapon, transport, a repository for the shaman's helper spirits, and a map of the spirit world. Understandably the costume needs to be made, worn and treated carefully to ensure that it does what it is supposed to do (see for instance, Diószegi 1996 for a highly detailed account of the manufacture of Tofa costumes and the rituals surrounding their making, wearing and upkeep). But not always – Korean shamans, for instance, treat their costumes and equipment as tools to be used and buy them ready-made from specialist shaman shops.

Recently there has been a trend toward looking at the typology of shamanic costume in the belief that tracing their development will enable us to postulate archaic forms that might shed light on the origins of shamanism. Elena Prokofyeva has traced Eurasian shamanic costumes to an archaic type intended to represent an animal or bird – mainly deer, bear, wolf, otter, crane, eagle and owl. Archaic types consisted of the whole animal skin, with the skin of the creature's head used as a head-dress. Originally, the animals were clan 'totems', but later the shaman 'became' a particular beast while shamanising. Larisa Pavlinskaya broadly agrees with Prokofyeva, but observes that later shaman costumes, with metal pendants sewn onto animal skin, fall into two main types. In one the metalwork depicts the whole animal, while the other portrays only the animal's skeleton. Pavlinskaya suggests the skeletal image is more ancient, citing the 'x-ray' style that occurs in ancient and recent indigenous art across Eurasia and found as far apart as Alaska and Australia. She postulates that before metallurgy the skeleton would have been embroidered or painted onto the animal skin. The motif derives from 'a cult of the dying and resurrected animal, which is a characteristic of hunting peoples' – one which persisted in Siberia until modern times. Pavlinskaya points out that costumes with a metal skeleton depict only two types of animal, bear and deer. The deer skeleton costume was worn for journeys to the upper world, the celestial realm; the bear skeleton costume was for travelling to the underworld. Bird images are also prominent and often combined with deer. Pavlinskaya links these images with Siberian mythological patterns. The deer symbolises the sun and is a central figure in the widespread myth of the 'Heavenly Hunt', while the bird has a role in creation myths of the 'earth diver' type found throughout Siberia and as far afield as Polynesia. 'The three images – the deer, the bear, and the bird – are dominant on the shaman's ritual costume and create a symbolic image of the universe' (Pavlinskaya 1994: 262).

There is nothing especially radical or challenging about these ideas, although Pavlinskaya's typology of shaman costumes forces us to think more carefully about why a particular style of image or object forms part of a costume when others might do just as well. But can shaman costumes so readily be categorised and assigned to particular Eurasian cultural eras? There is good reason to doubt that they can. For one thing, some Eurasian shamans do not wear costumes at all, though a Saami *noaide* may wear a special magic belt (Manker 1996) and Chukchi shamans perform almost naked. As far back as the medieval Norse sources, through Scheffer in the late seventeenth century to the present day, there is no evidence that they ever did wear animal disguise or symbolic representations of animals or birds. Elsewhere in Eurasia shamans might wear a variety of specialised head-dresses, masks, coats, gloves and footwear – some shamans wear all of these, others wear only one or two items – of varying degrees of importance and with different styles of decoration. Though there tend to be broad similarities between costumes of shamans in closely related ethnic groups or ethnically different groups in close proximity to one another costume can vary greatly even between neighbouring peoples or from one clan to the next, as the following examples will show.

Nganasan shaman costumes

Dolgikh (1996) gives a detailed description of the costume of a Nganasan shaman. The outfit consists of a parka, apron, mittens, head-dress and boots. The shaman's knee-length parka is made of deerskin, decorated with triangles along the hem and border, with a line of black triangles (to fortify the shaman's own spine) along the spine. It has three triangular flaps attached to the back. These represent bird tails and their function is to act as seats for souls being rescued from disease spirits and to help the shaman when he goes underwater while visiting the gods. The coat is festooned with soft leather bands, cloth twisted into cords and bundles of polar fox and wolf hair. The hair bundles are to guarantee success in hunting those animals. The cloth cords are there for the soul of a sick child to hold onto while the shaman is bringing it back from the underworld. The soft leather strips, with others sewn onto the sleeves, are for the shaman to prevent sickness coming from a hole in the ground. Sleeve and glove decoration is designed to resemble the hair of deer, so the shaman's arm resembles a deer's leg. (Similarly the mittens have three holes cut in each to make it easier for the shaman to hold his drum, but also so that they look like deer hooves.) Metal ornaments are sewn onto the parka – iron sheets to break ice during the descent to the lower world; small iron tubes representing deer hair; and bent pieces of iron representing the heads of six geese, which the shaman needs to fly to the upper world.

The shaman's apron is also made of deer hide, with the flesh side facing outward. It has a line of black triangles round the edge and a doubled line up the middle. In the centre is a black oval representing the shaman's navel. The apron has a fringe of soft leather strips and fox and wolf hair; two copper half-moons, one covering the shaman's navel and one further down, and two small copper chains. The half-moons are for the shaman to lie down on and to break the ice when entering the underworld – the chains are to bind souls to stop them straying. The head-dress comprises a headband with two ribbons crossing on top of head, with a fringe of red and blue striped tassels covering the face.

Not all Nganasan shamans have one costume. Graceva (1996) describes a shaman with three costumes. The heaviest and most ornate is for journeying to the lower world, with a lighter, less intricate costume for travelling to the upper world. The lightest is worn for divination. The Nganasan have no fixed number of costumes – the need and occasion for making a costume of a particular type are dictated by the spirits.

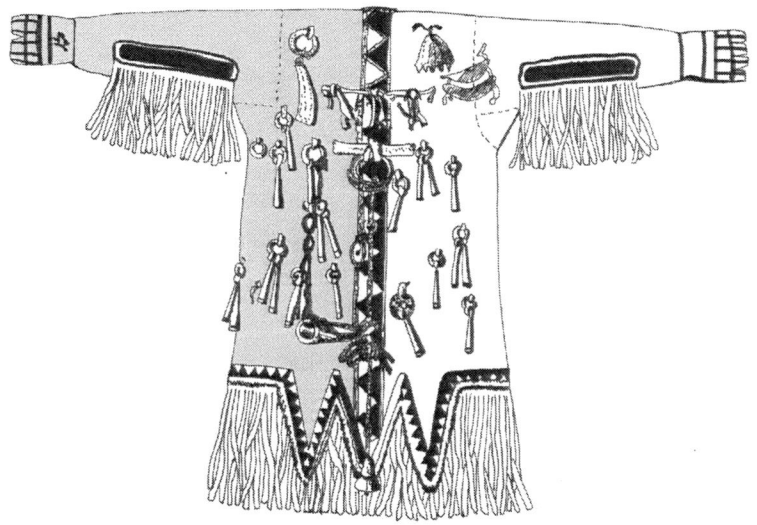

Front view of Nganasan shaman's coat donated to ethnographer A.A. Popov in the 1930s. After Graceva (1996).

An Enets shaman's outfit

The Enets have three categories of shaman, of which only the *budtode*, a powerful shaman who has the power to contact celestial spirits, has a special costume. Prokofyeva (1963) discusses one such costume belonging to a female shaman. The coat is deerskin with the fur inside, the flesh side painted red and decorated with deer fur and hide. The coat has fringes of polar fox fur, leather, metal buttons and bells, straps for the shaman's assistant to hold so that the shaman does not fall – a potentially fatal occurrence if the shaman is in the spirit world. Like the Nganasan shaman's parka it has three triangular flaps at the rear, representing a bird tail. Metal pendants represent deer, on which the shaman journeys to the sky, and a mythical bird called the bird (probably an eagle). Other creatures featured are an otter, a crane and a double figure of a man and woman. The coat is also hung with bells and a representation of a bird's wing-bone. The sleeves are fringed with fox and squirrel fur, representing feathers, and each sleeve has an iron band, representing wings, each with seven holes. There is no set number of pendants or fringes an Enets shaman's coat may have, but the only animals permitted are the ones listed here. The coat is augmented with a breast piece representing a bird's breastbone, decorated with tassels, bells, pendants, iron discs and other ornaments.

The shaman's head-dress is a cap comprising a headband with straps crossing at top of skull. The cap has four 'earrings' of dog and fox fur. At the front is a curved brass plate with nine projecting faces – these are the shaman's helper spirits. Also at the front is a brass projection representing the tip of a deer antler, a weapon against hostile shamans that is also used to part storm clouds. Hanging from the front is a fringe of leather strips. In addition to this the shaman has a blindfold, a piece of oval deer hide dyed red with a black border and two black spots for eyes – these represent the shaman's ability to see the spirit world.

Evenk shaman costumes

According to Shirokogoroff (1936: 288–9) the Evenk recognise two types of shamanic costume – the duck and reindeer, which are used in different types of performance. The duck is used for a shaman's journey to the upper world, the reindeer for travelling to the lower. The duck costume includes a deerskin or elk skin coat decorated with white reindeer hair, a long tail and leather fringes on the sleeves to represent wings. The coat may have coloured geometric designs – such as lines, circles or crosses – and may also be decorated with embroidered or metal representations of the skeleton of a duck, either the entire skeleton or a couple of bones representing the whole bird. The duck costume might also bear images of reindeer, elk, bear, wild boar, birds or human figures, and metal pendants. The costume usually has rows of bells arranged at front and back. The reindeer suit is made of the same material but without a tail. This type of coat is required to bear a complete skeleton of a reindeer made up of iron bones. Like the duck outfit the reindeer has images of various animals and anthropomorphic figures, but may also have a boat, a harpoon, a bow and arrow, representations of sun, moon, stars, thunder and the rainbow.

Both types of costume have soft leather strips symbolising snakes, usually with one at the back larger than the rest – the largest is the shaman's most important helper spirit. The other animals also represent spirits, and other images stand for things the shaman must negotiate on his spirit journey.

Tungus (Evenk) shaman. From Johann Gottlieb Georgi,
Bemerkungen einer Reise im Russischen *(1775).*

The costume of a female Tuvan shaman

A costume obtained from the grave of a Tuvan female shaman who died in 1958 is described by Diakonova (1996). The costume includes a small conical felt cap, lined with cloth. The top is trimmed with orange cloth and decorated with brocaded ribbon. A fringe made up of strings of coral, cornelian and blue glass beads, with a deer tooth at the lower end of each string, hangs from the fur brim. From the back of the cap dangle two ribbons tied with complete skins of ground squirrel and squirrel, with coloured cloth strips tied to each skin. At the front of the cap is a stylised face made from two cornelian beads for eyes and a nose of copper sheet rolled into cone. Two small copper triangles represent ears, with buttons and beads making earrings. Close to the ears are antlers made of copper tube, and a pair of eagle feathers. On the crown are nine cloth cylinders tipped with eagle-owl feathers, a row of four at each side and one at the apex.

The shaman's coat is a traditional Tuvan deerskin robe, with copper buttons and a number of plaits made of woollen thread twisted with different fabrics. The plaits represent snakes, which are helping spirits that expel disease spirits. They are red and black, signalling that the shaman has both good helping spirits and evil ones. The coat is also hung with three coloured pouches containing tobacco to aid ecstasy, copper pendants, tubes and bells, rattles, and the skin of a mink. The costume also has representations of wings.

Tuva shamans may also wear feathered headbands with or without human faces embroidered. These are found among other Mongol groups such as the Tofa (see below) and Uigurs (Diószegi 1961).

Tofa costume

The Tofa (also known as the Karagas) shaman wears a gown made from the skin of tame reindeer. Diószegi (1996) reports that one Tofa clan used three reindeer skins to make the basic gown. The gown is decorated with embroidery or appliqué, with metal, reindeer leather or cloth pendants. Some shamans have the cloth pendants permanently attached to their gowns, whereas others only attach them when about to shamanise. The metal pendants might be plates, bells or curved rods with tin cones or arrows hanging from them.

One of three types of head-dress may be worn: cap, crown or head band, of which the last is most common. Tofa head-dresses come in a range of colours and decoration. Headbands may be trimmed with white rabbit or lynx fur, or wild duck feathers, and topped with a row of three, seven or nine feathers from capercaillie, grouse, eagle, wild goose, crane or hawk. The type of feather varies from one clan to another, but all clans use eagle-owl feathers. Rolls of cotton or reindeer skin tipped with tassels decorate the sides. The bands themselves are decorated with embroidered or appliquéd faces, geometric designs or (occasionally) birds, though some are plain. Caps are made of triangular pieces of reindeer hair and white blue or yellow cotton, topped with duck feathers and trimmed with rabbit fur, with long ribbons hanging from the rim. Crowns are made up of a cloth headband and two iron bands that cross at the top of the head, with a plume at the point where they cross. Rolled cloth strips hang from the sides and wide ribbins depend from the back. Diószegi tells us that the type and decoration of Tofa head-dresses may depend on the shaman's clan. For instance, only two of the five Tofa clans wear the crown; while the type of feather worn on a headband is also determined by clan.

The decorations on Tofa shaman's gowns, according to, Diószegi

> ... constitute an integral unit... as a whole, they symbolized the human skeleton, consisting of the backbone, the chest, the shoulder-blades, the pelvis and bones of the arms and legs. The motifs on the fur-trimmed head-bands decorated with straight feathers symbolized parts of the human face and are probably the natural complements of the skeleton depicted on the clothing. (Diószegi 1996: 221–2)

In addition to these skeletal and facial features, the decoration includes the nipples and navel. Decoration on shamans' boots continued the skeletal theme. Diószegi also notes the leather plaits and ribbons attached to the gown were thought of as bird tails and wings, while some costumes had bunches of feathers attached to the back – these were also bird wings and tails.

A Sakha shaman suit

Vladimir Diachenko (1994) tells us that the costume of a Sakha shaman is designed to represent a horse. The shaman wears a horse skin cap and a robe made of the skin of a foal or fully-grown horse, with metal pendants and a long fringe. The robe has metal rings at the back to which reins are fastened for the shaman's assistants to hold during the performance, as the shaman gallops and bucks like a horse.

The Shaman's Costume

Sakha shaman, early twentieth century.

The shaman's drum

In addition to the costume, shamans have a variety of other tools at their disposal, of which the most important is usually the drum. When people think of shamanism, more often than not they will think of drums. Not all varieties of Eurasian shamanism make use of the drum, but where they do the instrument is invested with great power and importance. Eurasian shaman drums tend to be of one basic type – a shallow, circular or elliptical hooped wooden band over which animal skin is stretched. The wooden rim is braced with a cross piece which also serves as the grip. Usually the drum skin is illustrated with pictures of people, spirits or animals, or cosmological scenes.

The following examples will give a good idea of the typical Eurasian shaman drum. A Nganasan drum is an ovoid frame covered with wild deer skin. The grip is tied to four iron staples on the hoop; representing the shoulder blades of a wild deer – indeed, the drum is actually considered to be a wild deer. The skin of one drum has red drawings representing the shaman and his sons and daughters (though not his wife), polar fox, and sledges; and black drawings of a wolf and a cross which represents the drum grip. The picture of a wolf showed that the shaman had killed a wolf and so could protect deer against wolves. Nganasan drumsticks fall into two types. Each is like a bent wooden shovel with a human face painted on the grip. One type is partly covered with skin from the leg of a wild deer, and is supposed to help in descent to the lower world. The other is covered with the skin from a deer horn, and is meant to assist the ascent to the upper world. The drumsticks are used for divination: if the shaman throws the stick and it falls face up, it is a good omen (Dolgikh 1996). Tuvan drums are also elliptical. The handle is a carved representation of a shaman holding a drum, with a head dress and wide open mouth. The drum skin is painted red. Seven pendants hang from the crosspiece, three and four on either side respectively (Diakonova 1996). The Tuvan drum is considered to be a horse: a special ceremony for enlivening the drum treats the instrument as horse to be tamed (Vajnštein 1996a). The Tuvan drumstick is a spoon shaped object made from birch wood. The end is covered in skin from a wild goat's leg; inside bowl are metal strips arranged like the branches of a fir tree, with three sets of discs attached by rings (Diakonova 1996). Among the Enets the shaman's drum is ovoid, made of larch and deer hide – the skin of a doe for a female shaman, buck for a man. The drumhead is illustrated inside and out with red and black pictures – a large circle representing the circle of the of world, mountains, sun, moon and 'sky people'. Because of its power the Enets do not usually refer directly to the drum; it is usually spoken of elliptically. The shaman drum of the Saami is especially interesting. Drums used by the Saami *noaide* are cosmological diagrams, illustrated with pictures of the cosmic tree, the horizon and constellations, along with deities, animals and spirits. As well as being an aid to shamanising the drum is used for divination. Objects such as rings or pieces of reindeer antler are placed upon the skin and their movement among the pictures is noted when the drum is beaten.

In terms of execution and sheer variety of pictorial content Saami drums are probably the most consistently elaborate – in sharp

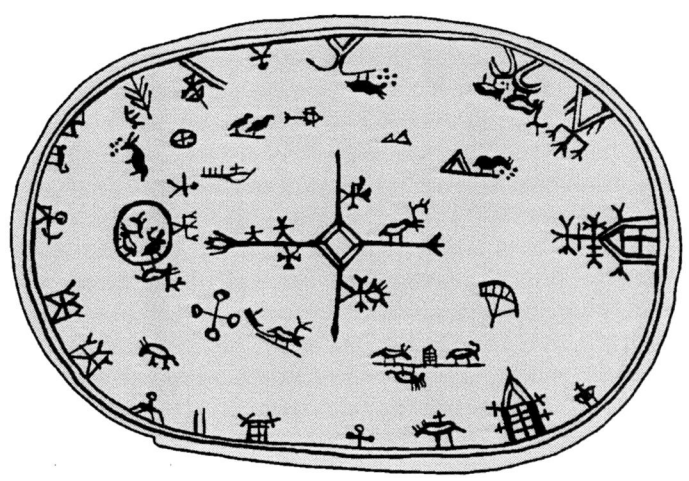

Saami shaman drum of c. 1700. After Rydving (1991).

contrast to other ethnically Uralic peoples, whose shaman drums are usually plain. They may include animals such as bear, reindeer, fox, lynx and various species of bird. Hunting and fishing scenes are fairly common (Kjellström 1991), while painted snakes and zig-zags and other designs parallel motifs from Finnish rock art (Autio 1991). Some drums portray figures and scenes from everyday settlement life, a type that appears to be connected with Saami resistance to Christianisation in the seventeenth and eighteenth centuries (Rydving 1991). These and less confrontational drums may also show figures from Saami myth. But the most striking type of representation is astronomical. Bo Sommarström (1987, 1991) has shown that many Saami drums are stylised star maps that may have been used for orientation. Those constellations recognised by the Saami are placed around a cross that seems to represent simultaneously the cardinal points and the horizon bisected by the World Tree, with its top in the heavens and its roots in the underworld. According to Sommarström this could be used for locating the direction of game animals, so that the drum functioned as a kind of compass, adding a further aspect to its divinatory function. During performance the Saami *noaide* would drum until a state of ecstasy was reached then lie prone covered with the drum.

Why is the drum so important to some shamanist peoples? Uzbek and Khazak shamans do not use drums at all but play stringed instruments while performing their shamanic duties. Some shamans employ rattles or, like the Darkhat, the Jew's harp (Diószegi 1963). Others use drums but place much less importance on them – drums may be communal rather than being the special property of one shaman. However, most Eurasian shamans – as well as the Inuit of North America – prefer the drum. Those that do attribute magical properties to the instrument, and to them it is highly significant. Eliade notes the importance of the materials of which drums are made. The wood is taken from a tree which is analogous to the World Tree, the cosmic centre; the drum skin is taken from an animal which may represent an ancestral creature, a tribal or clan emblem, or may be associated with travel to the spirit worlds. These are important factors. The drum skin is ritually activated, brought back to life as the animal ancestor, and the shaman becomes this creature during performance. The drum's components and symbols allow the shaman to fly to the Cosmic Tree, where the wood has its primal origins and where the shaman's animal ancestor lived in mythical times, in a subterranean area close to its roots. For Eliade, the implications are profound:

> ... by virtue of his mystical relations with the 'reanimated' skin of the drum, the shaman is able to share in the nature of the theriomorphic ancestor; in other words, he can abolish time and re-establish the primordial condition of which the myths tell... we are in the presence of a mystical experience that allows the shaman to transcend time and space. Both metamorphosis into the animal ancestor and the shaman's ascensional ecstasy represent different but homologizable expressions of one and the same experience – transcendence of the profane condition, re-establishment of a 'paradisal' existence lost in the depths of mythical time. (Eliade 1964: 171)

This probably tells us more about Eliade's personal preoccupation with 'transcendence of the profane condition' than it does about the properties attributed to the shaman's drum. For one thing, not all drums bear 'ascensional symbols' and not all drums are identified with a clan totem or animal ancestor. For another, a spirit journey is as often to the land of the dead as it is to the celestial realms. Some images painted on drum skins are indeed 'ascensional' but others are associated with descent to the underworld or are significant in an entirely different way, such as the wolf on the Nganasan drum mentioned above. However, despite his overblown

The Shaman's Costume

Left: *Teleut shaman drum now in the Museum of Anthropology and Ethnology, St Petersburg.*
Right: *Khakas shaman drum, nineteenth century.*

fantasy of the transcendent nature of the shaman's ecstasy Eliade is correct to make so much of the drum. It is often the steed on which the shaman makes a spirit journey. Among the Sakha, Buryat and Tuvans the drum is regarded as a horse, while other peoples such as the Tofa call it a deer, and these are believed to be the animals ridden by the shaman in ecstasy. (The drum's role in inducing ecstasy is discussed in chapter 5.) The drum is also frequently a representation of the cosmos, a map to help guide the shaman in the spirit realms. While rarely as ornate or visually striking as the more impressive types of shaman costume, it is generally accorded a healthy respect by the laity and is treated with great care, as befits such an important item of the shaman's magic toolkit.

The shaman's staff

Another important magical item is the shaman's staff. The staff could be utilised in performance instead of a drum, though it could also have other functions. Among the Enets, for instance, the shaman's staff – made of iron, with the lower end usually shaped like deer hoof – was used to treat sick and conduct dead to lower world (Prokofyeva 1963). Less impressively, Goldi shamans use staffs that resemble the sticks used for driving dog-drawn sleighs (Shirokogoroff 1935: 295).

There are three main types of staff used among the Darkhat, though all are made of juniper or birch. One type has two branches, like a pitchfork, joined by a cord and decorated with metal rings, coloured cloth strips and tassels, and metal cones. Another type has three forks like a trident, with similar decorations. The third kind of staff is carved into the likeness of a horse's head at the top and with legs and hooves carved at appropriate positions. These usually have a bundle of cloth at the neck and are hung with metal cones. Some of these staffs are double headed. Such implements are used in the same way as drums by new shamans who are too poor to afford a costume, though they also wear a ritual head dress. Tuvan shamans use a three-forked staff similar to the Darkhat one. Each tine has a metal ring attached, from each of which hang three metal cones. The staff has nine notches in the shaft. Two rolled strips of cloth are attached to the place where the forks meet – these are the reins of the staff, which is imagined as the shaman's steed (Diószegi 1963). The staff is the first item received by a new Tuvan shaman, but is superseded by a drum as the shaman's powers increase (Vajnštein 1996a).

Shirokogoroff (1935: 291, 296) tells us that Evenk shaman staffs are considered either horses or reindeer. Diószegi (1968a) points out that the shaman staff is not found among all branches of the Evenk. He adds that they sometimes represent men and may be made of wood or iron. The wooden staffs are made in pairs. They are decorated with iron rings and cones, ribbons and fringes. As with the Tuvan staff, the Evenk ones are supposed to be the beast the shaman rides in ecstasy. The preponderance of horse imagery on the Siberian shaman staffs of Mongol and Tungusic peoples is interesting – horse staffs are also used by Buryat shamans, for example – and speaks of the key role played by animals important to the traditional economies of various ethnic groups. The reindeer herding Evenk of the forests prefer reindeer imagery, while related peoples on or closer to steppe opt for the horse. However, the Siberian shaman's horse staff suggests the horse head 'sceptres' – stone heads apparently designed to fit onto a wooden staff or handle – associated with the Eastern European Eneolithic, in the fifth and fourth millennia BCE. Evidence suggests that they could be the earliest known representations of domesticated horses. Dragos Gheorgiu (1994) links these artefacts with the Indo-European Divine Twins, who were associated with horses and seem also to have been linked with ritual transvestism – for instance, Tacitus (*Germania* 43) reports that among the Naharvali priests of the Alci, the Germanic Dioskuroi, were ornamented like women. The context of horse domestication and ritual transvestism hints at a common origin for the Indo-European and Siberian horse-headed staffs or sceptres. The pairing of horse and reindeer staffs among the Evenk and the double-headed horse staffs of the Darkhat is a further pointer in that direction. Although at present it is unclear where this clue might lead – if indeed it leads anywhere – the obvious suspects are the nomadic, equestrian steppe cultures from whom later sprang peoples such as the Scythians and Mongols. As things stand it is anyone's guess as to whether either kind of horse staff derives from shamanism or was simply a by-product of horse domestication. Diószegi (1968a) concludes that the Evenk shaman staff was adopted from the neighbouring Buryat, along with a ritual whip that was derived ultimately from Tibetan Buddhism. However, he does not expand his investigation of the staff beyond the Evenk and Buryat regions.

Spirits

Shamans generally command at least a few spirits. Some shamans might have a veritable army of spirits at their disposal. While some, like the spirits inherited by a Saami *noaide*, are invisible – or perhaps merely notional – most are visually represented in some way. We have already seen how some are represented as part of the shaman's costume. In many cases it would also be accurate to say that the shaman's drum or staff are also spirits. Aside from these, representations of Siberian shamans' spirits come in a fairly wide range of forms. Just as their names and images vary, so do their functions. Shamans' spirits may be animal helpers, protectors, warriors or even ancestors, especially ancestral shamans. Sometimes shamans will take certain spirits into their own bodies and address those present at a performance (see chapter 5 for a discussion of apparent possession in Eurasian shamanism). But it is more usual for the spirits just to do the shaman's bidding or act as 'minders' while the shaman is travelling in the spirit worlds. There are many types and styles of spirits and their images across the range of Eurasian shamanism and it would require a lengthy catalogue to do them justice. Here are just a couple of examples.

Among the Tuvans the term *eeren* is used to denote both a spirit and its material representation, though the representation alone is known as a *lekan*. The *lekan* is usually figurative rather than abstract. An *eren* may be animal or human, and its *lekan* can be made from animal skin, cloth, felt, metal or wood. The *eeren* is treated with great respect, honoured with decorations of ribbons, plaited hair and beads, and given offerings of food and drink. Some natural phenomena, such as rainbows, and ritual objects are also thought to be *eerens*. Most are animals, however. The role of the *eeren* is to ward off or expel the disease spirits. Not all *eerens* belonged to shamans, though some – such as that of the powerful bear spirit – could only be owned by a shaman, and a strong one at that (Vajnštein 1996b).

The Evenk, along with the Buryat and other Mongol peoples, make use of masks to represent a particular type of spirit. The Evenk call it *abagaldai*, while the Buryat know it as *awagaldai* (it is also known as *šowoki* and related words meaning 'god,' 'idol,' 'guardian-' or 'master-spirit,' 'icon' and so on, though *abagaldai* and its cognates seems to be the main name). The name is of Mongol origin, from *abaga* 'uncle' and the personal name suffix *–ldai*. It has no etymology in the Tungusic languages, which suggests that the *abagaldai* originated in Mongol shamanism. Although they come in different sizes *abagaldai* are usually made of sheet copper, some with rolled copper cones in place of ears, slits for eyes and mouth, a rudimentary nose and sometimes decorations such as tassels and fringes. Occasionally these mask spirits are made of wood, painted and decorated with beards and other features. Some Buryat have a similar mask spirit known as a *börtö*, though this sort is usually wooden and may comprise a carved head rather than a mask. Traditionally the *börtö* represents the clan's ancestor whose head was preserved by his son, a shaman. A *börtö* may be owned by anyone, not just shamans – it is a clan protector rather than a shaman's tutelary spirit. The *abagaldai*, on the other hand, has an important role in shamanising; the shaman may wear an *abagaldai* mask and impersonate the spirit. The *abagaldai*'s background is unclear, but it seems to represent the spirit of an ancestral shaman (Diószegi 1967).

Opening the sacred wardrobe

These few examples show clearly that shaman costumes have no fixed composition, even where basic structure is very similar. The starting point is evidently normal ethnic costume – for instance, the Tuvan example is built around an everyday robe, although it may be cut differently from a normal one (Diakanova 1994). The Saami shaman wears the same clothing as everyone else, except for a magic belt, and may perform stripped to the waist, as in one account of around 1700 (Hultkrantz 1992). The Inuit shaman (*angakok*) has been known to perform naked or wearing only a belt, though masks and other props are employed and the *angakok* might perform hidden from view under a blanket, hood or cloak (Hunt 14-43; Merkur 1985). Evidence is difficult to find for Prokofyeva's idea of the complete animal skin as an archaic mode of costume, except that some of the costumes described above are made of deerskin that might conceivably belong to only one deer. And in Eurasia there is no definitive sign of the complete skin from an animal's head being used as a shaman's headgear. Truly ancient and shaman costumes are conspicuously absent from the archaeological record and illustrations from as long ago as Witsen's book of 1692 clearly do not show costumes made from complete animal skins as Prokofyeva asserts. Although Witsen's Evenk shaman is shown with a headpiece – evidently created from the upper half of a deer's head, complete with horns, ears and eyes – it is not the complete skin of the head. (Witsen's shaman also has what appears to be boots made from a bear's feet. But they are shown as if they are the shaman's own feet, in much the same vein as René Magritte's famous painting of a pair of boots which look like naked human feet – which conflicts with Pavlinskaya's ideas too.) It is hard to accept Prokofyeva's claim.

While there are clearly distinct types of shaman costume, they do not appear to fall into such easy categories as Pavlinskaya believes. For a start, the skeletal design of Tofa costumes is neither bear nor deer: it is human. Enets shamans only wear costumes to travel to the sky. Nganasan shamans might have up to three different costumes each, and Diakanova (1994) tells us that Tuvan shamans can have two, with one reserved for really important work. Furthermore, the Yakut shaman costume is closely identified with the horse, not deer or bear – a new suit is 'broken in' like a wild horse, and when forged the metal pendants are tempered in mare's blood. During performance the shaman acts like a horse and his assistants hold onto the reins attached to his robe. In fact, equine themes pervade Yakut shamanism. This reflects the importance of horses to Yakut life and economy. For instance, the horse plays a part in creation mythology and is central to indigenous Yakut religion; Yakut shamans do not perform without the actual or symbolic presence of a horse. In effect, the horse plays the same part in Yakut religion as the deer does for some other Siberian peoples.

Plainly, the shaman's costume is a matter of local culture and tradition – but local custom might not necessarily require a strict adherence to time-honoured formulae. In various Siberian contexts there is free and open borrowing between ethnic groups – for instance, Nganasan shamans are known to sometimes adopt Evenk paraphernalia, just as Nganasan novice shamans have been known to study under experienced Evenk shamans. Quite clearly the shaman's costume is of vital importance to shamans within traditions where costumes are important, for the reasons suggested by Eliade, Diakonova and other scholars.

But where does that leave those shamans for whom costume is not especially important, such as the Saami, Inuit and Teleut? Or those like the Chukchi, whose costume consists of little more than ornaments held together by a few strips of fabric? Why should the eminently useful magic costume of the sort worn by Tuva, Nganasan or Evenk shamans be absent among practitioners who perform exactly the same feats as shamans in those cultures and who even have ethnic affinities with one or other of them? Eliade neatly sidesteps the problem:

> The important point is that the experience does not take place with the shaman wearing his profane, everyday dress. Even where a costume does not exist, it is replaced by the cap, the belt, the drum, and other magical objects, which form part of the shaman's sacred wardrobe and which substitute for a costume proper. (Eliade 1964: 146)

This is not a satisfactory answer. If the magical objects Eliade suggests are really substitutes for a proper costume, why are they too present – and evidently considered necessary, not mere accessories – for shamans who do wear a full costume of special head-dress, gloves, boots and a coat with perhaps dozens of magic pendants and other components? In the context all Eliade is really saying is that people whose profession is religion or magic usually have some item worn during ritual or performance that protects, helps control spirits, or enables transformation and spirit journeys. They also set the practitioner apart from the rest of the community during ritual or performance – in Eliade's view, dividing the sacred from the profane. There is also a degree of truth in Mikhailowski's claim that the costume and its accoutrements are designed to instil awe – and Shirokogoroff (1935: 302) and Eliade (1964: 147) agree. But this does not explain the enormous differences between shamans' ritual dress, or lack of it, in different cultures. Almost all shamans use the drum in the shamanist *locus classicus*, Siberia and Central Asia, where it is emphatically *not* a substitute for a costume but a potent object in its own right. As the drum has almost exactly the same function among the Evenk and Nganasan as it does for the Saami and Inuit there is no

The Shaman's Costume

Goldi shaman coat now in the American Museum of Natural History.

basis for assuming it to be a mere substitute for a costume among the latter two peoples.

According to Pavlinskaya's view the shaman costume is based on a symbolic system that can be traced back to ancient rock art. This is obviously relevant to the idea that the Palaeolithic cave paintings of Europe represent an ancient magico-religious system that has survived to some extent among present-day hunting peoples, a mainstay of recent studies of ancient rock art and a perennial favourite among shamanologists and historians of religion. Whether the ancient art in question really is related to shamanism as it is known and studied by modern anthropologists is a question that will be addressed later in this book. Siberian rock art is another matter entirely, as it certainly relates to peoples ancestral to many historical Siberian ethnic groups. However, although numerous figures with bird or animal heads and other non-human features are depicted in Siberian rock art there is usually great uncertainty as to their date and no way of telling if they were intended to represent costumed shamans or something else entirely. And the further removed in time the more difficult it is to interpret whatever symbolic meaning they might once have had or to reach even tentative conclusions concerning their relationship to known shamanic imagery among specific ethnic groups in more recent times (Hoppál 1985: 132-149).

The problem of interpreting the structure and symbolism of Eurasian shaman costumes is compounded by the fact that some peoples, particularly those of South Siberia and Central Asia, have incorporated non-shamanist elements into their costumes. For example, Mongol shaman coats sometimes have triangular flaps hanging from the underside of the sleeves and high collars, derived from the cloaks of Tibetan lamas, and some head-dresses have borrowed pennons from Lamaist headgear (Diószegi 1961). Presumably these items were adopted for specific reasons, but it must be recognised that these loans are themselves part of a magico-religious costume, the vestments of Lamaism. The sleeve flaps are much like wings; and the pennons could double for feathers. As for the Lamaist collar, perhaps we should bear in mind that in their basic design shamans' coats are not so different from the coats worn by ordinary people. Without meaning to be glib – after all, the type of clothing worn by the indigenous peoples of Eurasia has changed over the millennia – the collar could just be a ritual fashion statement.

Power dressing

The shaman costume is a set of garments that has multiple functions. Typology and putative prehistoric origins aside, even the six ethnic costumes described as examples here show that not all costumes do the same things. Some are designed for upper world travel, some for journeys to the lower realm. Some have more spirits associated with them than others have. Some have symbolic weapons and others do not. Historically, many shamans have worn iron breastplates that were considered to possess great power, though these now are uncommon. There are many permutations, variations between ethnic groups and between clans; and one group may have several different types of shaman, each with their own style of costume.

A costume may be a suit of armour, a means of transport, a repository of helpful spirits, a map of the worlds in which the shaman travels, a disguise, a means of transformation – even an image of the shaman's person. At its most elaborate the shaman's costume can be all those things. It is also an emblem of liminality, signifying that the shaman is a person who is outside the normal social and cosmic rules. Even where the shaman's costume consists only of nakedness it emphasises the shaman's status as a dweller between worlds, an 'attribute of the state of being outside society (Hoppál 2001).

Eliade makes an interesting suggestion:

> In itself the costume represents a religious microcosm qualitatively different from the surrounding profane space. For one thing it constitutes an almost complete symbolic system; for another, its consecration has impregnated it with various spiritual forces and especially with 'spirits'. By the mere fact of donning it – or manipulating the objects that deputize for it – the shaman transcends profane space and prepares to enter into contact with the spiritual world. (Eliade 1964: 147)

This brings a startling but not wholly inappropriate image to mind. The more elaborate shaman's costume is in effect a device for travelling to other worlds, a kind of metaphysical inter-dimensional craft with the shaman at its controls, built-in weaponry, protective structures, navigation systems and even stealth capability. I am not for one moment suggesting that Doctor Who is a shaman – though in some respects there is an uncanny resemblance – nor that shamanic costume is a relic of colonisation by ancient space-travelling aliens or the degenerate memory of the technology of a lost civilisation. I am merely pointing out that the underlying concerns are exactly the same: taking precautions and developing procedures for existing in a hostile and largely unknown environment. The shaman's costume is strange enough to inspire dread and awe in equal measures but it is a fact that no part of a costume is specifically designed to do that. Everything is there to ensure the shaman's survival as far as it is possible to do so, to give the shaman power over spirits and to perform other functions so that the job can be done. Even the Saami and Inuit shamans, with no costume to speak of, have the tools they need painted on their drums and represented in other paraphernalia.

In this respect shamanism is really all about dressing for success. Each element of costume and equipment has a specific significance, but the ethnographies make it abundantly clear that in terms of the shaman's tasks the significance is wholly practical. It also communicates to the shaman's people the nature of the ritual and the power of the shaman. 'A shaman's equipment is an extension not only of the shaman's person but in particular of his or her capacity to act' (Vitebsky 2001: 82). The whole ensemble is certainly more than the sum of its parts.

5: JOURNEYING TO OTHER WORLDS

Performing rites

To begin with I will use the term 'ecstasy' as a convenient way of referring to trance, ritual intoxication and the various forms of what Harner (1980) calls the 'shamanic state of consciousness' – the defining characteristic of shamanism.

When Harner uses that term he is drawing partly upon his personal experience with the drug *ayahuasca* among the Shuar. But he is also following the shamanic gospel according to Eliade, like very nearly everyone who has ever studied shamanism since the 1950s. For Eliade, ecstasy is a timeless, free-floating state of communion with divinity. But for a shaman ecstasy is really only a means to an end. It is a method for entering other worlds, the realms where spirits and gods dwell, the land of the dead. The true central part of shamanism is the journey made by a shaman's spirit to those places that are believed to exist somewhere outside or alongside the world humans normally inhabit. This is where shamans do their real work. A shamanic performance – which anthropologists often called a séance – is designed to place the shaman in a peculiar state that allows them to journey to the supernatural worlds. The shaman needs to do this so that they can retrieve the souls of sick members of their community, neutralise the spirits that cause disease, commune with gods and spirits on behalf of their people, and influence the spirits that control the fertility of herds and game animals. Shamans may also travel to the spirit worlds to do battle with hostile shamans.

The means of inducing ecstasy varies according to the shaman's culture. The most common methods are drumming, dancing and chanting. Some shamans use alcohol or psychoactive plants to induce the desired state. Some use more than one of these methods together. Other shamans do not claim to enter an altered state at all, but mime the spirit journey and what takes place along the way. A shaman might be transformed into the likeness of an animal, as a disguise or to better navigate the spirit world. This might be believed to be an effect of their altered state of consciousness, or it might be facilitated by the images on a shaman's costume. The shaman needs some form of transport to the sky or the lower world and either the costume or drum may function as a vehicle or steed. The costume and drum, together or separately, also serve as the shaman's map of the cosmos and allow navigation to and within the other worlds. However, the main element is the ritual itself, the shaman's performance, which is invariably conducted before an audience. That is where all elements of costume, paraphernalia, method and purpose come together with the shaman's unique nature in the context of a social event when the shaman attains ecstasy and temporarily leaves this world for another.

The importance of public performance to shamanism should not be underestimated.

> The shamanic séance is not only a public ceremony, but a real theatrical event in its own right, in which many spectators participate with great apprehension, in so far as they expect a result of special importance for the whole tribe. (Corradi Musi 1995: 35)

The similarity of shamanic performance to a theatrical production has often been remarked. Tae-gon Kim breaks shamanic performance down into five elements: taboos and purification relating to the ritual space; ritual timing; offerings; the performance itself; the 'break rite', the ceremonial conclusion of the performance (Kim 1995). It is immediately evident that this structure corresponds well with what happens in modern theatre. The taboos and ritual preparation of the shaman's performance space is similar to the organisation of a theatre for a play – construction of scenery, the rituals performed by actors, a notoriously superstitious profession. For ritual timing read 'opening night,' 'last night' and so on. The offerings made by the shaman, assistants and clients are paralleled by good luck messages and the box-office takings. The play equates to the shaman's performance. And the 'break rite' for the theatre is made up of applause and curtain calls, flowers for the cast, and the first night party. All that is missing from the shaman's performance is the critic – though there are always anthropologists.

This similarity is hardly surprising. Modern Western theatre has its origins in ancient Greek theatre, which was originally a form of religious celebration, as is well documented; and the medieval mystery plays, in which actors played out Biblical tales, also as an act of worship. Although modern plays have a wholly different purpose – they are essentially entertainment, no matter what some critics might think – there is a degree of similarity between actor and shaman. Both engage in transforming themselves into something or someone else. And while performing each exists in a place that is simultaneously in this world and somewhere beyond it. But while they are immersed in their make-believe world actors do not do the things that a shaman does. Likewise, the theatre audience might suspend disbelief but they do not actually believe that what is happening on stage is real. When the play is over and the after-show drinks are finished, they go home having been entertained – no lives have been saved, no sickness healed, no herds protected, and the actors have not risked life and sanity in the service of their community.

However, some scholars play down the importance of performance in shamanism. Jonathan Horwitz even claims that 'there is no performance in the shamanic healing ritual':

> ... if the division between the audience and the actors disappears, where then is the performance? It, too, has disappeared. That is, in order to have a performance, it is necessary to have both actors and audience. If the *audience* becomes actors – that is, *participants* – then there is no performance, and this is exactly the case with the so-called shamanic healing performance. (Horwitz 1995: 240)

Horwitz' claim is based on the idea that in shamanic rites there can be a high level of interaction between shaman and onlookers. The audience might join in the ritual songs, welcome the returned soul of a sick person, or be healed as a community. Furthermore shamans do not see themselves as separate from the audience in the way actors do. But this is a questionable viewpoint. For one thing, healing is only one of the things a shaman does. We should perhaps not expect quite the same party atmosphere for a Siberian shamanising designed to counter hostile magic as for the Amerindian medicine ceremonies Horwitz cites in evidence. And while I agree that shamans are not the same as actors putting on a play, participation has nothing to do with defining performance. Evidently Horwitz has never seen or heard of *The Rocky Horror Show* – every night of which is a celebratory event in which audience participation both defines and enhances the performance. (There are numerous other examples of this in theatre and the analogy should perhaps be extended to include sporting events.) Horwitz is assuming that 'performance' is used of shamans solely in the theatrical sense – yet it is clear that in ethnography and studies of shamanism the word is used in several senses, all of which are contextually valid.

Anna-Leena Siikala asserts that 'the shamanizing séance, the ritual performance embodying the shaman's public activity, is the key to understanding the whole ideology behind shamanism' (Siikala 1987: 28). This may be going a little too far, but the performance is certainly of crucial importance to an understanding of shamanism. Whatever the purpose of a performance might be, the performance itself is the culmination of long and arduous initiation, learning, practice and preparation. It is the shaman's *raison d'être*, the dangerous and difficult activity for which only a shaman is fit and ready. As we have seen in previous chapters the shaman's costume and paraphernalia are laden with symbolism and magical power. The whole assemblage is itself an embodiment of the rules by which a shaman practises, an aid to magical travel and a means of empowerment within the strange worlds the shaman experiences while in a state of ecstasy.

The whole point of the shaman's performance is that it is a public display of the shaman's magical skills, the exercise of those abilities on behalf of and in front of the shaman's community. The most important of those abilities is ecstasy, the release of the shaman's spirit and its journey to the spirit worlds. Ecstasy is a thorny issue. It is popularly believed to involve an alteration in the shaman's consciousness through a natural predisposition to enter trance, or a technique of inducing an altered state by drumming and dancing, or the use of hallucinogenic substances. Many anthropologists and other academics make the same assumption. Another view is that the shaman's performance is merely clever play-acting, a display of thespian skill and legerdemain aimed at fooling people into believing that something magical is really taking place. While this may seem to offer a fairly straightforward choice between genuine ecstasy and shamming shamans, things are not quite that simple.

Hultkrantz (1979: 91) has identified types of shamanic performance that he calls 'imitative' and 'demonstrative' shamanism. (Hultkrantz is discussing Native American shamanism, though the idea is just as applicable to the Eurasian forms.) In the first the shaman does not usually claim to actually attain an altered state of consciousness as we might superficially understand the term. The journey and what occurs along the way are acted out for the audience. The shaman might mime climbing a tree or paddling a canoe, for instance. Yet during performance the shaman's community accept that an otherworld journey is indeed happening.

Journeying to Other Worlds

A seventeenth century depiction of the Saami noaide *in action.*

Demonstrative shamanism may or may not involve ecstasy, but it also includes actions that show to the audience that something of a supernatural nature really is going on. The shaman might produce objects by sleight of hand, or indulge in voice throwing or imitating the voices of spirits or animals. At the end of the performance an object meant to be a retrieved soul or vanquished disease spirit might be held aloft for all to see.

Imitative shamanism (or demonstrative shamanism, where it takes place without an accompanying alteration of consciousness) clearly conflicts with Eliade's axiomatic identification of shamanism as religious ecstasy. According to that view they should not be classed as shamanism at all. Yet if all other features of 'classical' shamanism are present imitative shamanism can be in essence identical in every respect but one – the ecstatic state – to what Eliade and most other scholars of the past century consider shamanism to be. With that one exception imitative shamanism can meet all the criteria of even the most stringent definitions of shamanism.

So is imitative shamanism – or imitative shamanism with a demonstrative element – really shamanism? The answer to that question depends on establishing the nature of the shaman's state of consciousness during performance. What is ecstasy? Is ecstasy the same as trance? What relation does ritual intoxication have to these? And how do these relate to performance?

Trance, ecstasy and altered states of consciousness

The interpretation of shamanic ecstasy has bifurcated since the end of the nineteenth century. One school, represented by the likes of Eliade, Campbell and Harner, sees it in religious terms, communion with a spiritual realm that can be accessed by manoeuvring the mind into a receptive state. The other considers ecstasy as the creative use of a neurological malfunction – for instance, Lewis (1989) discusses shamanic trance and ecstasy in mainly medical terms. However, the two forked paths have now come together again. Instead of the mystical and the medical as two polar opposite explanations for ecstasy there is now a school of thought that sees ecstasy as a neuropsychological condition, perhaps genetically determined, that allows us to interface with 'God,' whatever that might be (Newberg, d'Aquili and Rause 2001).

The use of the word 'ecstasy' can be misleading. English speakers tend to use the word fairly casually to denote extreme happiness or intense sensations of physical pleasure rather than in reference to the experience of being outside one's body. With regard to shamanism the word is used by English-speakers more specifically to refer to the perception of the consciousness (or personality, or spirit) being separated from the body and the normal world. The word 'trance' is also used to denote the same state. But the two words have different meanings. *Ecstasy* (from Greek *ekstasis*, 'standing apart') literally refers to the perception that one's consciousness or personality is no longer attached to the body but is located outside it.

Trance (from Latin *transire*, 'to go across', used in late Latin as a euphemism for death) basically signifies a death-like state, stupor, insensibility. These meanings are mirrored in Modern English usage. We speak of being 'beside oneself' with an extreme emotion, and the dead are said to have 'passed over.' Moreover, we know exactly what we mean by ecstasy and trance: for most people ecstasy is a state of unusual emotion or stimulation, usually pleasurable, in which we feel that we have transcended our normal existence. But we would say that someone dull, unresponsive and sluggish was 'in a trance.' In short, ecstasy is an out-of-body experience while trance is a state of sensory inactivity that resembles death.

This brings us to a major problem. There is clearly more than one kind of shamanic state of mind. Saami shamans are described as entering a death-like state in performance: from an account of around 1700 the shaman 'falls down dead to the ground and remains lying there breathless for three quarters of an hour' (Hultkrantz 1992), a typical description. It is while in this physically inert state that a Saami shaman journeys to the spirit world. Yakut shamans, on the other hand, are supposedly actually in an ecstatic state and their spirits are in another world while they dance and drum (Zornickaja 1996). Most people who write about ecstasy and trance in relation to shamanism use the words interchangeably and generally treat them as synonyms. Where a distinction is attempted further confusion is likely to arise. For instance, in a discussion of trance and ecstasy the French scholar Roberte N. Hamayon includes her compatriot Gilbert Rouget's distinction between the two conditions. According to Rouget, ecstasy is indicated by 'immobility, silence, solitude, no crisis, sensory deprivation, recollection, hallucinations'; while the characteristics of trance are 'movement, noise, in company, crisis, sensory overstimulation, amnesia, no hallucinations' (Hamayon 1995; Rouget 1985: 11). These definitions are the exact reverse of what we would expect from a consideration of the English nouns. Just to complicate matters further, Hamayon also cites Éveline Lot-Falck's division of trance into two types, 'dramatic' and 'cataleptic' (Hamayon 1995), which correspond pretty much with the contrasting Saami and Yakut examples given here. The taxonomic variation exemplified by these two typologies does not exactly help Hamayon's discussion. But at least Lot-Falck and Rouget recognises that more than one psychological and/or physical state may be involved. There are many possible other categories of trance or ecstasy as they occur in shamanism in Eurasia and North America. Hultkrantz (1996) wisely points out that much of the confusion and contradiction with regard to these phenomena is down to semantics, with for instance 'the term "ecstasy" being used by students of religion and ethnology, the term "trance" by psychopathologists and parapsychologists' – they are really one and the same thing. But what is it? And how can one neuropsychological state express itself in so many different ways?

Nowadays neuropsychological explanations are invoked for these phenomena, or they are related to brain structure and function. For instance:

> Our usual conception of the shaman is, indeed, that he employs monotonous effects to fall into ecstasy and arrive at the state of trance: he sings and dances alone, or along with others. The auditory stimulations and the motoric movements, in increasing intensity, and the emotional induction from the crowd around him result in his falling into a trance in the end, and the disconnecting of higher cerebral centers: his 'soul' journeys, released from the body. (Nordland 1967: 168)

In Nordland's view the shaman experiences 'the unreal' as a result of self-inflicted sensory and social deprivation allied with lengthy repetition of a physical task, a dissociated, dream-like condition much like 'cabin fever,' 'mountain fever' or the 'runner's high.' We would nowadays add other potential factors to Nordland's model, such as increased endorphin production, reduced blood sugar or hyperventilation. However, shamanism is not always a physically demanding occupation. What are we to make of types of shamanism where there is no great physical exertion on the shaman's part and no intoxicants are consumed but where trance or ecstasy are believed to take place? Uzbek shamans perform while seated but still attain ecstasy – and as some Uzbek shamans are elderly women it is not surprising that there isn't much jumping and running around involved.

Conversely, there are a many instances of shamans who perform strenuously but evidently do not experience any alteration of consciousness other than those normally experienced through physical exercise and deep concentration. Consider this report of Oken, a Kazakh shaman from the late nineteenth century:

> As he played he became more and more inspired and moved his bow more strongly; perhaps, he already had forgotten us and all that surrounded him... It seemed he already played

unconsciously and came into ecstasy... he shook in convulsions and wriggled badly, uttering at the same time crazy sounds and hiccuping loudly as if he had eaten a whole ram with bones... he twitched his shoulders, and there was foam on his twisted mouth. Now he was completely mad; he crept along the floor and sometimes cried out incantations in a threatening way; suddenly he pulled his head back and showed the whites of his eyes. (Quoted in Basilov 1994: 288)

Instead of a drum Oken played a stringed instrument with a bow, but it is evident that he exerted himself considerably. Yet Basilov notes that his ecstasy 'was not really an unconscious state with a lack of control over his actions' – the music that accompanied Oken's performance changed according to which spirits were being summoned and included a recognisable popular melody. Similarly, shamans apparently in ecstasy are suspiciously capable of fairly elaborate sleight of hand, or keeping up a complex narrative in words and mime, things we might not expect of someone whose mind has temporarily vacated their body.

Studies of shamanism provide plenty of evidence for physical expressions of both 'ecstasy' and 'trance' as Rouget describes them. But there is also ample evidence for the 'imitative' and 'demonstrative' shamanism identified by Hultkrantz, in which there is no real change in the state of a shaman's consciousness, except that they may be playing the role of someone in ecstasy, someone who is journeying to the spirit worlds. Scientific studies of people who enter ecstatic states or trances do appear to show that there are measurable changes in neural activity. These tend by and large to be studies of people practising yoga, meditating or at prayer – quiet, contemplative activities involving focused concentration on an idea or object, or aimed at reducing brain activity (see for instance, Ahlberg 1982; Björkqvist 1982; Kasamatsu and Hirai 1966; Anand, Chhina and Singh 1961). To the best of my knowledge no one has yet connected a dancing, leaping Yakut shaman to an EEG machine. It seems to me that meditation and shamanic states attained during performance are not comparable things. There have also been many studies of changes in brain activity, cognition or visual imagery in people under the influence of various psychoactive drugs. The last has resulted in controversy in the field of shamanology, and will be discussed below and in chapter 8. But as relatively few shamans in Eurasia use drugs to achieve ecstasy there is again a sense that these experiments might not have much to tell us about shamanic ecstasy.

And once again there is always that vagueness as to what ecstasy and trance actually mean to neurologists and psychologists.

This brings us back to that old favourite, mental illness (including neurological dysfunction). As we have seen, Eliade and others have pretty well put paid to the idea that shamans are neurotic, hysterical or psychotic. The shamanic lifestyle requires a high degree of physical fitness, resilience, concentration and control that would not be compatible with such conditions – though it might not rule out temporary instances of such states. But there is a possibility that some shamans at least might suffer from a condition that really does result in genuine ecstatic states: limbic system or temporal lobe seizures associated with epilepsy. During such seizures people experience profound feelings that are frequently reported in religious terms, such as a sense of being intensely aware of, or at one with, the universe (Newberg, d'Aquili and Rause 2001). Epileptic seizures of this type would normally prevent a person from the kinds of controlled, strenuous activity associated with shamanic performance – though such episodes might be induced through shamanising, which would accord with the Saami shamans' post-drumming stupor. However, epileptic episodes (which may happen once or twice without necessarily being indicative of a long-term epileptic condition) would be a good candidate for shamans' initiatory experiences. Similarly, bizarre experiences – unseen but otherwise sensed entities, visions of strange, spectral figures, sensations of physical distortion and dismemberment, or being tortured – can be induced by passing minute electric currents across the temporal lobes (Cook and Persinger 1997). Again, they are more in keeping with initiatory experiences than actual shamanising.

The bottom line seems to be that it is not necessary for trance or ecstasy to be genuine neuropsychological phenomena in shamanism. Many shamans in Siberia and North America do not experience any change in consciousness during performance – and there is no evidence that those who appear to do so genuinely enter altered states of consciousness. Shamans' communities have a rather different expectation and understanding to that of anthropologists with regard to what happens inside a shaman's head:

> ... shamanistic societies do not make use of native terms homologous to 'trance'... They do not refer to a change of state to designate the shaman's ritual action, though they may qualify his behaviour as enraged or furious during that time. It

even seems that the very notion of 'trance' is irrelevant for them. (Hamayon 1995: 19–20)

In other words the genuineness or otherwise of ecstasy or trance – in the sense of them being actual psychosomatic changes – is of no great import. The shaman does what a shaman is expected to do and as long as it is done in the right way it does not matter one way or another if the shaman is sane, sober, entranced, ecstatic, high as a kite or just plain crazy.

Hamayon points out what should have been obvious all along, that it is not necessary to believe in order to participate in a religious event, and furthermore cites Johan Huizinga's observation that 'it is possible to be both "knowing and dupe" at the same time.' Why should we assume that indigenous peoples do not have the wit to distinguish reality from a dramatic representation? When Westerners go to the theatre or cinema, or watch a fictional production on television at home, they are fully aware that it is not real – but are quite willing and able to *suspend disbelief* for the duration. Indigenous peoples, who are neither primitives nor simpletons, do exactly the same, only they do it for the wellbeing of the community, not for individual entertainment.

Crazy rhythm
The drum is so important to Siberian shamanism that it is virtually emblematic of the phenomenon. We have already seen that the drum is not just a musical instrument. It is also a map of the cosmos and may function as the vehicle that transports the shaman to other worlds. But its primary function is to beat out the rhythm of the shaman's performance – the tempo and complexity of its rhythm change to reflect the mood of the shaman's otherworldly adventures and to create the required atmosphere. And it is thought by some to be of critical importance as an aid to ecstasy.

Siikala (1978: 44–6) cites research published in 1962 by Andrew Neher that supports the idea that drumming can result in altered states of consciousness. According to Neher, the multiple frequencies emitted by drumbeats stimulate a larger area of the brain than instruments that emit notes in a single frequency. Furthermore, drumbeats tend to be of lower frequency, and the human ear is more resistant to damage caused by lower frequencies than it is to the effects of higher frequencies. 'Therefore, it should be possible to transmit more energy to the brain with a drum' (Siikala 1978: 45).

This is backed up by other research conducted from the 1950s to the 1970s into the effects of rhythmic stimulation upon epileptics, hysterics and people with family histories of neurophysiological disturbance: such people have a greater than normal response to rhythmic stimulation.

> Susceptibility to rhythmic stimulation can be raised considerably, effecting several of the senses simultaneously. If the drumming is also accompanied by dance movements, not only the auditory but also the tactual and kinesthetic senses are the receptors of signals. The exhaustion and agitation connected with frenzied dancing, which reduces the glucose content of the blood and increases the production of adrenaline, further promotes susceptibility to stimulation. (Siikala 1978: 46)

This sounds pretty convincing and it is an attractive idea. The idea that drumbeats can stimulate greater than normal electrical activity in the brain, and the possible effects of such intensified activity, would fit in with Persinger's use of electric current to stimulate hallucinations and otherworldly experiences in otherwise sober and healthy people (Cook and Persinger 1997). Yet it is far from settled. There can be no quibble with the supposition that music, especially rhythmic drumbeats, can enhance mood and stimulate our pleasure centres. After all, it happens to most of us on a daily basis. Even classical music can induce reverie or daydreaming. There is also good circumstantial evidence to support the idea that music was used in Neolithic Europe and elsewhere in the ancient world to induce trance or other receptive states for ritual purposes (Devereux 2001). But can music really bring about the kinds of alteration in consciousness that appear to occur in shamanic ecstasy? And can it alter someone's state of mind so radically that they experience a journey to a strange world inhabited by spirits? Neher's research may have shown that electrical activity in the brain changes to the beat, but there is still a long way to go before that translates into a spirit journey. What is more, Siikala refers to other research conducted upon people whose neurophysiology predisposes them to particular experiences. Various types of epilepsy may cause fugue, automatism and hallucination, and the same is true of so-called 'hysterical' conditions. However, as we have already seen, shamans tend not to fall into those categories. Most shamans are neither epileptic nor neurotic – nor are they mentally ill or neurologically dysfunctional in any other way.

Rouget researched this issue extensively, from the point of view of a musicologist, not an anthropologist or neurologist. He observes that music 'has often been thought of as endowed with the mysterious power of triggering possession' – in which he includes trance and ecstasy. The musicians are seen as 'the withholders of some mysterious knowledge that enables them to manipulate this power.' His conclusion is momentous: 'There is no truth whatsoever in this assumption' (Rouget 1985: 325). Rouget arrived at this conclusion by observing that there is no one kind of music that induces trance. Types of 'trance' music and the instruments that are used to make them vary widely between cultures around the world. Music that is used to induce trance in one culture is ineffective in another. The association of a particular music with trance is something that is learned – the trance (whatever that word may signify) occurs through association and not by stimulating brain activity. But it is not merely a conditioned reflex. Rather, it seems to be a culturally determined response to the onset of a genuine change in the brain's functionality.

Corradi Musi argues that the shaman's drumming 'evokes and creates an emotive atmosphere which is different from the usual one... which creates in the spectators an atypical feeling' – it is done as much for the audience as it is for the shaman, perhaps more so:

> The musical rhythm is not only socializing, but is emotively captivating. The rhythm of the drum corresponds to the rhythm of the blood, and its physical effect is so strong that the body feels it and provokes the beating of the foot. Music, dance and singing create a highly charged emotion and make visible an internal dangerous state which can lead to a loss of control, and thus a in a certain sense exorcize it, thanks to the cleverly orchestrated directions of the worker of sacred acts... The rhythm of the drum does not condition ecstasy, which can occur even without it... The shaman uses the drum as a means of transport, because its rhythm transports man away from himself, but he knows how to direct it wherever he likes, how to control it by manipulating the emotions of the bystanders in the same way. (Corradi Musi 1995: 37)

In other words, the shaman uses the drum to create the receptive mood of choice in those looking on. Corradi Musi's view boils down to an echo of the old hippie dictum 'free your ass and your mind will follow' and for good reason: the music excites the body and conditions the mood. This agrees more or less with another of Rouget's conclusions, that while music does not of itself induce trance, it may be used to determine the shape of the experience. This would be true for both the shaman and audience.

So which do we choose to believe – the scientist in a laboratory measuring the effects the music has on his subjects, or the ethnomusicologist with his wide knowledge of music and an understanding of differing traditions of trance and ecstasy? Actually, there is no reason why we should not believe them both, as they are not mutually exclusive. Neher managed to reproduce in laboratory conditions the psychosomatic experiences associated with drumming in a more natural social settings, ceremonies involving drumming. These experiences consisted of increased electrical activity in the brain, 'unusual observations' made by the subjects, and twitching muscles. Crucially, Neher does not report that his subjects' vacated their bodies and went off to supernatural regions where they had adventures involving spirits and gods. While Neher has indeed demonstrated that drumming has definite psychosomatic effects, they are quite clearly not in the same league as a shaman's ecstasy. Rouget, on the other hand, recognises that there are different types of intense behaviour that occur against a background of which music is an important element, but concludes that music does not induce that behaviour, though it may shape it. That is precisely what happens in Siberian shamanism. Whatever trance and ecstasy might or might not be in neuropsychological terms, the shaman's drumming sets the pace of the performance, helps illustrate what the shaman is supposed to be doing and experiencing, and in addition creates an atmosphere in which the spirit journey is more believable.

Drugs
In the last few decades shamanism has increasingly been associated with drugs, specifically plants with psychoactive properties. Since the acid-drenched late 1960s a number of influential writers have preached the gospel of psychedelic shamanism. Carlos Castaneda has been by far the most popular. From the moment in 1968 that the first of his books based on the alleged adventures of a first-person anthropologist entering the weird and wonderful world of the Yaqui *brujero* Don Juan proved a great success with young seekers after native wisdom. And of course with those who saw them as an endorsement of the spiritual qualities of psychedelic drugs.

Castaneda was not the first to proselytise the mystical properties of drugs, of course. Aldous Huxley had already published *The Doors of Perception* (1954) concerning his experiences with mescaline; William Burroughs and Allen Ginsberg's *Yage Letters*, about their dealings with *ayahuasca* appeared in 1963. More cogently, Aleister Crowley, who in the 1960s was enjoying a posthumous reappraisal as an icon of spiritual rebellion, had been an advocate of almost the full range of drugs available in his lifetime as aids to religion. And in 1970 Timothy Leary's era-defining *The Politics of Ecstasy* appeared. Given the times, it is hardly surprising that shamanism was caught in the fun and the shaman's spirit journey adopted as just another type of trip. Of course, this was popular culture at its most open-minded and absorbent. But beneath the fun and games of recreational drug use and playful mysticism there was serious anthropological work going on with regard to the traditional ritual or religious use of drugs, particularly with regard to practices now classed as shamanism.

That work had been going on for some considerable time. The eating of the hallucinogenic mushroom *Amanita muscaria* (fly agaric) in Siberia has been recorded on and off by anthropologists and travellers for centuries. In the eighteenth century Strahlenberg, Steller and Krashenninikov recorded the purely recreational use of this mushroom in Kamchatka, among the Kamchadal, Koryak and Yukaghir; and Georgi observed it among the Khanty and Sakha. Bogoras reports extensive fly agaric use among the Chukchi (Bogoras 1904). Karl von Ditmar (von Ditmar 1900) observed a Koryak woman shamanising while intoxicated by the mushroom. Other witnesses in this region report that people attending shamanic performances consumed *Amanita muscaria*. Indeed, practically all accounts agree that in Kamchatka the fly agaric was a popular and common intoxicant, preferred to alcohol by some tribespeople (usually excluding women). It was not solely associated with shamanism, though some would use it to prepare for shamanising. 'Many shamans, previous to their séances, eat fly-agaric in order to get into ecstatic states,' writes Jochelson (1905: 583) of the Koryak. Fly agaric intoxication has also been observed in shamanism further to the west. Ostyak shamans obtained supernatural knowledge by eating three or seven mushrooms then going to sleep, during which the spirits communicated with him in a dream (Eliade 1964: 220–1). Saami shamans were said formerly to have consumed mushrooms with seven white spots. Mansi, Nenets, Selkup, Yurak and Khanty shamans also consumed the mushroom (Balázs 1996).

The interesting thing to note here is that among some Siberian peoples almost everyone used fly agaric to get intoxicated. It was not confined to shamans. Koryak shamanising in particular seems to have been an ecstatic free-for-all. The effects of large doses of fly agaric intoxication include tremors, physical agitation and restlessness, hallucinations, extremes of terror and joy, and macropsia (objects appearing much larger than they really are), followed by stupor and possibly convulsions. Small doses result in euphoria, suppression of fear, and a feeling of increased strength. R. Gordon Wasson (1971) identified fly agaric as the enigmatic *Soma*, the divine intoxicating plant of ancient India – the effects are certainly close to those described in the *Rig Veda* – and its Iranian counterpart *Haoma*. The literature of *Amanita muscaria* generally agrees that the more a person takes, the more intense the ecstasy. But to take enough to hallucinate or experience otherworld journeys requires the same sort of dose that would rend the user useless for anything but the most rudimentary ritual activity. Small doses produce euphoria but not ecstasy, and there are no hallucinations.

Not all shamans among the fly agaric-using peoples use it for shamanising. And there is some evidence that shamans who used the mushroom to achieve ecstasy were considered second rate. Furthermore, there seems to be little evidence of fly agaric use among Tungusic or Mongol shamans, though vodka and tobacco are recorded among the Evenk (Shirokogoroff 1935: 306) and Manchu shamans are reported as using 'drugs and medicines' to perform (Shuyun 1995: 61).

Amerindian peoples make ritual use of a wide range of psychoactive plants. *Banisteriopsis* is the key ingredient, with other psychoactive plants, of a hallucinogenic beverage (commonly known as *yagé*, *ayahuasca* or *capi*) consumed in Brazil, Colombia, Ecuador and Peru. A typical *Banisteriopsis* brew can contain harmaline and related alkaloids, dimethyltriptamine and other hallucinogens, making for a heady cocktail. Inevitably, *yagé* allows Amerindian shamans to perceive the spirit world and interact with its inhabitants. Effects include tremors, hallucinations (coloured snakes, bright light, gardens, animals, spirits and villages), euphoria and sensations of moving very quickly. Among the Cashinahua of Peru, *yagé* is taken and used communally to contact the spirit world – individual shamans are only called in when the communal rite fails to produce a result (Kensinger 1973). The Tukano of Colombia use *yagé* communally in initiation ceremonies (Reichel-Dolmatoff 1972). *Yagé* use among the Sharanahua of Peru is also communal, though it is particularly connected with the shamans (Siskind 1973) – a similar situation exists among the Campa of Peru (Weiss 1973). The Shuar (Jivaro) of Ecuador do not use *yagé* communally, but considering that 'approximately one out of every four Jivaro men is a shaman' (Harner 1968) there would seem little need to make a point of it.

Peyote, a hallucinogenic cactus from the arid regions of Texas and Mexico which contains mescaline, is perhaps the best known of the psychoactive plants native to the Americas. Archaeological evidence shows that peyote has been used in Mexico for at least three thousand years. Like *yagé* its use is not confined to shamans, though it is certainly considered a sacred plant which gives access to the spirit world. The Huichol undertake pilgrimages to obtain peyote. Although most Huichol do not participate these are open to anyone of all ages and either sex, and any pilgrim could consume it and perceive the spirit world, though only the shaman can make contact with the gods (Furst 1972). In the late nineteenth century peyote was adopted by the Mescalero Apache, resulting in a wholesale transfer of authority from traditional medicine men, until then the only members of the tribe who had been able to make contact with the spirit world.

> In ordinary shamanistic practices, a single shaman is the principal figure and the experiences of attendants at ceremonies is subordinate. Religious ecstasy, visions and communication with supernaturals are the shaman's prerogatives and validate his power and efficacy. The use of peyote by other people at ceremonies made its psychological and physiological effects common, and the uniqueness of the shaman's experiences disappeared. The peyote meetings became places in which shamanistic rivalries and witchcraft flourished. Disruption resulted, rather than cohesiveness through shared experience.
> (Boyer, Boyer and Basehart 1973: 56)

These tensions ultimately caused the Mescalero to stop using peyote and to forbid further consumption. However, peyote use spread among the Plains Indians, and the version of the peyote rite practised by the Comanche and Kiowa reached as far as southern Canada (La Barre 1989).

A host of other drugs, both hallucinogenic and narcotic, are used ritually in the New World, including tobacco. As with *yagé* or peyote there is no regular pattern in their use – they may be taken communally or by the shaman alone, or both communally and by the shaman alone on special occasions or for specific purposes. Psilocybe mushrooms – which are often depicted in Aztec art – are consumed by most of the Mazatec (Huautecan) of Mexico for contacting the spirit world and obtaining knowledge. But only shamans ingest them on a regular basis, and the main reason for that seems to be that they are the people strong enough to do so (Munn 1978).

In general the circumstances of drug use in shamanism are much the same in Siberia as in the Americas. A drug may be used by almost anyone with no ritual restrictions, and at all kinds of ceremonies and celebrations, though a shaman might consume more of it and do so more often than anyone else. Moreover, Amerindian tribes to the north of the home range of peyote appear to have been introduced to hallucinogens as an aid to shamanising only recently. Until the sudden growth of the peyote cult among the Apache around 1870 there is no evidence for use of strongly hallucinogenic plants in most North American shamanism, though plants like tobacco and jimsonweed were used extensively by 'medicine societies' (Hultkrantz 1979: 75–6). This suggests that in the Americas hallucinogenic plants only became an important part of shamanism – in its broadest, popular sense – when their properties were discovered. In other words, when shamans found that it was possible to really perceive dreamlike other worlds where spirits could be encountered. But that also meant that anyone could do it, not just the shaman. That might explain the difference in status between shamans in most of North America, where ecstasy was restricted to a few specialists, and their counterparts in the south, where shamans are often part-time ritual overseers or where sometimes even a small community might have many shamans.

The Siberian use of fly agaric seems to fall into a slightly different pattern. A key factor here is that among the Koryak and other peoples of the north fly agaric was the local intoxicant of choice, whereas peoples like the Tungusic and Mongol tribes favour *kumiss*, fermented mare's milk. Critically, the forest reindeer herders used the mushroom, while the horse tribes of the steppe drank alcohol. Tungusic shamans drank *kumiss* and vodka, and smoke tobacco along with everyone else, just as Koryak shamans consumed fly agaric in a communal intoxication. Evidently the choice of intoxicant is dictated first by a people's ecological history, then by tradition. External influences also come into play: fly agaric use in Eastern Siberia declined as alcohol and tobacco became more readily available following Russian colonisation (Rudgley 1993: 42).

Naturally Eliade is in no doubt that ecstasy through intoxicants is a poor substitute for the real thing:

> Intoxication by mushrooms also produces contact with the spirits, but in a passive and crude way... this shamanic technique appears to be late and derivative. Intoxication is a mechanical and corrupt method of reproducing 'ecstasy', being 'carried out of oneself'; it tries to imitate a model that is earlier and that belongs to another plane of reference. (Eliade 1954: 223)

Eliade is convinced that 'the magico-religious value of intoxication for achieving ecstasy is of Iranian origin' (Eliade 1964: 401). Further to this he suggests that the infernal aspect of shamanic journeys – visions of hellish regions – entered Siberian shamanism from the Middle East via Iranian-speakers. His conclusion is based on the derivation of words for *Amanita muscaria* and intoxication in Uralic languages from Iranian *bangha*, denoting cannabis. However, the reverse appears to be true. The Uralic words supposedly derived from *bangha* – and cognates in other languages of Eastern Siberia – are widely enough distributed to make borrowing from Iranian-speakers unlikely. Moreover, they seem to share a common origin with Indo-European words like Latin *fungus* and English *punk* (Wasson 1971: 164–71). This means that it is far more likely that either the Iranians named hemp after a fungal intoxicant they had once known but perhaps could no longer obtain, or (less probable) they borrowed the name from Uralic-speakers (Balázs 1996). Or perhaps the word was part of the language family ancestral to both Uralic and Indo-European.

Even if the *bangha* argument stood up to scrutiny, Eliade's argument is pretty weak. Especially when we learn that for all his harping on about the purity and primacy in shamanism of that mystical communion with the divine, drug-free ecstasy, he writes:

> In any case, it is plain that real shamanic trances are comparatively rare, and the majority of séances involve only an ecstatic journey undertaken by the spirits or the fabulous account of adventures whose mythological prototypes are already known. (Eliade 1964: 228)

This completely undermines Eliade's idea of shamanism as a primal mystical technique. By his own admission, most shamanic journeys do not involve a real alteration of the shaman's state of consciousness – they are mostly either symbolic or enacted as a kind of pantomime. It also casts doubt on Harner's idea of a 'shamanic state of consciousness': shamans do not need to enter into 'real' ecstasy in order to do their work. And it weakens the idea that use of hallucinogens to become ecstatic is an important part of shamanism globally – it is not the drugs that are important to shamanic ritual but the cultural patterns imposed on the experience coupled with the community's expectations of the shaman. Shamans might make use of hallucinogenic plants, but the ritual use of hallucinogenic plants, especially where their use is common and recreational, is not inherently shamanic. Arguably, ritual practitioners in cultures where recreational use of hallucinogens is open to all are not really shamans, not unless their status is confirmed in some other way, such as initiatory and social processes that define a shaman's condition, along the lines of those discussed in chapter 3.

In recent years there has been an increased popular identification of shamanism with the use of hallucinogenic plants. The impetus for this has not come entirely from Central and South American native ethnography, though there are plenty of *bona fide* anthropological studies that detail the psychedelic rituals of Mexico and points south. As we have seen two of the main pillars of late twentieth century dissatisfaction with modernity were – and to a large extent still are – the appearance of drugs (notably strong hallucinogens like LSD) in unprecedented quantities as an integral part of pop culture, and religious experimentation. These trends met at and crystallised around the books of Carlos Castaneda. But two other important books are worth noting – R. Gordon Wasson's study of the Vedic wonder beverage *Soma* (Wasson 1971) and John M. Allegro's *The Sacred Mushroom and the Cross* (1970), which explored the idea that Christianity might be based on a sacred mushroom cult. Allegro's controversial book in particular received massive publicity. Although Wasson and Allegro did not deal with Amerindian shamanism, they certainly contributed greatly to the growing belief that first-hand experience of the divine might be just one small tablet away. However, Wasson and Allegro wrote about forms of worship that appeared to be long gone. This was remedied by collections of essays edited by Harner (*Hallucinogens and Shamanism*, 1973) and Furst (*Flesh of the Gods*, 1972), both of which dealt mostly with indigenous practices in Central and South America. Here were living traditions that (for Americans at least) were close to home.

The extent of ritual drug use in the Americas is unparalleled, almost certainly because, as Weston La Barre (1970: 143) observed, no other continent has anything like the same number or variety of narcotic and hallucinogenic plants. However, not much of it occurs in shamanism as a Siberian would understand it – and the further south we look, the less Amerindian ritual resembles Siberian shamanism. If ever there was shamanism in those regions that in any way resembled the classical Siberian model, the ready availability and sheer variety of so many powerful substances, and their communal consumption, must have changed it beyond all recognition.

Drug use among Siberian shamans has been largely neglected since Eliade. General studies of psychoactive plants in culture usually do not dwell on Siberia (for instance, Rudgley 1993 and Devereux 1997, though both briefly discuss fly agaric use in Eastern Siberia), while recent studies of Siberian shamanism rarely mention drug use.

Ascent and descent

While in an ecstatic state the shaman's spirit is supposed to journey to the spirit worlds. Throughout the Eurasian shamanic continuum there are only two types of journey: the descent, in which a shaman travels to the land of the dead; and the ascent, which involves flying to the celestial realm where the gods live. While the shaman's ecstasy is outwardly much the same for each type of journey, there is little similarity between them in terms of the internal experience.

The Evenk underworld is peculiar to each clan. Anisimov (1963a) tells us that the Evenk land of the dead is reached by a mythical 'clan river' which unites all the lower and upper worlds with the middle land inhabited by the living. This river (*mumongi khokto bira*, 'watery river road') is the route taken by the shaman when consulting the *mangi*, the shaman's chief ancestral spirits, to determine the cause of an illness; or conducting the dead to their final home, the clan underworld. Conceived of as an ordinary Evenk clan camp, the *khergu* ('land of the dead') lies at the mouth of the clan river. A shaman must persuade the female ruler of the dead to accept the recently departed into her clan. Evenk shamans travel to the lower world with an entourage of helping spirits, who act as guardians and helpers to the *khargi*, the shaman's spirit in the form of an animal. Drumming and dancing, the shaman enters an ecstatic state then acts out the *khargi*'s journey and gives a running commentary, assisted by their (human) helpers, who revive them when they fall into a stupor and call the shaman back to the human world. The shaman reaches the lower world by way of the *turu*, a larch pole at the centre of the shaman's tent, reaching from the fire to the smoke-hole, representing the World Tree, which is analogous to the clan river. The Evenk shaman does not enter ecstasy while treating a patient – their helping spirits do whatever travel to the upper or lower world is necessary. Only when a disease spirit is removed and caught does the shaman enter the lower world again, to dispose of it.

Following a successful treatment, a reindeer is sacrificed and shared out among the attendees, its skin hung on the *turu* as an offering to the gods. The shaman goes with the dead animal to thank the gods in person:

> In a special song addressed to the gods, the shaman thanked the protectors of the clan for the help received. He then performed a special dance symbolizing his journey to the gods of the upper world. He climbed up, supposedly, by the *turu* into the upper world and walked along the earth of the upper world, passing the heavens one after the other, to the *Amaka sheveki*, the supreme god. The shaman gave him for safekeeping the soul of the patient – a small wooden image of a man attached to the top of the *turu* larch. The *Amaka* entrusted the guarding of the patient's soul to the spirit of the shaman. The shaman's return journey to the earth of the *dulu* (middle world) was represented in the form of a strenuous, joyous, noisy dance of ecstasy. (Anisimov 1963a: 105)

Shirokogoroff (1935: 304–14) describes Evenk shamanic performances that differ in some respects from the one recounted by Anisimov. The shaman's ascent to the sky and descent to the underworld are also different. For example:

> During this journey the shaman must go down a mountain range (in a northwestern direction), where he may meet with difficulties caused by the spirits of other shamans and other spirits which are in conflict with his own spirits. On his way he has to go through a small hole, near which the spirits and other shamans may capture his soul. The journey is reported by the shaman... At his arrival to the entrance to the lower world the shaman has to cross three rivers, where he meets with the spirits of the lower world. Finally he enters the world of

darkness, and the assistants must produce with steel and flint sparks to light his way... (Shirokogoroff 1935: 307)

Anisimov's description of the Evenk shaman's ascent and descent is interesting for several reasons. Firstly, it underscores the idea that, no matter what may seem to be happening, the shaman retains self-control and at the same time maintains control of the entire event. Although the shaman may dance and drum with increasing fury, and appears to fall to the ground insensible and foaming at the mouth, in need of help from their apparently frantic assistants, everything goes according to plan. Secondly, it reiterates the close connection between shamanic symbolism and social context. The shaman's underworld journey is carried out in a spirit world exclusive to the clan, reaffirming social cohesion and promoting the group's identity under patronage of its very own mistress of the dead. And the clan underworld is populated entirely by clan members.

But the most important thing to note here is that despite an underlying ethnic unity, different Evenk communities each have their own unique take on what the spirit worlds are like and what the shaman experiences in them. Other shamanist peoples also have their own versions of what the lower and upper worlds are like. For instance, some Altai shamans descend to a lower world that comprises seven levels, at each of which an obstacle must be overcome. At the lowest are the mouths of nine rivers, where Erlik Khan, lord of the underworld, has his palace. To reach the underworld the shaman must travel south from the *yurt* to the Altai mountains, after which a series of wide steppes are crossed until the shaman reaches the Iron Mountain, which is strewn with the bones of shamans who failed to climb it. Once across, the shaman travels to a hole through which the lower world is reached. Below ground, the shaman must cross a plain, then a sea spanned by a bridge only as wide as a hair. Through the water can be seen the bones of shamans who failed the test. Crossing the bridge the shaman witnesses the torment meted out to sinners. At the other side is the palace of Erlik Khan, which is guarded by dogs and a porter who must be bribed before the shaman can enter. Erlik is offered gifts and wine, and becomes intoxicated and happy, giving the shaman his blessings. Throughout the performance the shaman tells the audience what is happening and mimes the action (Eliade 1964: 200–3).

In a Goldi shamanising to escort a dead soul to the lower world, the shaman faces west while sitting on a board representing a sled, with a supply of food and representations of two spirits. When the spirits have hitched a team of dogs to the sled the shaman sets off. At first easy, the road becomes more difficult as the journey progresses. A wide river must be traversed. The land of the dead is much like this one – the dead live in yurts with fires in the hearth and they herd reindeer. Relatives of the deceased greet the shaman and the soul being escorted. Yurak shamans and their departed charges are also greeting by the dead person's relatives (Eliade 1964: 211–13).

The Evenk underworld is much like this world, with the dead living in a clan camp much like any earthly Evenk camp. This close resemblance between the land of the dead and the realm of the living is found in the beliefs of other shamanist peoples. According to Jochelson (1905: 47) the underworld consists of villages like those in this world, with each family having its own house. Chernetsov tells us that among the Mansi,

> The way of life of the dead also remains very close to that of the living. They form a world in all respects similar to the world of the living, in whose immediate neighbourhood they are located. In this world they "live," like people, in clans... The world of the dead is the same as the world of the living, but transferred, if we may so express it, into some "fourth dimension" and, therefore, usually invisible and imperceptible... The similarity of the world of the dead to that of the living extends even to the point that the dead have their shamans and spirits. Moreover, people are invisible to the dead... (Chernetsov 1963: 8–9)

Living humans entering this realm are considered by the dead to be spirits, and are expelled by the helper spirits of dead shamans. Chernetsov likens the land of the dead to a 'mirror-image of that of the living.' In another reversal, the Yurak dead live as they did while alive, except that all become young after death.

On the whole, Siberian concepts of the lower world tend to be quite banal – these underworlds are pretty much the same as the mortal world. There is sometimes a distinctly topsy-turvy feel about them, but that only serves to sharpen the idea that they represent nothing more than a transposition of life to death and satisfy the ordinary human anxieties about what happens after death by insisting upon both continuity and easement. No real imagination is required to construct such an afterlife. Central Asian shamanism, on the other hand, is rather more interesting with regard to what lies beyond the

Journeying to Other Worlds

grave. Altai shamans visit a realm not unlike the Christian Hell, though it is more closely akin to the afterworld portrayed in ancient Iranian texts. The bridge is an interesting feature: Zoroastrian myth tells of the Cinvat ('separation') bridge, 'the holy bridge made by Mazda' that stretches over hell to paradise. It is 'the route of every one, righteous or wicked; the width across the route of the righteous is a breadth of nine spears, each one the length of three reeds, but the route for the wicked becomes like the edge of a razor' (*Denkart* 9.3). A variation on this motif occurs in North American native myth: the Telumni Yokuts believe that the land of the dead is reached by crossing a stream by way of a shaking bridge that the living cannot use (Eliade 1964: 311; Hultkrantz 1957: 218). Similar bridges occur in Arthurian romance, Norse myth and Malaysian tradition (Stone 1996). Eliade (1964: 396–401) observes that in Iranian tradition a crossing of the Cinvat by a living man is associated with an ecstatic state similar to shamanic ecstasy brought on by an intoxicant. This suggests a connection between the Iranian afterworld and shamanism. Eliade (1964: 104) comments that the Altaic underworld probably 'had Indo-Iranian models' but the distribution of the 'perilous bridge' theme makes it unlikely to have originated among the Iranians. Norse cosmology and Arthurian legend have points in common with Iranian tradition, and the early Iranians certainly had some contact with shamanist Uralic and Turkic tribes. Islamic inflence would also perhaps explain the theme's presence in Malaysia. But the Amerindian instance gives us pause. If the Yokuts' shaking bridge shares a common origin with the Cinvat then the motif must be of great antiquity.

Shamans also ascend to the sky. In cultures across Eurasia this follows a similar course to the Evenk ascent mentioned above, and usually occurs in conjunction with animal sacrifice to the sky gods. For example, the spirits of Altai Tatar shamans accompany the spirits of horses sacrificed to Bai Ülgän, the sky god. (This also requires the soul of the person who holds the horse's head during the sacrifice.) In one account (Eliade 1964: 190–7), the shaman summons his helper spirits and mounts a dummy goose, miming the flapping of wings; he then summons 'the mother of nine eagles', dropping a shoulder to show that the bird has perched on it and imitating an eagle's cry. The shaman circles his tent to pray for a guide. When enough spirits have been mustered the shaman pretends to climb the notched birch pole at the centre of his tent. He mounts a horsehide covered bench, representing the spirit of the sacrificed horse, then climbs to the second notch of the birch pole, announcing he has entered the second celestial level. This goes on for some time, with the shaman miming his ascent and reciting a commentary. This includes goose noises, a conversation with the creator god Yayutsi, bowing to the moon and sun, and other business. The Tatar heaven has quite a few levels, and the more powerful shamans are, the higher they fly. When the shaman reaches his limit he stops and asks Bai Ülgän for good fortune for the community. Bai Ülgän informs the shaman if the horse is acceptable, makes predictions and tells the shaman what sacrifice he next expects. At the end the shaman collapses exhausted and appears to fall into a deep sleep.

The differences between ethnic and local versions of otherworld geography are numerous. For instance, the entrance to the Evenk lower world is in a northerly direction, the Altaic version is to the south. Some underworlds have one level, like that of the Evenk; others have three, or seven, or nine. The 'perilous bridge' motif is present in some versions but not in others. The Evenk underworlds are ruled by women, like those of the Saami and other Uralic peoples, while the Altaic version are ruled by a male. The Altaic lower world is a place where sinners are punished, but the Evenk one is much like the land of the living, only in a different place. As for shamanic ascents to the sky, there is not much geography to speak of in any of them, just a succession of levels with the supreme celestial deity conveniently present at the topmost level the shaman has power to reach. The number of heavenly levels differs from one people to another – the range is from one level to twelve or more.

Anyone hoping to find a cohesive 'shamanic' cosmos in these, or an inspiration for otherworld organisation in internal comprehension of brain structure during altered states of consciousness, is doomed to disappointment. The only constant feature is the basic threefold division, and that is not a product of any 'shamanic' state of consciousness but of simple observation of the world such as anyone might make by looking around them. The sky, for one thing, is simply there for anyone to see – and it is the abode of the benign gods in most cultures. It can be divided into as many levels as necessary for whatever purposes local custom requires, as indeed can the invisible realm of the dead. A basic layout for a generalised land of the dead can be discerned in traditions spanning most of the Northern Hemisphere – but the structure is a stylised version of the human world, with the same kinds of physical features and familiar settlements.

The problem of possession

Possession by spirits has long been a contentious issue in shamanology. Eliade asserted that there is a clear distinction between ritual possession and shamanism, though he acknowledged that possession does sometimes occur.

> It will easily be seen wherein a shaman differs from a 'possessed' person... the shaman controls his 'spirits', in the sense that he, a human being, is able to communicate with the dead, 'demons', and 'nature spirits', without thereby becoming their instrument... To be sure, shamans are sometimes found to be 'possessed', but these are exceptional cases for which there is a particular explanation. (Eliade 1964: 5)

For Eliade the situation is clear-cut. The shaman controls the spirits, not the other way round. True shamanism does not involve the shaman being possessed by spirits, though shamans may sometimes take spirits into themselves while healing someone, and this can be dangerous. Vulnerability is implicit in a shaman's nature: 'frequently, through his constant struggling with evil spirits, he falls into their power, that is, he ends by being really "possessed"' (Eliade 1964: 236).

However, ethnographers before Eliade had often observed that Siberian shamans became possessed while shamanising. For instance, Shirokogoroff (1935: 311–14) refers to a number of case studies in which spirits enter Evenk shamans. For the most part these are the shamans' own helper spirits, but in one instances where a shaman was old and sick a malign spirit entered her and required casting out.

Debate about possession in shamanism began in earnest when Hans Findeisen (Findeisen 1957) declared that possession by spirits is the main feature of shamanic ecstasy, describing the shaman as a 'possessed priest,' whose body is occupied by spirits while its own is elsewhere. Findeisen roundly equates shamans with Western spirit mediums. This was countered in a review of Findeisen's book in the journal *Ethnos* by Ivar Paulson, who observed that when a shaman 'takes into himself, as the term often runs, the spirits, he nevertheless retains his own personality at that. He is the master, and not the slave or a passive instrument of the spirits, as is usually the case with a spiritualistic medium.' Findeisen replied to Paulson in the same journal, asserting that 'possession is the phenomenological centre of shamanism – without possession no shamanism.' Findeisen's response was in turn fiercely criticised by Engelbert Stiglmayr, who suggested that possession was indeed a characteristic of North Asian shamanism, but that it was devoid of the spiritualistic overtones that Findeisen claimed. (See Hultkrantz 1996 for a summary of this debate.)

Perhaps the foremost recent proponent of the idea that possession is central to shamanism is Ioan M. Lewis, whose *Ecstatic Religion* was first published in 1971 and is now in its third edition. Lewis claims the that Finnish scholar Anna-Leena Siikala's assessment of shamanic ecstasy supports his contention that 'we are correct to argue that far from being opposed or mutually exclusive phenomena... shamanism and spirit-possession regularly occur together, the shaman being essentially a master (or mistress) of controlled spirit-possession' (Lewis 1989: 8). Lewis goes on to rebuke timid British anthropologists for not being so bold as their American counterparts as to using the word 'shaman' in cases where it is appropriate, to traditions of spirit possession in Africa, for instance. This does seem to be supported by some of Siikala's remarks. For example:

> Common to the central and eastern parts of Siberia, for example, among the Yukagir, the Evenki, the Yakuts, the Manchus, the Nanais, and the Orochi is the possession séance, during which the shaman's chief spirit helper enters his body and speaks through him. The shaman fully identifies with the spirit; he in fact turns into the spirit and manifests this change in his gestures, movements, and speech. Another person at the séance, usually the shaman's assistant, then becomes the shaman, talking to the spirit. (Siikala 1987: 11)

However, things are not quite as they seem with regard to Lewis' embrace of Siikala's notions. For one thing, Lewis approaches trance, ecstasy and possession in terms reminiscent of older ideas of 'Arctic hysteria' and psychopathy as explanations of shamanism. He is almost entirely concerned with psychiatric and psychoanalytical interpretations of these states, treating ecstasy and possession as though they were one and the same thing. This does not sit easily with the idea of imitative shamanism, and is certainly at odds with the performance aspect of shamanic ecstasy. But nor does it gel with a closer look at Siikala's interpretation. Siikala cites Theodore R. Sarbin's investigations into the psychological and physiological effects of role-taking. Sarbin's role theory can be summarised fairly crudely: the more intense and physical the performance, the further an actor is removed from their ordinary persona.

> A role performance demanding a person's total effort is precisely 'special, temporary orientation', and concentrating on this effaces his 'generalized reality-orientation'. Consciousness changes as reality takes shape according to the new role. Sarbin stresses that the role-expectations of every role determine a suitable organismic involvement. The shamanic rite demands such intensity of performance that it leads to an altered state of consciousness. (Siikala 1978: 63–4)

Here we should bear in mind that shamanic performance usually entails much physical exertion, including mime. It is possible that the shaman's repeated performances of the same physical actions could intensify the role. Felicitas Goodman (1990) is of the view that certain postures can be used to initiate trance to the extent that a spirit journey is possible.

The 'altered state of consciousness' Siikala refers to is clearly not the same sort of thing demanded by intoxication, which may really be one or more of variety of chemically-determined changes of cognition and perception. It is not a pathological personality change brought about by disease or trauma. Nor is it the same as possession as students of religion would understand it. Essentially it is a modification of identity similar to the kinds of role-playing we all engage in during the course of our daily lives: change and adaptation according to the requirements of whatever social situation we may find ourselves in at any given moment. For instance, when alone with close friends or family we may quite naturally speak and behave very differently to the way we do at work. The shaman's life involves much the same thing, but at a level elevated and magnified by ritual and public display, in much the same way as an actor on stage. It is an extreme of empathy but it does not mean that the shaman's body is taken over by a spirit. For instance, honking like a goose and flapping wings does not come naturally to humans – when a shaman does it the action is volitional, not the natural consequence of thinking like a goose. The inhabiting spirit – the major part of the shaman's modified persona – is still the shaman's own, even if it is not behaving in its usual way.

Elsewhere Siikala writes:

> I have tried to show that the journey of the shaman and possession, the entering of the spirit into the shaman's body, are simply functional alternatives describing the communication between the shaman and the other world... The shaman's journey is, however, still a special feature of shamanism and is not connected with other kinds of mediumistic traditions. (Siikala 1989: 21-22)

Siikala is clearly saying that she regards possession and ecstatic journey as very different things, and particularly that the shamanic spirit journey is distinctive to shamanism. Elsewhere she refers to spirit possession in Siberian shamanism as 'the shaman's identification with a spirit role' (Siikala 1982). Siikala is obviously well aware that for the most part shamanic ecstasy does not involve any change in consciousness on the part of the shaman and that what goes on at a shamanising is often little more than intense play-acting. Put simply, the ecstatic journey involves a shaman miming a descent to the underworld or an ascent to the heavens; the so-called possession involves a shaman acting the part of various spirits. The shamanic rite is a social ritual, a public performance, and it would be a pointless exercise if everything took place in stillness and silence. No one would know what was going on.

Examples of shamans who are obviously playing roles crop up time and again in the literature, as do examples of shamans whose 'trance' or 'ecstasy' does not extends so far that it gets in the way of the performance. Furthermore, the spirits who are actually said to 'enter' the shaman are almost always the spirits that belong to that shaman, including his personal spirit. This is not the same order of possession as we find in Haitian *voudun*, for instance, where a person may voluntarily – but not volitionally – be completely taken over by a *loa*, a divine spirit whose characteristics and personality the possessed person assumes completely. Occasionally a vulnerable Eurasian shaman might be so infested, but nearly always involuntarily.

In the 1960s Ernst Arbman examined the evidence for spirit possession in shamanism and found it wanting (Arbman 1963–70). Hultkrantz, who endorses Arbman's view – though with reservations – summarises:

What may sometimes appear as true possession among such tribes as the Yakut, Tungus, Goldi, Yukagir and Chukchee is basically a role play in which the shaman impersonates the spirits, sometimes in dialogue form. Sometimes... this conscious, deliberate action passes over into an unconscious ecstatic automatism, a visionary dream, which may be mistaken for a possessional state. It is not possession, however, for the shaman may impersonate one spirit after another, and even if one of them, his main helper, is supposed to have taken up his abode within the shaman all the rest are outside him. (Hulktkrantz 1996: 20–1)

What seems at first sight to be possession by spirits is really something closely akin to method acting: a close identification with the part being played, in which the shaman *becomes* the spirit rather than being possessed by it. The difference is subtle but important.

Out of this world?

In studies of shamanism ecstasy and trance are unsatisfactorily defined – and will probably remain indefinable. There are many different types of 'altered states of consciousness,' including differing states induced by different types of drug, exhaustion or neurological dysfunction. But what is 'normal' consciousness anyway? Many of us experience 'ordinary' reality through a filter of nicotine, alcohol or caffeine. Even the food we eat can have psychoactive properties. What is more, our so-called 'ordinary' state of consciousness is affected by chemicals produced by our bodies and as such is highly dependent on mood, activity, time of day, social or sexual stimulation, the weather, and so on. What we think of as our ordinary consciousness changes from one moment to the next – it is a range of states, not one immutable mode of consciousness. Similarly, it is clear that there are many types of consciousness that may be experienced by shamans during performance, not a single neuropsychological state called ecstasy.

Scientific research into religious ecstasy and trance has historically been concerned with examining abnormal psychology or neurology, or healthy people in abnormal circumstances. Nils G. Holm recognises that ecstasy is something more than a neuropsychological anomaly. It is the product of intensified mental states shaped by cultural factors.

> Research of recent years... has emphasized the possibility of understanding distinctive phenomena from the perspective of normal psychology. It is common to speak in terms of an intensification of certain mental mechanisms and processes towards a certain upper limit. In addition, the cognitive content – the system of religious concepts – has received attention as a contributory factor in the process. Without the conceptual world that is specific to every culture, we do not, it is felt, find any ecstatic phenomena. (Holm 1982: 23)

In other words, whatever else may be happening with regard to a shaman's neuropsychology, the shamanic experience plays out according to the symbolic content and structure prevalent in the culture. The deepening or intensification of the shaman's mental state is only a preliminary stage – the shaman's beliefs and cosmological expectations do the rest.

Contrary to Eliade's view of ecstasy the method of achieving ecstasy is ultimately irrelevant to shamanism. The reality or otherwise of ecstasy, or what it signifies in neurological or psychological terms, is not important. Shamanism is essentially an interaction between shaman and community. The circumstances of psychedelic shamanism in the Americas and parts of Siberia are clear: the ingestion of drugs is generally a communal act, and the shaman performs against the backdrop of mutual intoxication. Imitative and demonstrative shamanism may be little more than religious pantomimes, but they are no less valid for that. Shamans who attain a genuine alteration in their consciousness through lengthy spells of drumming or dancing, without recourse to drugs, also engage in a narrative for the benefit of onlookers. Shamanic performance tells a story, the story of the shaman's ascent to the sky or descent to the world below, and how a soul was rescued, how the shaman dealt with the spirits encountered along the way, and how the return was achieved. The story told in shamanic performance is based on the myths, beliefs and cosmology of the shaman's people. Even where the shaman takes a powerful hallucinogen, it is not the change in conscious that is important. It is *what the shaman is believed to experience while in that state* that is of interest to their community, many of whom will also be under the influence. The shaman does not need to literally leave this world in order to enter the next. The journey to the spirit world is informed by cultural expectation – and the expectations are those of the community as a whole. And the community's participation is vital. It effectively dictates the action.

Horwitz has completely missed the essence of audience participation. In theatrical productions participation is not just about applauding the hero, jeering the villain and singing along to the music. In most theatre, cinema or television drama the audience participates in a different and subtle way. The different elements – scenery, action, script – are transformed into a unified whole, a story. That transformation does not take place on stage or screen, but in the mind of the audience. And its effectiveness hinges on expectation. We go to the cinema with a preconceived idea – because of the director, actors and genre – about how the film should look and the story should develop. Within these parameters almost any denouement or plot thread is satisfying. But the tighter the parameters the more the finished product must meet our expectations. How many of us have come away from a theatrical adaptation of a book dissatisfied because the plot, characterisation or dialogue has been changed? This happens because we have expectations and want to see them fulfilled. Shamanism is much the same. It relies on the shaman fulfilling the expectations of the audience, the traditional beliefs of how the spirit world is set out, what spirits do, what happens to the soul during illness, and how the shaman is expected to perform. Like a theatre audience, the shaman's community participates by suspending disbelief while the shaman performs. And, as Arbman's interpretation of possession might suggest, the more intense the performance the more effective it will be in promoting suspension of disbelief. Outside their minds, in the material world, the performance might be just someone dancing around in a strange costume, banging a drum, chanting rhymes, performing crude conjuring tricks, and apparently going mad. That is certainly how anthropologists saw shamanism, before observer participation became fashionable and deeper understanding began to dawn. But the community sees something different – in their mind's eye the shaman really is crossing the barriers between this world and others, struggling with hostile spirits and doing deeds of magical heroism. In a very real sense, the ecstatic journey does not take place inside a shaman's head but in the mind – the imagination – of the observer.

Wallis objects that shamanic experiences

> ... are not make-believe – shamans/neo-Shamans believe the 'spirit world' they interact with is real, very real indeed – and shamanism studies has in some more theorised quarters moved beyond conceptions of shamans as theatrical charlatans. Using 'performance' and other metaphors for understanding and

interpreting shamanisms/neo-Shamanisms therefore runs the risk of ignoring their seriousness and discredits practitioners. It may in part derive from a peculiarly atheistic, scientific perspective and reflects a deep-seated need on the part of Westerners to retreat into the comfort of metaphor rather than address the 'reality' of 'spirits' to shamans/neo-Shamans. (Wallis 2003: 69)

This is a reasonable objection, though we might argue that the 'reality' of what happens to one shaman might not necessarily be true for another. But even if it were true, describing shamanising as performance is not the same as claiming that it is charlatanism. Theoretical studies on shamanism do still frequently discuss shamanising in terms of performance, but the word is not used as Wallis seems to imply, in a derogatory sense, as a metaphor for either charlatanism or simple-minded fantasising. The word 'performance' is not used as a metaphor in any sense – its is simply a neutral term that describes what is happening at a shamanic séance with regard to the interaction between shaman and onlooker. That interaction is facilitated by two things: belief on both sides in spirits and a spirit world, and what a shaman does – shamanising, the performance. In any case, Wallis appears to forget that many onlookers take performance very seriously indeed, even when it has no more serious purpose than entertainment.

Basilov (1997) reports how Uzbek women attending shamanic performances he witnessed in the 1970s would fall readily into ecstasy, though his presence distracted them. I wonder how closely their 'ecstasy' resembled the state of absorbed theatre or cinema audiences – we often use the words 'entranced' and 'spellbound' of people wholly absorbed in plays or films. Depending on how absorbed they are in the characters and story, people may weep at tragic romances, experience genuine fright during horror films, and so on. Basilov also cites a nineteenth-century account of Nenets onlookers being drawn into their shamans' ecstasy, grimacing, shaking, foaming at the mouth, with bulging, bloodshot eyes and their hair standing on end. This is reminiscent of the behaviour of fans at boxing matches and other sporting events involving adversarial physical contact, who have often been known to emulate the performers by fighting among themselves. This mimicking of those who are the focus of our attention is known in other areas. For instance, men and women will often unconsciously mirror the actions of people to whom they are attracted. People watching football on television may find themselves automatically making kicking movements at critical moments in the action. We speak of being 'caught up' in the action, in the moment, or whatever – what we really mean is that we are acting outside our conscious control in accordance with what is going on externally. We even do it with actions that are generally wholly outside conscious control, such as that incredibly infectious phenomenon, yawning. The drawing into ecstasy of the onlooker at a shamanic performance appears to be similar to these phenomena. Like them, its form is dictated by what is being observed, and it occurs and develops within a culturally determined framework.

Humans are essentially gregarious creatures that tend naturally to fall into step with one another. One reason for this is that we generally read and return the signals given out by others on a variety of levels. Dramas, rituals and other performances involve the manipulation of those signals for artistic or religious purposes. Victor Turner suggests that rituals and dramas alike consist of the orchestration of separate elements – culturally resonant signs and references – that encode meaning. 'Their full meaning emerges from the union of script with actors and audience at a given moment in a group's ongoing social process' (Turner 1987: 24). Performance – whether religious, artistic or sporting – is something done in front of other people, the ones who as observers ultimately give it meaning. This is the case with traditional shamanism.

This is where many forms of neo-shamanism part company most significantly from the traditional shamanisms of Eurasia and America. They are so often presented as solitary pursuits that are primarily of importance to the practitioner as an individual or to a small group of fellow practitioners. Similarly, analogies made between shamans and ritual magicians in the Western occult tradition (such as in Drury 1982) fall at this critical hurdle. This is not to say that ecstasy alone or in small groups of fellow voyagers as an exercise in understanding and improving oneself, whether it is achieved through an actual change in brain chemistry or by means of guided imagery, with or without a drum and costume, is wrong. If it suits the individual and leads to no harm, then clearly it is not. But, bereft of social context, lacking the requisites of shared tradition and divorced from the essential nature of shamanising as performance, it is not shamanism as a shamanist culture would understand it.

6: THE PREHISTORY OF SHAMANISM

Something old?

How old is shamanism? When and where did it come into existence? These are not easy questions – nor are they new ones. Speculation on the antiquity of shamanism goes back to 1775 when Johann Gottleib Georgi suggested that shamanism was a very ancient and influential form of religious expression:

> The shamanic religion belongs to the religions of the ancient world. It is the oldest in the Orient and the mother of the Lamaist, Brahmanic, and other heathen sects. (Quoted by Flaherty 1992: 85)

For Georgi, the pagan religions of Europe were degenerate descendants of shamanism. However, he stopped short of saying that shamanism was the world's oldest type of religion, preferring instead to suggest that it derived directly from the religion of Moses, with which he thought shamanist tradition had much in common (Flaherty 1992: 86). While there was no firm consensus of opinion as to the actual age and precise origins of shamanism, by the early twentieth century there was a general agreement that shamanism went back quite a long way and was once very widespread. Furthermore, it was widely seen as an expression of primitive spirituality:

> ... if it was not once 'the common cult of all the Turanian (*i.e. Altaic-speaking* – AS) peoples' or even the 'very earliest religion of the world', as some are inclined to think, it seems certain to be a phenomenon of great antiquity and of relative primitiveness. (Casanowicz 1925: 434)

However, there were differing views. For instance, in 1891 Dordji Banzarov, a scholar of Buryat extraction, denied any ancestral relationship between shamanism and other Asian religions. He claimed that shamanism originated among the Mongol and related peoples. Shamanism reflected their 'primitive way of observing the outer world – Nature – and the inner world – the soul' (quoted by Czaplicka 1914: 167). Banzarov stressed the primitive nature of shamanism but unlike Casanowicz – who was writing at a time when the term 'shamanism' had gained currency among anthropologists operating among peoples outside Eurasia, particularly in the Americas – he preferred to see it as a phenomenon specific to one particular cluster of closely related ethnic groups. Shirokogoroff, on the other hand, took a rather different approach. He suggested that shamanism arose relatively recently, probably during the first millennium CE, as a consequence of the interaction between Buddhism and native animist religious beliefs. Shirokogoroff based his idea on three main strands of evidence that seemed pertinent in the context of his observations of shamanism among the Evenk and Manchu. These were the supposed derivation of Tungusic šaman from Sanskrit sraman, by way of Pali saman, meaning a Buddhist monk; the oral traditions of the Manchu and other shamanists that placed the beginnings of shamanism early in the second millennium; and material relating to shamanism in Chinese historical texts (Shirokogoroff 1923, 1935: 276-285).

However, the likes of Banzarov and Shirokogoroff were minority voices. The prevailing view was that shamanism originated in remote antiquity and was a primitive expression of religiosity that had been retained by cultures which had failed to progress to civilisation. (The same view is still prevalent today. Though nowadays scholars tend to reject the word 'primitive' in favour of supposedly non-evolutionist labels such as 'pre-industrial,' or 'pre-literate' – which, as their prefixes indicate, amount to much the same thing – or contextually meaningless terms like 'tribal,' 'indigenous' and the like.) This belief was mostly based on little more than preconceptions of European superiority or a simplistic application of Darwinian ideas to human societies. Not until the middle of the twentieth century was any hard evidence cited to support the idea of shamanism's great antiquity.

The invention of Palaeolithic shamanism
In 1912, while the three young sons of Comte Henri Bégouen were exploring a system of caves on their father's estate in the French Pyrenees, they discovered an array of art – engravings, paintings and sculpture – dating from the Upper Palaeolithic Magdalenian Culture. The cave – soon to be named Les Trois Frères after the Bégouen brothers – contained a picture (in a mixture of paint and engraving) of a strange creature, a composite of human, owl, lion, stag, wolf and horse. The figure also appeared to have part of its skeleton

superimposed. Bégouen had a keen amateur interest in archaeology and was friendly with some notable figures in the French archaeological world, among them the Abbé Henri Breuil, whose illustration of this fantastic figure would become famous. Breuil dubbed this oddity the 'God of the Cave,' but by 1929 to everyone else it had become a 'sorcerer.' In line with prevailing theories of Palaeolithic cave art as hunting magic Comte Bégouen suggested the figure was meant to be a sorcerer embodying the attributes of the animals (Bégouen 1929).

Surprisingly, in view of the figure's superficial but striking resemblance to the antlered and bear-footed Evenk shaman illustrated in Nicolas Witsen's book of 1692, the sorcerer of Les Trois Frères went unremarked by shamanologists for a number of years. The first person to use the word 'shaman' of this cave painting seems to have been E.O. James, albeit in an offhand manner while discussing Bégouen's interpretation (1957: 173). A few years later the Hungarian János Makkay made a more detailed comparison between Siberian shamans and the figure from Les Trois Frères (Makkay 1963). The idea was also taken up by Andreas Lommel (1967) and others.

In the meantime, shamanism had been invoked to explain other figures in Palaeolithic cave art. In 1952 Horst Kirchner concluded that a painting from the cave at Lascaux, of a rigidly posed male human figure with a bird-like head, depicted with a bison and what looks like a bird sitting on a pole, was intended to portray a shaman in trance (Eliade 1964: 481). Since Kirchner other strange cave figures – such as the bison headed figure of Le Gabillou and similar ones at Les Trois Frères and elsewhere have also been interpreted as shamans. In general, identification of these figures as shamans has tended to focus on their apparent composite nature – they are part human and part animal. More precisely, they are human in basic shape but have animal attributes or features. The Lascaux figure looks vaguely as if it has the head of a bird, while the Gabillou and other figures are bison-headed. At a greater extreme, the sorcerer of Les Trois Frères has a human outline with clearly outlined male genitalia, but features assigned to several different animals. These therianthropic features are frequently compared with the animal elements of shamans' costumes.

At first sight this blanket identification of composite cave figures with shaman costumes seems perfectly reasonable. If the shaman wears an animal disguise or magical costume with animal elements, and shamanism is associated primarily with hunting peoples close to our own time or contemporary with us, it makes sense to assume that

Therianthropic figure, Le Gabillou.

we are witnessing evidence for something very similar in the Palaeolithic. But on closer inspection we find that things we might take for evidence of Palaeolithic shamanism are nothing of the sort. The emblematic 'sorcerer' of the cave of *Les Trois Frères* is ambiguous and unclear, and its association with shamanism is largely dependent first on the Abbé Breuil's drawing of it, then on a secondary interpretation of various aspects of the figure. Makkay's analysis of Breuil's illustration of the Les Trois Frères sorcerer is illuminating in this respect.

> All details of the head are covered by an animal mask. Through this only the eyes and nose are transparent, or retaining human features respectively. There were holes for the eyes and the nose on this mask. The person wearing it must have seen and breathed continually during his movements or dance... His head is decorated with a mask with stag-horn, his face reminds us perhaps of an owl, his ears are like a wolf's. His hands are imitated by the paws of a bear or lion, his costume was doubtless completed by a horsetail in the back. (Makkay 1963: 58)

At this point Makkay speculates on the nature of the figure's painted stripes, which allow two possibilities – that they were intended either to represent the man's own skin beneath the costume, or to represent his skeleton. Makkay plumps for the latter. 'The most important proof of this assumption is the... self-standing presence of the left patella and portrayal of the feet... painted stripes mark the five toes of each foot separately, inside of the unitary outlines.' He goes on to compare this with the representations of skeletal bones on Siberian shaman costumes.

Makkay's analysis only holds up if in the first place Breuil's illustration is accurate and if identification of the figure's animal traits and other features is reasonable. Breuil's picture is actually an elaborated version of what is visible on the cave wall – to be diplomatic, it shows both more and less than there actually is. Photographs of the sorcerer of Les Trois Frères show just how imaginative Breuil's drawing is (see, for example, Bahn and Vertut 1997: 165). Importantly, photographs clearly show that the so-called skeleton is nothing of the sort. The toes and outline of the feet are not tarsal and metatarsal bones. There is no free-floating patella. The other painted 'bones' are clearly outlines of the figure's back, limbs and belly. They do not in any way resemble a skeleton. This

Abbé Breul's drawing of the therianthropic figure of Les Trois Frères.

effectively kicks into touch a major part of Makkay's argument. Whatever the sorcerer was intended to represent it was not a Siberian-style shaman with externalised skeleton. Moreover, the alleged animal features are indistinct and ambiguous. Even assuming that it was always intended as a unified design incorporating paint and engraving, rather than a painting executed over an existing

Therianthropic figure with bison, Les Trois Frères.

engraving, the exact nature of those features is difficult to determine. The sorcerer of Les Trois Frères might well depict someone in a ritual animal costume, though it could equally have been intended to portray a god or a powerful spirit. It might even have been intended as a metaphorical portrait of an esteemed or powerful individual. The plain truth is that we don't know what the artist intended. But one thing is sure – it gives no unequivocal evidence for Palaeolithic shamanism. Likewise the bison-headed human figures of other caves: they could be dancers or celebrants in ritual costume – perhaps even shamans – but they could just as easily signify something else entirely.

The 'bird-headed' man of Lascaux, which Kirchner interpreted as a bird-masked shaman in trance, is intriguing. It forms part of a scene with an eviscerated bison, a woolly rhinoceros (often downplayed or omitted from discussion of this scene), a bird on a pole, and a spear with an apparently discarded spear-thrower. Kirchner's idea would sit comfortably with the unconsciousness of Saami and Siberian shamans at certain points of their performance. However, the scene is patently a hunt – the gutted bison and hunting gear are clear enough – rather than a ritual. The 'shaman' has also been interpreted as a hunter, dead or dying from the bison's attempts at self-defence. (Another suggestion is that the bison has been fighting with the rhinoceros and that the human has moved in to take advantage of the carnage, which illustrates the range of possible interpretations of this particular scene – see Ruspoli 1987: 149–51).

The Prehistory of Shamanism

'Entranced' human figure with bison and bird, Lascaux.

The figure's bird-like features might well represent a bird-mask. But the figure is hardly naturalistic – a rectangle with stick-like arms and legs, most unlike the magnificent bison – and its head is not even especially convincing as a bird. The supposed mask could quite easily just be a sketch of human features. The bird on a pole – the shaman's detached spirit perched upon the pole that features in some shamanic rituals, according to the shamanic interpretation – could be just a bird. Kirchner's interpretation depends on accepting three things as fact: that the human is an entranced shaman; that his face is a mask; and that the roosting bird is his roaming spirit. None of these is worth anything more than a doubtful 'maybe' – and there are other possible explanations for the scene as a whole that do not rely upon interpreting a few selected elements of the scene as symbols for something else. For instance, the rhinoceros is usually ignored as though it had been tacked on as an afterthought, yet it looks to have been an integral part of the scene.

The case for these composite cave figures being shamans rests on slender evidence that is not really evidence at all – only interpretation. That interpretation is based on a comparison of selected trappings of shamanism recorded within only the last five hundred years with a few selected features of art that is at least ten thousand old and is also a long way from where shamanism has historically been practised. Identifying the Les Trois Frères figure as a shaman means a further interpretation of an initial interpretation of features in Breuil's drawing – a picture that is inaccurate and misleading. Kirchner's contentious analysis of the Lascaux painting aside, the other Palaeolithic composite figures resemble shamans in one respect only: they look like people in animal costumes, and shamans often incorporate animal images into their ritual attire. If that is the main criterion for shamanism, then we might as well apply it to a pantomime horse, with equal justification. Kirchner's interpretation of the Lascaux scene relies on selecting only four of its elements – the supine human figure, the man's face, the bird, and the pole the bird is perched upon – and arbitrarily deciding to ignore ambiguity and lack of clarity, and to reject plausible alternative interpretations. Kirchner then chooses to relate them to elements of shamanism recorded a continent away more than ten thousand years after the painting was made. The methodology is frankly unconvincing. Whatever the figures were intended to represent – and while they might well have been intended to represent shamans it is equally possible that they could have been intended as humour, for instance – such interpretations are not evidence for Palaeolithic European shamanism. Nor do they necessarily constitute evidence for the types of religious practice that existed at that time and place. All they really demonstrate is that the populations of Palaeolithic Europe included some highly skilled artists and that they were capable of imagining, for reasons as yet unclear, composites of human and animal.

Art and altered states

The composite cave figures do not constitute firm evidence for shamanism in Palaeolithic Europe. A recent theory relies on other evidence from cave art for the supposition that shamanism was practised in Palaeolithic times. Certain images from the Palaeolithic caves – abstract designs including waves, zig-zags, hatching and other geometric shapes – had long been assumed to be either decoration or idle doodles, or perhaps unknown magical or religious symbols. In 1988 J.D. Lewis-Williams and Thomas A. Dowson proposed a radical new explanation – that these designs represented images actually seen by Palaeolithic shamans in trance states.

Lewis-Williams and Dowson studied rock art associated with two present-day peoples, the San of southern Africa and the

Rain animal with winged or feathered beings, including one with a nosebleed. Southern African San rock painting. After Lewis-Williams 2002.

Shoshone of the Coso Range in the California Great Basin, each of which included 'shamanism' in their culture. This built upon earlier studies by Lewis-Williams, which suggested that motifs in San rock were derived from trance visions, and research on altered states of conscious which suggested that their effects were constant in all cultures and times, hard-wired into the human nervous system. From these researches Lewis-Williams developed a model of 'entoptic phenomena' – also known as phosphenes, images recurring continually in altered states thanks to the commonality of the human neurological structure – to interpret rock art motifs. Entoptic images fall into seven geometric forms: the lattice or grid; parallel lines; dots; zigzags; concentric curves; meandering lines; and spirals. Lewis-Williams and Dowson concluded that a close correspondence between San and Coso rock art supported their hypothesis: entoptic images matched motifs in the rock art. They also found a correlation between these images and geometric designs from the Palaeolithic caves of Europe. Critical to this theory was the idea that there were three basic stages of trance, characterised by visual phenomena developing from flashes of light and simple shapes to complex hallucinations, and that these were reflected in the art (Lewis-Williams and Dowson 1988).

Since 1988 Lewis-Williams and Dowson have expanded and refined their hypothesis, separately and in collaboration with other scholars (see for example, Clottes and Lewis-Williams 1998; Lewis-Williams 1997, 2001, 2002, 2002a). Their idea has acquired many supporters, such as James L. Pearson (2002) and Jean Clottes. The hypothesis has moved on a quite a bit from the initial concern with geometric art. Now, other features of rock art – such as elongated or floating human figures and images of people, therianthropism and with nosebleeds – have been confidently identified as shamans in trance. Elongation is seen as a representation of the change in bodily self-perception in trance, while the floating figure is taken as an obvious representation of someone in ecstasy. Therianthropic figures depict the hallucination of changing into an animal. The nosebleed occurs because of the great exertion required by trance dancing. San informants have substantiated their identification of these figures as shamans.

While it is not yet the predominant paradigm in rock art research, the trance model is catching on fast – for instance, Andrzej Rozwadowski (2001) has invoked entoptic images to explain motifs in Central Asian rock art, including 'solar headed' figures otherwise explained as sun gods. Most archaeologists and anthropologists remain cautious, however, and following the example of a severe criticism of the trance model by Anne Solomon (1997) some have gone on the offensive. Two of the theory's chief opponents are the archaeologist Paul G. Bahn and the anthropologist Alice Beck Kehoe. Bahn at first cautiously welcomed the trance model, but grew increasingly disillusioned as he learned more about shamanism and altered states of consciousness. Bahn's disillusionment found expression in a series of scathing criticisms of the theory and the attitudes of some of its proponents. Kehoe began her criticism of the trance model in a polemical study of the way shamanism has been used and abused by Western scholars but has since made more specific attacks.

Bahn's view of the trance model is based on several key points (Bahn 2001). He observes that proponents of the trance model base their understanding of shamanism on Eliade, whose idea of shamanism is distorted by personal bias in favour of a mystical interpretation, selective use (and misquotation) of ethnographies, lack of historical perspective and omission of key factors, such as the lack of a clear distinction between the ritual and secular in animist societies. Bahn also cites evidence that the three-stage model of trance is unsupported by clinical research except in association with drugs such as mescaline and LSD, that entoptic imagery is not indicative of trance but can occur in many other contexts, and that in any case trance (as clinically defined) is at best rare in Eurasian shamanism. Furthermore, the oral traditions that appear to confirm the shamanic nature of rock art in California and southern Africa were obtained from peoples with no actual connection with that rock art or any other. In Africa the traditional lore of people whose ancestors probably *were* responsible for the art flatly contradicted the shamanic trance hypothesis. The art represented mythology and was not a record of trance experience. Kehoe (2000: 72-74) agrees that there is no sure connection between rock art and shamanism. The 'shamans' cited by Lewis-Williams and Dowson do not produce art themselves, let alone rock art. With Patricia A. Helvenston, Bahn has produced a further assault on the trance model (Helvenston and Bahn 2002). They observe that only mescaline, LSD and psilocybine produce an altered state that resembles the three-stage model. As far as is known, only the fungus ergot would have been a natural source of such a drug in Palaeolithic Europe – but ergot is highly toxic as well as hallucinogenic and is unlikely to have been used. The other native plants containing powerful hallucinogens, fly agaric and henbane, do not induce a trance consistent with the three-stage model. No natural source of such drugs occurs in Africa. Other scholars have tested the trance model among Amerindian populations (Quinlan 2001; Steinbring 2001), in Spain (Díaz-Andreu 2001) and Central Asia (Francfort 2001) and found it wanting – though Francfort (1998) does find shamanist content in terms of iconography rather than altered cognition.

Over the last decade or so the argument for and against the trance model for explaining prehistoric rock art has bounced back and forth between its proponents and opponents. For instance, in a short response to a paper in *Antiquity* by Mairi Ross (2001) that mentioned the trance model in fairly neutral terms as an 'emerging trend' in rock art research, Kehoe (2002) observed that one such trend that Ross had failed to mention was that of opposition to the trance model. Kehoe also briefly pointed out a few of the trance model's shortcomings, not least that it relies on the assumption that today's 'primitives' mirror those of long ago. Lewis-Williams (2003) responded vigorously by reiterating the main points required for the model without really modifying his stance on any of the issues that had attracted the most criticism. It was also clear that he was, at second hand, still heavily reliant on an idea of shamanism that derived ultimately from Eliade.

In terms of the overall argument, this exchange – and others like it –resolves nothing. But it does illustrate the extent of the division between the two sides. (Not to mention the painfully slow process of debate in academic circles.) The bottom line is that supporters of the trance model persist in asserting the truth of a pernicious factoid – the universality of trance in shamanism – in the context of a view of shamanism that is fundamentally flawed, supported by evidence that is contextually irrelevant. Helvenston and Bahn (2002) have suggested that there may be ways to test the trance hypothesis for rock art. Even so, it is abundantly clear that shamanism is wholly irrelevant to the rock art theory.

Shamans of prehistory?

The interpretation of images in prehistoric art as shamanic depends on several preconditions. The first precondition is that particular states of mind are identical with trance or ecstasy as they occur in modern forms of shamanism. The second is that those states of mind involve perceptions that are reflected in shamanic ritual and belief. And the third precondition is that images from prehistoric art also reflect those states of mind and perceptions arising from them.

As we have seen in chapter 5, the nature of shamanic ecstasy is very much in doubt. It may be a genuine altered state of consciousness brought on by the ritual or it might be due to ingestion of hallucinogenic or narcotic plants. But more often than not there is no altered state as such, simply a *performance* of ecstasy. Where members of a shamanist people do enter altered states – usually by consuming psychoactive plants – it does not necessarily take place within the confines of shamanic ritual and it is not exclusive to the shaman. Even when drugs are used it is usually the case that both shaman *and* onlookers are under the influence, so that the shaman is no more of an ecstatic than anyone else, if alteration in consciousness is the criterion for ecstasy. Altered states of consciousness – trance, ecstasy or hallucination induced by whatever means – are not in themselves characteristic of shamanism. Shamanic ecstasy, journeying to the spirit realms, is conceptual rather than actual. In short, evidence of altered states of consciousness is *not* evidence of shamanism. If the images and decorative motifs of Palaeolithic cave art can be interpreted as representations of altered perception during drug or performance induced trance states, that does not automatically qualify them as evidence for shamanism.

It is clear that except for Central and South Amerindian peoples, where religious belief and ritual have become inextricably bound up with hallucinogens, the effects of drugs have little in common with shamanic imagery in most of Eurasia. Psychoactive mushrooms feature in the shamanism of the Chukchi and other northern Siberian peoples, but their spirit realms are much the same as other shamanist peoples among whom drugs are not used. The mushroom spirits of the Chukchi are an exception in Siberia, and besides they are not of the same order as other spirits in Eurasian shamanism. The nature of the supernatural worlds a shaman visits is actually more akin to that experienced in dreams than it is to the visually astonishing and emotionally disturbing worlds of hallucination experienced during psychedelic trips.

The relationship of Paleolithic art to the imagery of altered states of consciousness is ultimately unknowable. We have seen that the trance model of prehistoric rock art is in serious doubt and that the fantastic 'sorcerers' are an interpretation based on the assumption that shamanism has remained essentially unchanged for many millennia among certain peoples. And that depends upon accepting a further assumption that shamanism is as it is imagined by the archaeologists who project it backward onto ancient culture. Their conception of shamanism has been coloured by an identification of shamanism with trance and other altered states of consciousness, rather than the things that define shamanism in the first place, and by an over-reliance on the authority of Mircea Eliade.

Of course it is possible that something very much like historical shamanism existed in Palaeolithic Europe. But if the cave paintings as they stand in our present state of knowledge are evidence of anything it is not shamanism as history knows it. It might perhaps some form of magic or religion, possibly one among many, that could have developed into shamanism among some peoples and into other forms of magic and religion among other peoples. Why should we assume that the magico-religious practices of shamanist peoples have not changed since the days of the European Upper Palaeolithic? Much else in their lives has changed over the millennia – their economy, technology, religion, language, political connections and location – so why not their expression of religious ideas? For instance, we know that Buddhism has had an enormous impact on Siberian religion, influencing shaman costumes, cosmology and ritual. At the heart of the web of assumptions that underpin the idea of the 'shamans of prehistory' lies the same idea that has bedevilled anthropology for more than a century, that these are primitive peoples who represent an earlier stage of human development.

> The nineteenth-century comparative method noted that Siberian small nations subsisted primarily on reindeer, and archaeological finds indicated that Stone Age Europeans killed quantities of reindeer; therefore the Siberians could be living fossils for European Palaeolithic research. Siberian nations have shamans, therefore this perishable part of their societies could be attributed also to their fossil analogs, never mind that no drums or shamans' costumes, nor any paintings or carvings of these, have been discovered in Palaeolithic sites. Jean Clottes and David Lewis-Williams did not invent the hypothesis that Palaeolithic communities had shamans resembling those in historic Siberia, they merely utilize the nineteenth-century comparative method, modifying the nineteenth-century interpretation that Palaeolithic art is about hunting magic, to claiming it records *shamans'* visions of hunting success. They accept the nineteenth-century understanding that their human 'living fossils' are *less evolved* than civilized people. (Kehoe 2000: 94)

The degree to which Clottes and Lewis-Williams (Kehoe might have named more than a few others) really accept that understanding is questionable. The reality is probably that they are simply going with the flow of post-processual archaeology, which from the last couple of decades offers many examples of comparison between aspects of present-day indigenous cultures around the world with evidence from prehistoric sites in Europe. The idea is that ideas and beliefs that underlie the form and function of the practice that is known can shed light on the one that is not. But that does not affect the gist of what Kehoe is saying, that Western archaeology and anthropology are still handcuffed to an outmoded equation in which 'uncivilised' = 'primitive,' 'primitive' = 'early,' and 'early' = 'universal' – and that consideration of one part of the equation may elucidate another.

The way forward to the way back
Rather than persist in reverse engineering a prehistoric shamanism from modern examples of trance and hallucination that are not

wholly appropriate to shamanism, we should be endeavouring to investigate properly the way shamanism has developed and attempting to trace its origins through a more satisfactory method. The best and most obvious place to look is the *locus classicus* of shamanism, Eurasia – especially those parts of Siberia, Central Asia and northern Scandinavia that have inhabited for a long time by peoples that were historically shamanist. In those regions we can actually track shamanism quite a long way into the past. Information about Saami shamanism in Old Norse and medieval Latin sources confirms that it existed as a major cultural factor in Scandinavia at the beginning of the second millennium CE. As it surely did not arise fully-fledged precisely at the time Scandinavians began writing about it, we can be sure that it had an existence for some time prior to that point in time. Chinese sources that mention or describe in unambiguous terms the shamans of peoples ancestral to today's Mongols and Manchu go back to around the same time, but again we can presume that shamanism existed prior to that.

However, what we must not assume is that the ancestral shamanisms of the Saami, the Evenk or any other Eurasian people had remained unchanged for millennia up the point at which they entered the historical record. The known adoption of lamaist paraphernalia and costume by Mongol shamans is absolute proof that they did not. Similarly, the Evenk adoption of Mongol shamans' equipment is ample evidence that mutual borrowing among Siberian peoples has been going on for some considerable time. Add to the introduction at various times of copper and iron instruments and decorations, the use of manufactured textiles instead of animal skins and free borrowing from Buddhist cosmology, and a different picture begins to emerge. Instead of a type of magico-religious practice that has remained fossilised since Palaeolithic times we find instead a tradition that is in a constant state of change. If there ever was an original template for shamanism it may have looked rather different to historical shamanism and may have involved different ideas with regard to cosmic structure, what happens after death and the nature of spirits. In which case it would not have been shamanism at all, but a magico-religious tradition from which Eurasian shamanism emerged along with other expressions of religious belief that gradually grew into the diversity of forms we know of today. Any evidence at all should be treated cautiously.

Textual evidence does not go back very far, so we are forced to consider material remains. The trouble is that apart from a few copper and iron components Shamanic costume and paraphernalia tend to be made of perishable materials – cloth, fur, feathers, leather and wood. Consequently shamans' gear recovered by archaeologists tends to be pretty recent. Ironically, most of the best evidence may be found in rock art, but not in terms that would fit the trance model of ancient rock art. Mihály Hoppál has examined Siberian rock art for traces of ancient shamanism. The artwork includes depictions of bird- and animal-headed humans, animals and birds, archers, 'solar headed' figures, faces or masks – and figures with costumes and drums in what appear to be ceremonies. However, these date only from around 2000 BCE at the earliest and many are from the historical period. Anatoly L. Martynov (1991) finds a range of influences and ideas preserved in ancient Siberian art, including shamanism, but does not make a great deal of it. Hoppál sees no clear evidence for shamanism in most of the rock art. He observes that even though Siberia 'is a place where a kind of continuity of population is beyond doubt... one must be cautious since not everything on the rocks has a connection with shamanism or religion' (Hoppál 1985). Ekaterina Devlet (2001) offers more evidence of shamans depicted in Siberian rock art – but again her examples date back only to the same period. Esther Jacobsen (2001) looks at the rock art of the Esagaan Salaa/Baga Oigor complex of north-western Mongolia, which may be up to 12,000 years old, but sees no evidence for shamanism as we know it. Anna-Leena Siikala sees evidence for shamanism in Finnish rock art that dates from 3000 BCE at the very earliest (but could be very much younger). There is no clear depiction of shamanic ritual or paraphernalia but she is satisfied that it has a shamanic origin 'on the basis of animal-ceremonial practices and the associated shamanistic view of the world' (Siikala 1984). As there are plenty of historical hunter-gatherers with no shamanist element that is not entirely satisfying. The same is true of Francfort's identification of shamanic elements in Central Asian rock art (Francfort 1998).

The only compelling evidence for continuity of shamanic tradition from ancient times to the present is that from Siberia examined by Hoppál and Devlet. The evidence consists of a number of pictures of shamans with costumes, drums and drumsticks, some in scenes that appear to represent shamanic performance, and at least one showing what seems to be a flying shaman complete with drum and drumstick. None are earlier than about 2000 BCE. The oldest of these particular artworks are located in the Altai, Tuva, Sakha and Khakas regions, along the Middle Yenisei and Middle Lena rivers, and Mongolia – a large but fairly compact area, roughly

'Solar headed' petroglyph of second millennium BCE from Tamgaly Valley, Kazakhstan. After Rozwadowski (2001).

an ellipse tilted from south-west to north-east with its focus to the north-west of Lake Baikal. This is where we find the best evidence for prehistoric shamanism, exactly where classical shamanism, with costume, drum and other paraphernalia, occurs in historical times. From this we might tentatively suggest that if Eurasian shamanism as we know it developed anywhere, it developed in that area.

The only hard evidence to indicate otherwise is an object from the Oxus Civilisation of Bactria and Margiana, which flourished between 2300 and 1800 BCE. This is a cylinder seal that shows what may well be a shamanic ceremony, with a hybrid human-animal figure beating a drum, with another holding a staff, two more holding a pole and other balanced atop the pole by its navel. A larger, horned figure is at the centre of the scene, beneath a creature that might be a wolf or dog. Above the drummer is another therianthrope holding two sistra, rattle-like instruments common in the Mediterranean and Middle Eastern cultures. Francfort (1994) thinks the hybrid figures look like apes but they seem closer to bears, or perhaps wolves, in human pose. However, he sees this as a shamanic ceremony focused upon a representation of the *axis mundi*, similar to the shamans' poles found in Siberia in recent times. Francfort cites other evidence of shamanism, mainly that for the ritual consumption of opium and ephedra, to support his contention that the religious and symbolic system of the Oxus Civilisation was primarily of Central Asian origin. Given the dates for the Oxus Civilsation, a Central Asian origin could cover a multitude of possibilities Altaic-speakers, Uralic-speakers or early Iranian-speaking nomads. Furthermore, in the light of chapter 5 we should seriously question this association of drugs with shamanism. Whatever the reality might have been, if the scene on the cylinder seal is acceptable as shamanic performance then it may well be the earliest evidence for Eurasian shamanism outside the Siberian area described here. Until and unless something else comes along, that is.

Although there are still many ifs and buts to deal with, this seems to be the best way forward for tracing the history and origins of shamanism – good, old-fashioned archaeological leg-work combined with cautious anthropological insight, common sense and a refusal to speculate too far outside the available evidence. It helps if we begin our search by looking at the places where *real* shamans have historically lived and plied their trade – that is where we are most likely to find any traces that might have been left by their putative shamanist ancestors. Most importantly, we should certainly stop looking at indigenous peoples as if they were fossils, unchanged through many thousands of years.

7: A NEW AGE OF SHAMANISM

Spiritual discontent and the archaic revival
The last three decades of the twentieth century saw a major surge of interest in shamanism in Europe and North America, one that continues unabated in the early years of the present century. There has been a concomitant increase in the number of published books and papers with the words *shaman* or *shamanism* in their titles or as their subjects. On the Internet there are now literally thousands of sites dealing with the subject. This burgeoning interest is not just the preserve of scholars, however. Many people are now actively participating in or practising a wide variety of beliefs, rituals and personal psychodramas that are claimed to be shamanic. Neutral observers usually refer to these collectively as neo-shamanism.

The roots of neo-shamanism are many and deep. It would take a fairly detailed history of late twentieth century counter-culture to do justice to the background, and this is not the place for such a diversion. But it is true up to a point that the main factors in the rise of neo-shamanism lie where popular anthropology and the drug culture meet. The beginning may perhaps be traced to the publication in 1954 of Aldous Huxley's *The Doors of Perception*, which brought a dimension of respectability to the idea that drugs could open the way to genuine spiritual experience. The erratic polymath Aleister Crowley had been advocating drug use for similar ends for a long time prior to that, of course. But in those days Crowley – the 'wickedest man alive' and self-styled 'Great Beast' – was not the kind of person whose words were given much weight outside strictly occult circles. Later in the 1950s writers such as William Burroughs, Jack Kerouac and Allen Ginsberg experimented with a variety of drugs to assist the creative process – Burroughs even tried the South American ritual concoction *yagé*. In the 1960s cannabis and LSD became more widely known through their association with high-profile users such as the Beatles and other pop stars. Drug use began to take off in a big way, especially among the young. Spiritual enlightenment was closely associated with drugs or their users. Timothy Leary preached the gospel according to LSD, while John C. Lilly explored inner space and tried to communicate telepathically with dolphins. Jim Morrison and the Doors (named after Huxley's book) sham-shamanised onstage, the Beatles went off to India with the Maharishi to seek enlightenment, the Rolling Stones were busted, and Brian Jones went to North Africa and discovered the trance pipes of Joujouka. Interest in Aleister Crowley was renewed, thanks in no small part to his appearance as a face in the crowd on Peter Blake's cover design for the Beatles' *Sergeant Pepper's Lonely Hearts Club Band*. Across the USA and Europe, young people were turning on, tuning in, and dropping out. The process continued through the 1970s and found new energy with the Ecstasy-fuelled dance culture of the late 1980s and the 1990s.

The other major catalyst for the rise of neo-shamanism was the publication within the space of ten years of a number of key texts by academics – anthropologists, historians of religion and an ethnobotanist. In the first place there was the publication of Mircea Eliade's *Shamanism* in English in 1964. In 1970 John M. Allegro published *The Sacred Mushroom and the Cross*, in which he argued that Christianity was based on the cult of a hallucinogenic mushroom. And in 1971 R. Gordon Wasson published *Soma: Divine Mushroom of Immortality*, a book arguing that the ancient Indian divine beverage *soma* had been a hallucinogenic mushroom. Allegro's book attracted wide media coverage – inevitably it was deemed blasphemous by many Christians, and just as inevitably that attracted even more attention, to the point where in 1973 an abridged paperback version was published for the popular market. While these books were not written to satisfy the demands of a youth culture that was increasingly fascinated by drugs and the quest for spiritual enlightenment, they certainly caught the *zeitgeist*. I have already discussed the influence Eliade's book had on the germination of New Age philosophy in conjunction with the ideas of C.G. Jung and Joseph Campbell. Wasson and Allegro were not on that particular wavelength, but there is no doubt that their association of drugs with the core beliefs of major world religions resonated with wider interest in more exotic spiritual ideas and helped pave the way for the coming New Age movement.

In 1968 Carlos Castaneda's *The Teachings of Don Juan* was published. Castaneda's evocative account of his growth to spiritual wisdom under the tutelage of the Yaqui *brujero* Don Juan was tailor-made for the time. An adventure of the mind involving exotic drugs, expanded consciousness and authentic-sounding Amerindian philosophy, *The Teachings of Don Juan* became an essential read on both sides of the Atlantic. Castaneda continued to write sequels into the 1980s, most of them becoming best sellers in alternative bookshops. Following hard on Don Juan's heels there appeared a pair of important collections of papers dealing mainly with the role of hallucinogens in Amerindian culture. Peter T. Furst edited *Flesh of the Gods* in 1972 – a year later came *Hallucinogens and Shamanism*, edited by Michael J. Harner. These collections included papers on the ritual use of *ayahuasca*, peyote and other hallucinogenic plants. The former included a paper by veteran anthropologist Weston La Barre, an expert on the Amerindian peyote cult, who suggested that hallucinogenic plants played a key part in the origins of religion. In the latter Harner proposed that hallucinogens were a factor in European witchcraft. The cumulative message was clear: drugs had an important function as a route to spiritual fulfilment, and that fulfilment lay in ecstasy.

Since the early 1970s many more books have been published dealing with the spiritual use of psychedelic drugs, shamanism, or both. Most books on neo-shamanism are frankly bad. The 'shamanism' they promote is often little more than a type of meditation fluffed out with a simplistic rehash of Eliade's mystical shamanic ideal and laced with mythological material that has no discernible relationship with any anthropological assessment of shamanism. New Age shamanism in particular is almost wholly concerned with personal empowerment and self-healing, and mainly based on a romantic vision of an Amerindian shamanism that has never existed outside the New Age movement. Many writers on Amerindian-based New Age shamanism – such as Harner (1990) – acknowledged but tend play down the use of drugs in Amerindian spirituality. Writers who are not in the business of promoting a specific worldview or belief system tend on the whole to be better researched and more measured than those that expound and promote the practise of New Age shamanism. For instance, Paul Devereux's *The Long Trip* (1997) is a thoughtful excursion through the role of hallucinogens in prehistoric spirituality by someone with first-hand experience of the historical and cultural *milieu* in which neo-shamanism has taken root. Others writers, such as Terence McKenna (1991, 1992) have adopted a more forceful stance which amounts to proselytising drug use. McKenna has been a major proponent of the 'archaic revival' – using supposedly age-old ecstatic techniques to get back to a closer relationship with one another and with the living earth. These represent the two poles of neo-shamanism: self-centred and clean living at one extreme, earth-centred and earthy at the other.

While it would be foolish to suggest that drugs and pop anthropology were the only factors that led to the rise of neo-shamanism, they were certainly significant and formative ones. But there were also growing movements into which neo-shamanism would come to take firm root. For example, by the mid-1970s witchcraft – the varieties that grew from the ideas of Gerald Gardner and his followers – was mounting a comeback. Many people were turning to other religions based on native Celtic and Germanic traditions, or to the veneration of a multiethnic Goddess, rather than the established faiths. We might also cite Goddess-centred beliefs as a factor in the rise of neo-shamanism, if only because one of the key Goddess texts has been Robert Graves' *The White Goddess* (1948), which refers to the use of hallucinogens in ancient European religions – and Graves had even taken hallucinogenic mushrooms. (For informative accounts of the rise of witchcraft and paganism in the late twentieth century, see Harvey 1997 and especially Hutton 1999, 1999a.) Another important element of the backdrop to the development of new Western shamanism was the environmental movement. Based on a growing concern that humans were fast making this planet uninhabitable through poor maintenance and wilful pollution, this gave rise to a number of inter-related organisations. For example, there were the Campaign for Nuclear Disarmament, the Ecology Party in Britain (later to change its name to the Green Party in line with its counterparts in mainland Europe), Friends of the Earth and Greenpeace. These organisations were initially characterised by a lack of political ideology – though the underlying themes were vaguely left-wing – until they recognised a need for wider policies as it became more likely that they could actually attain a degree of political influence. Since the late 1980s these organisations have largely been supplanted by a large, loosely knit collection of small groups and individuals focusing on issues rather ideology. In Britain these came into being at a time when major road-building schemes threatened ancient woodland, wildlife habitats and people's homes on a grand scale. At present the focus is more upon opposition to capitalism and an ill-defined globalisation, as well as single issues like war, genetically modified crops and nuclear power. But the shared vision is one of attachment to the earth. A less palatable phenomenon, but one no less important to the growth of neo-shamanism, is the resurgence of nationalism across Europe, especially in the wake of the demise of the Soviet Union and the fall of Communism, and in the West as a widespread 'native' response to immigration. In the former Soviet lands the emphasis is mainly on rediscovering ethnic or national identity after so many years of repression. In Western Europe and the USA, the drive is also essentially reassertive (see for instance, Crawford 1993), though for some groups its foundation is more in xenophobia and racism than in release from decades of spiritual constraint. The end result is similar, however – the revival, or more often the invention, of religious forms that are seen as more appropriate to the nationality or ethnicity of their adherents than religions imported from other cultures.

These factors are all relevant to the emergence of shamanism as a significant spiritual practice not only in the West, but also in the ancient shamanic heartlands of Eurasia. The search was on for a type of spirituality that could satisfy all or most of the needs of late twentieth century Western youth as well as older people yearning for something more fulfilling than the established religions had to offer. This is not to say that the decision to revive an old shamanism or invent a new one was entirely volitional or deliberately formulated to fit the multiple requirements of a particular mould. Rather that the *zeitgeist* – people's concerns, culture and personal interests – dictated the ultimate form of new spiritual movements and that some of those were based on various ideas of shamanism. The upshot is that there are now several main varieties of shamanism being practised in the West. There are also revivals of 'native' shamanism in the Americas, and particularly in Siberia. I shall briefly examine a few of these here.

Core Shamanism

Core Shamanism was developed by Michael J. Harner from workshops in shamanism held while he was a professor of anthropology in New York in the 1970s. In 1980 Harner published *The Way of the Shaman* as a manual for the many interested people who were unable to attend his workshops. The book is presently in its third, 'tenth anniversary' edition. Core Shamanism is based on indigenous shamanism, mainly Amerindian, but is stripped of elements specific to particular cultures. What remains is a generic technique for entering the 'Shamanic State of Consciousness' (abbreviated to SSC) and guidance on what to do while in that state. Core Shamanism is evidently founded on the platform of Eliade's assertion that genuine trance or ecstasy is common to all forms of shamanism and that it is a very ancient phenomenon. As I have suggested earlier in this chapter, Harner does not advocate the use of drugs to achieve the SSC – which is rather surprising considering that *ayahuasca* was pivotal to his acceptance of the reality of spirit worlds.

Although Core Shamanism is promoted in workshops and Harner's own foundation and its house journal, the essential teachings are expounded in *The Way of the Shaman*. The book begins with an account of Harner's shamanic awakening among the Shuar, and continues with a very basic introduction to shamanism, focusing almost completely on the SSC, which is attained by means of intense concentration on particular images to the sound of drumming.

> In the SSC, the shaman typically experiences an ineffable joy in what he sees, an awe of the beautiful and mysterious worlds that open before him. His experiences are like dreams, but waking ones that feel real and in which he can control his actions and direct his adventures. While in the SSC, he is often amazed by the reality of that which is presented. He gains access to a whole new, and yet familiarly ancient universe that provides him with profound information about the meaning of his own life and death and his place within the totality of all existence. (Harner 1990: 21–2)

This eulogy is followed by a selection of examples, both shamanic and non-shamanic (though no distinction is made between them), of how indigenous 'shamans' enter the spirit worlds. These are boiled down to the tunnel or hole, similar to those in modern stories of near death experience. Then Harner gives the 'first experiential exercise in shamanism,' a simple creative visualisation designed to be accompanied by a drumbeat. And so on.

Despite Harner's claim that Core Shamanism is the essence of shamanism stripped bare of cultural baggage, it is quite clear from the terms he uses that it is really a rendered-down version of several different varieties of Amerindian ritual presented as a way to self-realisation. For instance, Harner refers to 'power animals' and 'spirit canoes,' and ideas taken from Amerindian magic, such as 'tobacco traps' for disease spirits. There is hardly any discernible input from Eurasian shamanism. The emphasis is squarely on self-empowerment, healing and personal development. The exercises are essentially directed private reveries rather than socially functional performances, unless there is healing to be done. Even then the impression is that the healing rite is meant to be as closeted, discreet and confidential as a visit to a psychoanalyst or GP.

In 1985 Harner gave up his academic career and relocated to California, where his non-profit Foundation for Shamanic Studies still exists today. The Foundation's journal, *Shamanism*, ranges widely through the different forms of the technique and does not confine itself to promoting Harner's ideas (though it does promote his books, courses and drumming tapes). There is no question that Harner is sincere in his beliefs concerning shamanism, and no suggestion that he has anything but good intentions toward shamans and shamanism worldwide. To his great credit he has – through the Foundation – given substantial amounts of money to help preserve or restore shamanism in the Americas and Siberia. In spite of a critical view of Harner's ideas on what shamanism is, Kehoe (1999: 82) points out that he leads a relatively simple lifestyle and avoids the usual trappings of 'cult' leaders.

While Michael Harner is clearly a dedicated and conscientious man, his Core Shamanism is not similarly beyond reproach. In many respects it has no resemblance to shamanism as an indigenous shaman would really practise it. Harner's presentation of the SSC is more like a California dreaming than a Siberian one. Nevertheless, Core Shamanism has many devotees around the world, and through the Foundation has an enormous influence on revivals of shamanism among indigenous peoples. For example, the Foundation has helped fund the main organisation overseeing the revival of shamanism in Tuva (see below).

Seiðr and Seidr

Seiðr was a magical technique practised in medieval Scandinavia. Whether or not it was actually a type of shamanism – perhaps even borrowed from the Saami – is open to question. According to Snorri Sturluson's *Ynglingasaga* – a semi-mythological part of his historical cycle *Heimskringla*, written around the beginning of the thirteenth century – the god Óðinn was an exponent of *seiðr*. This magic was closely associated with women, to the extent that a man who practised it was stigmatised with something called *ergi*, a word that in other contexts seems to have signalled that the subject was someone taking the passive role in homosexual intercourse, an effeminate man. (The adjective formed from this word is *argr*.) Practitioners of *seiðr* were sometimes called *seiðberendr*, a compound of *seiðr* with a word used to denote female animals in heat (Ström 1974; Sørensen 1983).

Dag Strömback (1935) believed that *seiðr* was a variety of shamanism, but a different interpretation of textual evidence suggests rather that it was largely a form of hostile magic rather than what we might generally expect of shamanism (Stone 1994). Óðinn was associated with the *völva* women who were certainly shamans of some sort, if the description in *Eiriks saga rauða* is anything to go by – and there is a brief reference in the poem *Lokasenna* to Óðinn drumming with the *völva*. The *völva* (singular *völur*) have become inextricably linked with *seiðr* – though the link is slender – and whether or not *seiðr* really was a kind of shamanism the idea that it was has firmly embedded itself in present-day revivals of Germanic heathenism. For instance, Høst (2001) suggests that *seiðr* might not have been shamanism but uses the terms *seidhr* and shamanism interchangeably.

Modern seidr – I shall follow Wallis (2003) in using this form to distinguish it from the ancient Norse technique – is practised by members of present-day Heathen and Norse pagan groups, and by a some free-lance heathens. The extent to which it resembles any authentic magical technique from the ancient Germanic peoples is debatable. In the first place there is a serious doubt as to whether ancient *seiðr* was a shamanic activity. Moreover, while the Norse sagas and poems contain odd scraps of information about *seiðr* and references to its practitioners, there is simply not enough known about it to allow anything more than a very rough, partial picture of what it entailed. This has resulted in many variations on the theme, often with the yawning gaps filled in with ideas transplanted from medieval Icelandic poetry, interpreted in terms of shamanism, or taken from Siberian and – especially – Amerindian shamanism. Jenny Blain – a practitioner as well as an academic observer – observes that 'the seiðfolk do not reconstruct the past, though their practices are based in it' (Blain 2002: 158).

How does the practice compare with Eurasian shamanism? In terms of trance and ecstasy, not very well. Jenny Blain's study of seidr and its practitioners is revealing in this respect. Some practitioners talk about being possessed by the old Norse deities, who may dispense advice to those who are not possessed. That kind of possession is more like *voudun* than Eurasian or Native American shamanism. Similarly, the seidr spirit world is usually most unlike that experienced by Eurasian shamans – its features often have a fluidity that is distinct from the consistent structure of Siberian otherworlds – the animals may be unfamiliar, the geography changes. Furthermore, when practitioners interpret the events and characters they encounter in trance, the emphasis is either strongly on the kind of generalised spiritual profundity that characterises Eliade's approach, or on matters of personal spiritual development. In some respects the seidr trance seems to be an amalgam of magical meditation and role-playing adventure game. Some influences are easy to detect. For instance, an account of possession describes garments 'that are characteristic of Odin' – a wide-brimmed hat, eye-patch and cloak, perhaps also 'a tall staff... tobacco pipe and drinking horn' (Blain 2002: 66). While most of these things might well be associated with the god, Óðinn might be surprised to learn that he has taken up smoking. It seems pretty obvious that this particular version of Óðinn has acquired an attribute of Gandalf from Tolkien's *Lord of the Rings* – a character who was based on Óðinn in the first place.

Annette Høst, a Danish practitioner, describes how her own method of seidr uses the most common elements associated with *seiðr* in medieval texts: 'the staff, the song, the high seat and the circle of singers' whose song 'transports' the practitioner into 'an altered state of consciousness' (Høst 2001: 73). Høst's observations on that altered state are interesting.

> Sometimes, but not necessarily, the state which the *volva* is carried into includes a soul-flight. When there is a journey, there is a significant tendency for it to go to the middle world (including the 'big' middle world, that is to 'the end of the world' or 'east of the sun, west of the moon') or the lower world, but rarely to the upper world.
> But often the *seidhr* does not contain a soul flight in the familiar sense of the word. Rather, the practitioner might experience layer upon layer of realities at the same time... (Høst 2001: 75)

Høst seems to be saying that the type of ecstasy that characterises Eurasian shamanism is rare in her form of seidr. The usual effect is an intensely heightened awareness of the world coupled with a profound insight into the fluid nature of reality. When the altered state does resemble a shamanic spirit journey it is usually to someplace located within what the medieval heathen Scandinavians called Miðgarðr – the 'Middle Earth' where we live – or, less often, to the lower world. Like Eurasian shamanism, Høst's seidr makes use of the relevant local cosmology – in this case the three-layered cosmos of Norse myth – but unlike shamanism most of the action takes place in this world or those parts of it inhabited by supernatural entities. The traditional shamanic journey is to the upper or lower worlds.

Seidr is not the only form of neo-shamanism to inherit aspects of fantasy role-playing games, for which Tolkien's classic book was an early inspiration. Those aspects have blended seamlessly with meditation techniques originating in the Orient, the 'path workings' of recent Western occultism, and the idea of shamanic spirit journey, especially as it is portrayed in Core Shamanism. Although like an adventure game there is an element of the unexpected, there is a structure to these trance experiences in seidr. But it is the structure of Western ideas of 'vision quest' rather than the Eurasian shaman's journey to perform specific, functional tasks in a realm that is familiar and mapped. Where seidr does resemble Eurasian shamanism is in the often public nature of its workings. Seidr may be practised in private for purposes of an individual's spiritual self-development but in some branches of Heathenism it is primarily a public ritual, for oracular or healing purposes, performed to benefit the community.

One important aspect of seidr today is its implications for gay Heathens. Some Heathen groups frown upon homosexuality, but seidr looks back to a magical technique that was not only practised by the chief Germanic god but was also associated with homosexual behaviour. Unsurprisingly, some gay Heathens have taken up seidr, as have heterosexual men – though this may result in a modification of attitudes and behaviour (Blain 2002: 126–7). Unsurprisingly, there has been resistance, sometimes homophobic, to the interpretation of *ergi* as homosexual activity (Blain 2002: 116–29). Less depressingly, Høst (2001: 77) suggests that it could refer to the submissiveness required to enter trance, while Blain (2002: 140–1) suggests that the perceived 'unmanliness' of *ergi* might really refer to the vulnerability of a person in trance. These ideas are interesting, but they highlight the limitations of seidr as a coherent belief system. Both Høst and Blain stress that seidr is a modern practice that is not the same as the ancient *seiðr* even though it is based on ancient texts that mention the latter. I would argue that it is acceptable to base seidr on ancient texts – but not to interpret those texts in terms of ideas that are quite outside them. It seems far more likely that the medieval Norse writers knew exactly what they meant by *ergi*, and that the meaning was exactly the same as when the word was commonly used as an insult – effeminacy and womanly traits. That would certainly resonate with the transsexual shamans of the Chukchi and other Siberian peoples. On the other hand, ideas such as vulnerability and submission to trance are not found in the ancient texts in association with either *seiðr* or *ergi*, so there seems little point in suggesting that they might have been major considerations of the poets and saga-writers.

The Siberian revival: Tuva

Since the collapse of communism the member states of the former Soviet Union have been gathering momentum in the rediscovery and revival of suppressed elements of their indigenous cultures. Shamanism is one such element.

Tuva is probably the greatest success story in the Siberian shamanist revival. The indigenous people of this semi-autonomous region on Russia's border, with north-western Mongolia, who are related to the Mongols, have turned shamanism into a symbol of national identity. Tuvan shamanism was almost wholly extirpated during the Soviet era, so the Tuvans have had to start their shamanism almost from scratch, though the driving force behind the revival, Mongush Kenin-Lopsan, had been documenting the remnants of Tuvan shamanism for some time before that. Kenin-Lopsan, a descendant of shamans, was instrumental in the foundation of the Düngür Centre, the present focus of Tuvan shamanism, in the Tuvan capital Kyzyl in 1992. A respected authority on Siberian shamanism, Kenin-Lopsan has been designated a Living Treasure of Shamanism by Harner's Foundation for Shamanic Studies, which has also donated funds to the Tuvan cause.

One of the most illuminating accounts of the Tuvan revival is by Benedict Allen, who featured his own encounter with the Tuvan shamanist establishment in his BBC2 documentary series *Last of the Medicine Men* (Allen 2000). Allen describes a shamanism that is clearly based largely on Tuvan tradition, but which just as clearly has been augmented with ideas from further afield. The female shaman Ai-chourek, for instance, used as much New Age jargon as authentic shamanist terminology and her paraphernalia and costume indicated similar external influences.

In Tuva shamans are not supposed to practise without a license from the Düngür Centre, whose head – Kenin-Lopsan, the government-backed power in Tuvan shamanism – decides who is an authentic shaman and who is not, and whether or not a particular shaman can be interviewed or filmed. He even has the authority to decide whether or not a shaman may travel abroad to events and conferences on shamanism. Kenin-Lopsan comes across in Allen's account as authoritarian and manipulative, even slightly narcissistic, though impressively knowledgeable. Under Kenin-Lopsan's tutelage Tuvan shamanism seems to be increasingly commercialised and centralised.

One of the medicine-man's greatest roles is, of course, the priest. Once we are no longer hunter-gatherers, it seems that we humans get together to form a very fixed Church. Sooner or later, we have our first reformation, as Tuva was having now – the new pushing aside the old, the no longer relevant. The simple, spiritual inspiration of the medicine man was being sorted into an organized religion. Kenin-Lopsan was now a bishop, and soon there'd be sacred texts. One of his key *khams* – a man rumoured to have been taught his neo-shamanism by a New Age American lady – was presently proselytizing like a Christian evangelist in other parts of Tuva. (Allen 2000: 123)

Mihály Hoppál has a rather different view of Kenin-Lopsan – 'a living classic' – and has a more optimistic view of the future of Tuvan shamanism.

Current Tuva shamans, many of whom I have had the good fortune to meet, are characteristic figures in the history of shamanism in Siberia: many of them were imprisoned in the fifties, spending years in labour camps, and despite that they are again practising their craft. While speaking to them, their commitment and readiness to help could clearly be felt, as well as their pride in the fact that they are preserving and continuing genuine folk (ethnic) traditions. (Hoppál 1996: 3)

Only time will tell which of these forecasts is accurate. But we must remember that Siberian shamanism has always been subject to change and each ethnic group's shamanism has been influenced by ideas from outside.

From Siberia to Cyberia
The rise of shamanism as a spiritual force in today's societies, both East and West, has had a number of by-products. For instance, in addition to the examples discussed above, shamanism has now entered the mainstream – if that is the right word – of new religions based on old 'native' traditions, especially in the British Isles. In chapter 2 I briefly discussed the 'shamanisation' of historical European witchcraft among some academics and popular writers in

the course of the twentieth century. In line with that mood, and as part of the cultural changes discussed at the beginning of this chapter, Wicca and (generically) Paganism have become increasingly 'shamanised' over the last twenty years or so. Since the mid-1980s shamanism has featured regularly in the pages of 'pagan' and occult magazines such as *The Cauldron, Talking Stick* and *Moonshine*. This reflected a sea change in an area once dominated by Gardnerian witchcraft, Wicca and various occult orders more interested in the Western tradition of high magic, such as the Fellowship of Isis or the Druid orders. Even movements that had seemed to be settling in for a long and stable future embraced shamanism. For instance, the generic Celtic strand of Paganism took a hint from the possibility that druids were shamans and incorporated shamanist elements. (Though there is a tendency to see shamanism in terms of creative visualisation or guided imagery framed by an idealised Celtic mythology – see for example, Cowan 1993; Matthews 1991, 1991a).

In the 1980s *Moonshine* in particular featured a number of important articles on shamanism whose low profile does not justly reflect their influence. A series of articles by Phil Hine set the tone, advocating synthesis and claiming the individual's right to choose which tradition was suitable for them.

> We appear to have reached the point where, having broken all Western lines of Tradition and become divorced from them, we can try and access any other system on the planet. This is only to be expected when the very concept of national boundaries is teetering. The barriers to the cross fertilization of knowledge are being pushed back by the growth of information technology.
> (Hine 1988: 3)

Hine developed this theme, pursuing a vision of shamanism that was both eclectic and concentrated. That vision was also edgy and exhilarated, with nods to Dada and Surrealism, and a frank, gleeful acknowledgement of the dangers involved in Hine's extreme approach.

> Critics of the Western approach to magick often point out that it can become too much of a head-trip, concerned with abstractions and mental constructs. Shamanism however, is intensely physical, often to the point of intense discomfiture. Shamanic magick often involves pain, disarrangement of the

senses, delusions, hallucinations and states bordering on obsession and personality disintegration. It's a lot of fun, really. It's not very safe, there aren't (as far as I know) any short cuts, yet for some reason it is incredibly *trendy*, yet there doesn't seem to be much interest in Voodoo or Jivaro shamanism. Any ideas why? (Hine 1989: 9)

Phil Hine was one of the key figures in the development of Chaos Magick, an approach to spiritual and magical ideas that took its cue from postmodernism – see for instance Hine's *Prime Chaos: Adventures in Chaos Magic* (1999). Similar strands of thought have resulted in various forms of 'urban shamanism' (again with Hine as a key figure, but incorporating ideas from Antero Alli, Peter J. Carroll, Jan Fries, Terence McKenna and other 'alternative' writers on neo-shamanic themes) and 'techno-shamanism'. These forms of neo-shamanism are a far cry from Harner's gentle Core Shamanism with its blissful SSC, or the pastoral reveries of Celtic Shamanism. They are dirty and dangerous, and the spirit worlds they access are mean streets and virtual realities where the unexpected – and often the unpleasant – lurks around every corner.

Curiously, these new forms of shamanism in the West hark back to older ideas about what shamanism is. Hine's shamanism takes in Eliade's preoccupation with ecstasy and trance – though Hine gives it a mischievous twist – and the romantic idea of the shaman as a deranged and ideologically dangerous outsider, liberated from the restraints of ordinary reality and normal behaviour. In these respects, and in its eclecticism, Hine's chaotic shamanism is not so different from Harner's Core Shamanism – though they are polar opposites in terms of commitment and the physical level of participation. There is also that constant assumption that shamanism is a primitive form of spirituality and that practising shamanism is a way to recapture the primordial state of harmony with nature and the earth.

The agony and the ecstasy

Are neo-shamanism 'authentic' shamanisms? As we saw in chapter 1, Robert J. Wallis (2003: 21) thinks that they may be when enough people practise them and if they get results, and that in any case when people call themselves shamans it is self-defining. I would suggest that a neo-shaman is an authentic shaman if and when they perform and behave like people who are shamans in a tradition that is unarguably shamanistic. That means that they have to resemble one or other of the Eurasian shamanisms – and the same is true for so-called shamanisms among indigenous peoples elsewhere in the world. Nor is the number of practitioners or believers any guide to authenticity. And as for getting results – well, what are the results of shamanism? The ecstasy that actually seems to be quite rare in indigenous shamanism? The agony of initiation? The spirit worlds that in Eurasian shamanism are imaginal constructs rather than experience of different realities? The prestige and power indigenous shamans have among their own people? Or successful healing, which on its own is not an indication of shamanism?

Gordon MacLellan, a practising neo-shaman, suggests that a person is not self-defined as a shaman but defined by others and by circumstances.

> I'm called 'a shaman' – maybe by people who do not know any better – or even by those who should. But since none of us seems to be able to define exactly what makes the shaman, maybe when people feel the term is the right one, that is enough of a decision and that will have to do. 'Shaman' isn't a label that is achieved: not a status that can be measured, tested and awarded. Rather, it is something that comes upon a body and its appellation depends probably more upon the role that an individual plays within a community and, to some degree, how they achieve that rather than on any personal claim upon the title. (MacLellan 1996: 365)

MacLellan seems to be saying in a round about way that being a shaman is what makes someone a shaman. This might make perfect sense to a person in his position, but to those of us who prefer tighter argument it is a circular definition that doesn't help us get any closer to whether neo-shamans are really shamans.

From my own point of view, neo-shamans do indeed need to be measured and tested before they can be awarded the name shaman. There is no doubt that some practitioners are worthy of the title, displaying all or most of the characteristics of shamans in Eurasia as we know them from ethnography. Others are clearly not shamans in any but the loosest possible sense of the word. Given the readiness of many anthropologists and students of religion to accord shamanic status to every priest, herbalist and fortune-teller that comes their way, that ought to be enough. Yet it seems to me that the neo-shaman and the shaman may be growing closer together. For instance, the present-day practitioners of seidr include people who I would not hesitate to describe as shamans – although their techniques are probably nothing like the *seiðr* practised in medieval Scandinavia, they are rather like Eurasian shamans in function and form. Otherwise, we should remember that Western neo-shamanism is still in its infancy – just as real shamanism once was at some indistinct point in the past. Neo-shamanism today might grow into something very much like shamanism, especially as anthropological scholarship continues to feed back into neo-shamanist circles. Intriguingly, neo-shamans are now the subject of serious study by a growing number of anthropologists, some of whom – such as Jenny Blain and Robert J. Wallis – are also practitioners. The future of neo-shamanic studies looks very interesting indeed.

SUGGESTED FURTHER READING

The works cited as references in this book represent only a fraction of the publications on shamanism and allied subjects. Of those, many include papers not mentioned in this book but which give useful background information or theoretical discussion and are well worth reading. In addition to the books and papers listed in the bibliography I recommend the following books, all of which are in English and most of which have been published relatively recently and are still either in print or may be tracked down relatively easily on the Internet. In keeping with the spirit of the present work, recommended studies on shamanism among specific ethnic groups are restricted to peoples related to the Siberian and Central Asian peoples on whom I have focused.

Collections
CHILSON, Clark and KNECHT, Peter (ed. 2003), *Shamans in Asia*. London.
HALIFAX, Joan (ed. 1979), *Shamanic Voices: The Shaman as Seer, Poet and Healer*. New York.
HOPPÁL, Mihály (ed. 1984), *Shamanism in Eurasia*. Göttingen.
HOPPÁL, Mihály and HOWARD, Keith D. (ed. 1993), *Shamans and Cultures*. Budapest.
HOPPÁL, Mihály and PÁRICSY, Pál (ed. 1993), *Shamanism and Performing Arts: Papers and Abstracts for the 2nd Conference of the International Society for Shamanistic Research July 11-17, 1993. Budapest, Hungary*. Budapest.
HOPPÁL, Mihály and von SADOVSZKY, Otto (ed. 1989), *Shamanism Past and Present*. 2 vols. Budapest,
NICHOLSON, Shirley (ed. 1987), *Shamanism: An Expanded View of Reality*. Wheaton, Illinois.
PENTIKAINEN, Juha (ed. 1996), *Shamanism and Northern Ecology*. Berlin.

Amerindian shamanism
TAUSSIG, Michael (1987), *Shamanism, Colonialism, and the Wild Man: A Study in Terror and Healing*. Chicago.

Japanese shamanism
BLACKER, Carmen (1982), *The Catalpa Bow: A Study of Shamanistic Practices in Japan*. London.
HORI, Ichiro (1968), *Folk Religion in Japan: Continuity and Change*. Chicago.

Korean shamanism
COVELL, Alan Carter (1983), *Ecstasy: Shamanism in Korea*. Elizabeth, New Jersey.
WALRAVEN, Boudewijn (1994), *Songs of the Shaman: The Ritual Chants of the Korean Mudang*. London.
YU, Chai-shin and GUISSO, Rachel W.I. (ed. 1988), *Shamanism: The Spirit World of Korea*. Berkeley, California.

Mongolian shamanism
HEISSIG, Walther (1980), *The Religions of Mongolia*. London.

Saami shamanism
BÄCKMAN, Louise and HULTKRANTZ, Åke (1978), *Studies in Lapp Shamanism*. Stockholm.

Periodicals

There are a few journals and magazines dealing more or less exclusively with shamanism. Most are related to New Age or Core Shamanism, with the exception of *Shaman*, an academic journal published for the International Society for Shamanistic Research. The major journals are:

Sacred Hoop
Heddfan, Drefach Felindre, Llandysul, West Wales SA44 5UH.
www.sacredhoop.org

Shaman
Journal of the International Society for Shamanistic Research.
Molnar and Kelemen Oriental Publishers, Szeged, PO Box 1195, Hungary 6701.
www.arts.u-szeged.hu/journal/shaman.html

Shaman's Drum
PO Box 270, Williams, OR 9754A, USA.

Further reading

Spirit Talk
On-line magazine of Shamanic Circles.
shamaniccircles.org

In addition to these, articles and papers on shamanism and a range of associated subjects crop up occasionally in archaeological and anthropological journals, and in Pagan or Heathen magazines.

BIBLIOGRAPHY

AHLBERG, Nora (1982), Some psycho-physiological aspects of ecstasy in recent research.' Nils G. Holm (ed.), *Religious Ecstasy.* Stockholm, 1982.
ALLEN, Benedict (2000), *Last of the Medicine Men.* London.
ANAND, B.K., CHHINA, G.S. and SINGH, Baldev (1961), 'Some aspects of electroencephalographic studies in yogis.' Reprinted in Charles T. Tart (ed.), *Altered States of Consciousness.* 3rd ed. San Francisco, 1990.
ANISIMOV, A.F. (1963a), 'The shaman's tent of the Evenks and the origin of the shamanistic rite.' Henry N. Michael (ed.), *Studies in Siberian Shamanism.* Toronto, 1963.
ANISIMOV, A.F. (1963b), 'Cosmological concepts of the peoples of the north.' Henry N. Michael (ed.), *Studies in Siberian Shamanism.* Toronto, 1963.
ARBMAN, Ernst, 1963–70, *Ecstasy or Religious Trance,* Stockhom.
AUTIO, Eero (1991), 'The snake and zig-zag motifs in Finnish rock paintings and Saami drums.' Tore Ahlbäck and Jan Bergman (ed.), *The Saami Shaman Drum.* Stockholm, 1991.
BAHN, Paul G. (2001), 'Save the last trance for me: An assessment of the misuse of shamanism in rock art studies.' Henri-Paul Francfort and Roberte N. Hamayon (ed.), *The Concept of Shamanism: Uses and Abuses.* Budapest, 2001.
BAHN, Paul G. and VERTUT, Jean (1997), *Journey through the Ice Age.* London.
BALÁZS, J. (1996), 'The Hungarian shaman's technique of trance induction.' Vilmos Diószegi and Mihály Hoppál (ed.), *Folk Beliefs and Shamanistic Traditions in Siberia.* Budapest, 1996.
BALDICK, Julian (2000), *Animal and Shaman: Ancient Religions of Central Asia.* London.
BASILOV, Vladimir N. (1994), 'Texts of shamanistic invocations from Central Asia and Kazakhstan.' Gary Seaman and Jane S. Day (ed.), *Ancient Traditions: Shamanism in Central Asia and the Americas.* Niwot, Colorado, 1994.
BASILOV, Vladimir N. (1996), 'Vestiges of transvestism in Central-Asian shamanism.' Vilmos Diószegi and Mihály Hoppál (ed.),

Shamanism in Siberia. Budapest, 1996.

BASILOV, Vladimir N. (1997), 'Chosen by the spirits.' Marjorie Mandelstam Balzer (ed.), *Shamanic Worlds: Rituals and Lore of Siberia and Central Asia.* New York, 1997.

BALZER, Marjorie Mandelstam (1996), 'Sacred genders in Siberia.' S.P. Ramet (ed.), *Reversals and Gender.* London, 1996. Reprinted in Graham Harvey (ed.), *Shamanism: A Reader.* London, 2003.

BAYLIS, Philippa (1988), *An Introduction to Primal Religions.* Edinburgh.

BÉGOUEN, Count Henri (1929), 'The magic origin of prehistoric art.' *Antiquity* 3.

BJÖRKQVIST, Kaj (1982), 'Ecstasy from a physiological point of view.' Nils G. Holm (ed.), *Religious Ecstasy.* Stockholm, 1982.

BLAIN, Jenny (2002), *Nine Worlds of Seid-Magic: Ecstasy and Neo-Shamanism in North European Paganism.* London.

BOGORAS, Waldemar G. (1904-1910), *The Chukchee.* New York.

BOYER, L. Bryce, BOYER, Ruth M., and BASEHART, Harry W. (1973), 'Shamanism and peyote use among the Apaches of the Mescalero Indian reservation.' Michael J. Harner (ed.), *Hallucinogens and Shamanism.* Oxford, 1973.

BUTLER, Judith (1990), *Gender Trouble: Feminism and the Subversion of Identity.* London.

CAMPBELL, Joseph (1949), *The Hero with a Thousand Faces.* New York.

CAMPBELL, Joseph (2nd ed. 1969), *The Masks of God: Primitive Mythology.* New York.

CAMPBELL, Joseph (1984), *The Way of the Animal Powers: Historical Atlas of World Mythology, Volume 1.* London.

CASANOWICZ, I.M. (1925), 'Shamanism of the natives of Siberia.' Smithsonian Report for 1924.

CHADWICK, Nora K. (1936), 'Shamanism among the Tatars of Central Asia.' *Journal of the Royal Anthropological Institute* 66.

CHERNETSOV, V.N. (1963), 'Concepts of the soul among the Ob Ugrians.' Henry N. Michael (ed.), *Studies in Siberian Shamanism.* Toronto, 1963.

CHOUCHA, Nadia (1991), *Surrealism and the Occult.* Oxford.

CLOTTES, Jean, and LEWIS-WILLIAMS, David (1998), *The Shamans of Prehistory: Trance and Magic in the Painted Caves.* New York.

COHN, Norman (1975), *Europe's Inner Demons.* London.

COOK, C.M. and PERSINGER, Michael (1997). 'Experimental

induction of the 'sensed presence' in normal subjects and an exceptional subject.' *Perceptual and Motor Skills 85.*
CORRADI MUSI, Carla (1995), 'The shaman-actor in the Finno-Ugric area: Considerations on the ritual theatre.' Tae-gon Kim and Mihály Hoppál (ed.), *Shamanism and Performing Arts.* Budapest, 1995.
CORRADI MUSI, Carla (1997), *Shamanism From East to West.* Budapest.
COWAN, Tom, 1993, *Fire in the Head: Shamanism and the Celtic Spirit,* San Francisco.
CRAWFORD, Lucy (1993), 'Native shamanism.' *Talking Stick* 12.
CZAPLICKA, Marie Antoinette (1914), *Aboriginal Siberia: A Study in Social Anthropology.* Oxford.
DAVIES, Susan M. (1988), 'The Sami Nåjd.' *Shadow* 5/2.
DEVEREUX, Paul (1997), *The Long Trip: A Prehistory of Psychedelia.* New York.
DEVEREUX, Paul (2001), *Stone Age Soundtracks: The Acoustic Archaeology of Ancient Sites.* London.
DEVLET, Ekaterina (2001), 'Rock art and the material culture of Siberian and Central Asian shamanism.' Neil S.Price (ed.), *The Archaeology of Shamanism.* London, 2001.
DIACHENKO, Vladimir (1994), 'The horse in Yakut shamanism.' Gary Seaman and Jane S. Day (ed.), *Ancient Traditions: Shamanism in Central Asia and the Americas.* Niwot, Colorado, 1994.
DIAKONOVA, Vera P. (1994), 'Shamans in traditional Tuvinian society.' Gary Seaman and Jane S. Day (ed.), *Ancient Traditions: Shamanism in Central Asia and the Americas.* Niwot, Colorado, 1994.
DIAKONOVA, Vera P. (1996), 'The vestments and paraphernalia of a Tuva shaman.' Vilmos Diószegi and Mihály Hoppál (ed.), *Shamanism in Siberia.* Budapest, 1996.
DÍAZ-ANDREU, Margarita (2001), 'An all-embracing universal hunter-gatherer religion? Discussing shamanism and Spanish Levantine rock-art.' Henri-Paul Francfort and Roberte N. Hamayon (ed.), *The Concept of Shamanism: Uses and Abuses.* Budapest, 2001.
DIÓSZEGI, Vilmos (1961), 'Problems of Mongolian shamanism.' *Acta Ethnographica Ac. Sc. Hung.* 10. Reprinted in Hoppál 1998.
DIÓSZEGI, Vilmos (1962a), 'How to become a shaman among the

Sagais.' *Acta Orientalia Ac. Sc. Hung.* 15. Reprinted in Hoppál 1998.
DIÓSZEGI, Vilmos (1962b), 'Tuva shamanism: intraethnic differences and interethnic analogies. *Acta Ethnographica Ac. Sc. Hung.* 9. Reprinted in Mihály Hoppál (ed.), *Shamanism: Selected Writings of Vilmos Diószegi.* Budapest, 1998.
DIÓSZEGI, Vilmos (1963), 'Ethnogenic aspects of Darkhat shamanism.' *Acta Orientalia Ac. Sc. Hung.* 16. Reprinted in Hoppál 1998.
DIÓSZEGI, Vilmos (1967), The origins of the Evenki "shaman-mask" of Transbaikalia.' *Acta Orientalia Ac. Sc. Hung.* 20. Reprinted in Hoppál 1998.
DIÓSZEGI, Vilmos (1968), *Tracing Shamans in Siberia: The Story of An Ethnographical Research Expedition.* New York.
DIÓSZEGI, Vilmos (1968a), 'The origin of the Evenki shamanic instruments (stick, knout) of Transbaikalia.' *Acta Ethnographica Ac. Sc. Hung.* 17. Reprinted in Hoppál 1998.
DIÓSZEGI, Vilmos (1974), 'Shamanism', *Encyclopaedia Britannica.* Reprinted in Hoppál 1998.
DIÓSZEGI, Vilmos (1996), 'The problem of the ethnic homogeneity of Tofa (Karagas) shamanism.' Vilmos Diószegi and Mihály Hoppál (ed.), *Folk Beliefs and Shamanistic Traditions in Siberia.* Budapest, 1996.
DODDS, E.R. (1951), *The Greeks and the Irrational.* Berkeley, California.
DOLGIKH, B.O. (1996), 'Nganasan shaman drums and costumes.' Vilmos Diószegi and Mihály Hoppál (ed.), *Shamanism in Siberia.* Budapest, 1996.
DOUGLAS, Mary (1966), *Purity and Danger: An Analysis of the Concepts of Pollution and Taboo.* London.
DRURY, Nevill (1982), *The Shaman and the Magician: Journeys Between the Worlds.* London.
DUBOIS, Thomas A. (1999), *Nordic Religions in the Viking Age.* Philadelphia.
DUERR, Hans Peter (1985), *Dreamtime: Concerning the Boundary between Wilderness and Civilization.* Oxford.
ELIADE, Mircea (1958), *Rites and Symbols of Initiation: The Mysteries of Birth and Rebirth.* New York.
ELIADE, Mircea (1960), *Myths, Dreams and Mysteries: The Encounter Between Contemporary Faiths and Archaic Reality.* London.

ELIADE. Mircea (1964), *Shamanism: Archaic Techniques of Ecstasy.* Princeton, New Jersey.

ELIADE, Mircea (2nd ed. 1969), *Yoga: Immortality and Freedom.* Princeton, New Jersey.

FLAHERTY, Gloria (1992), *Shamanism and the Eighteenth Century.* Princeton, New Jersey.

FINDEISEN, Hans, 1957, *Schamanentum,* Stuttgart.

FRANCFORT, Henri-Paul (1994), 'The Central Asian dimension of the symbolic system in Bactria and Margiana.' *Antiquity* 68, 259.

FRANCFORT, Henri-Paul (1998), 'Central Asian petroglyphs: Between Indo-Iranian and shamanistic interpretations.' Christopher Chippindale and Paul S. Taçon (ed.), *The Archaeology of Rock Art.* Cambridge, 1998.

FRANCFORT, Henri-Paul (2001), 'Art, archaeology and the prehistories of shamanism in Inner Asia.' Henri-Paul Francfort and Roberte N. Hamayon (ed., *The Concept of Shamanism: Uses and Abuses.* Budapest, 2001.

FURST, Peter T. (1972), 'To find our life: Peyote among the Huichol Indians of Mexico.' Peter T. Furst (ed.), *Flesh of the Gods: The Ritual Use of Hallucinogens.* New York, 1972.

GENNEP, Arnold van (1903), '*Shamanism* is a dangerously vague word.' Translated from 'D'emploi du mot "chamanisme"' (*Revue de l'Histoire des Religions* 47/1) in Jeremy Narby and Francis Huxley (ed.), *Shamans Through Time: 500 Years on the Path to Knowledge.* London, 2001.

GENNEP, Arnold van (1960), *The Rites of Passage.* London.

GHEORGIU, Dragos (1994), 'Horse head sceptres – first images of yoked horses.' *Journal of Indo-European Studies* 22.

GINZBURG, Carlo (1983), *The Night Battles: Witchcraft and Agrarian Cults in the Sixteenth and Seventeenth Centuries.* London.

GINZBURG, Carlo (1990), *Ecstasies: Deciphering the Witches' Sabbath.* London.

GLAVATSKAYA, Elena (2001), 'The Russian State and shamanhood: The brief history of confrontation.'' Juha Pentikäinen, Hanna Saressalo and Chuner M. Taksami (ed.), *Shamanhood: Symbolism and Epic.* Budapest, 2001.

GLOSECKI, Stephen O. (1989), *Shamanism and Old English Poetry.* New York.

GOODMAN, Felicitas D. (1990), *Where the Spirits Ride the Wind:*

Trance Journeys and other Ecstatic Experiences. Bloomington, Indiana.
GRACEVA, G.N. (1996), 'A Nganasan shaman costume.' Vilmos Diószegi and Mihály Hoppál (ed.), *Shamanism in Siberia.* Budapest, 1996.
GRIM, John A. (1983), *The Shaman: Patterns of Religious Healing Among the Ojibway Indians.* Norman, Oklahoma.
HAMAYON, Roberte N. (1994), 'Shamanism in Siberia: from partnership in supernature to counter-power in society.' Nicholas Thomas and Caroline Humphrey (ed.), *Shamanism, History, and the State.* Ann Arbor, Michigan, 1994.
HAMAYON, Roberte (1995), 'Are 'trance,' 'ecstasy' and similar concepts appropriate in the study of shamanism?' Tae-gon Kim and Mihály Hoppál (ed.), *Shamanism and Performing Arts.* Budapest, 1995.
HAMAYON, Roberte N. (2001), 'Shamanism: symbolic system, human capability and Western ideology.' Henri-Paul Francfort and Roberte N. Hamayon (ed.), *The Concept of Shamanism: Uses and Abuses.* Budapest, 2001.
HARNER, Michael J. (1968), 'The sound of rushing water.' *Natural History Magazine* 77/6. Reprinted in Michael J. Harner (ed.), *Hallucinogens and Shamanism.* Oxford, 1973.
HARNER, Michael J. (1973), 'The role of hallucinogenic plants in European witchcraft.' Michael J. Harner (ed.), *Hallucinogens and Shamanism.* Oxford, 1973.
HARNER, Michael J. (3rd ed.1990), *The Way of the Shaman.* San Francisco.
HARRISON, Michael (1973), *The Roots of Witchcraft.* London.
HARVEY, Graham (1997), *Contemporary Paganism: Listening People, Speaking Earth.* New York.
HELVENSTON, Patricia A. and BAHN, Paul G. (2002), *Desperately Seeking Trance Plants: Testing the "Three Stages of Trance" Model.* New York.
HINE, Phil (1988), 'The shamanic survival.' *Moonshine* 11.
HINE, Phil (1989), 'Techniques of practical shamanism. Part One: Jack your body.' *Moonshine* 16.
HOLLIMON, Sandra E. (2001), 'The gendered peopling of North America: Addressing the antiquity of systems of multiple genders.' Neil S. Price (ed.), *The Archaeology of Shamanism.* London, 2001.

HOLM, Nils G. (1982), 'Ecstasy research in the 20th century – an introduction.' Nils G. Holm (ed.), *Religious Ecstasy.* Stockholm, 1982).
HOPPÁL, Mihály (1985), 'On the origin of shamanism and the Siberian rock art.' *Studia Hungarica.* Budapest, 1985. Reprinted in Anna-Leena Siikala and Mihály Hoppál, *Studies on Shamanism.* Budapest, 1998.
HOPPÁL, Mihály (1992), 'Pain in shamanic initiation.' Mihály Hoppál and Juha Pentikäinen (ed.), *Northern Religions and Shamanism.* Budapest, 1992.
HOPPÁL, Mihály (1996), 'Shamanism in a postmodern age.' *Folklore* (Estonia) 2.
Mihály Hoppál (ed.), 1998, *Shamanism: Selected Writings of Vilmos Diószegi.* Budapest.
HOPPÁL, Mihály (2000), *Studies on Mythology and Uralic Shamanism.* Budapest.
HOPPÁL, Mihály (2001), 'Cosmic symbolism in Siberian shamanhood.' Juha Pentikäinen, Hanna Saressalo and Chuner M. Taksami (ed.), *Shamanhood: Symbolism and Epic.* Budapest, 2001.
HORWITZ, Jonathan (1995), 'The absence of 'performance' in the shamanic rite.' Tae-gon Kim and Mihály Hoppál (ed.), *Shamanism and Performing Arts.* Budapest, 1995.
HØST, Annette (2001), 'Exploring seidhr: a practical study of the seidhr ritual.' Torben A. Vestergaard (ed.), *Shamanism and Traditional Beliefs. North Atlantic Studies* 4/1-2. Aarhus, 2001.
HULTKRANTZ, Åke (1957), *The North American Indian Orpheus Tradition: A Contribution to Comparative Religion.* Stockholm.
HULTKRANTZ, Åke (1973), 'A definition of shamanism.' *Temenos* 9.
HULTKRANTZ, Åke (1979), *The Religions of the American Indians.* Berkeley, California.
HULTKRANTZ, Åke (1992a), 'Aspects of Saami (Lapp) shamanism.' Mihály Hoppál and Juha Pentikäinen (ed.), *Northern Religions and Shamanism.* Budapest, 1992.
HULTKRANTZ, Åke (1992b), *Shamanic Healing and Ritual Drama: Health and Medicine in Native North American Religious Traditions.* New York.
HULTKRANTZ, Åke (1996), 'Ecological and phenomenological aspects of shamanism.' Vilmos Diószegi and Mihály Hoppál (ed.), *Shamanism in Siberia.* Budapest, 1996.

Bibliography

HUMPHREY, Caroline (1980), 'Theories of North Asian Shamanism'. Ernest Gellner (ed.), *Soviet and Western Anthropology*. London, 1980.

HUMPHREY, Caroline and ONON, Urgunge (1996), *Shamans and Elders: Experience, Knowledge, and Power among the Daur Mongols*. Oxford.

HUNT, Norman Bancroft (2002), *Shamanism in North America*. Toronto.

HUTTON, Ronald (1993), *The Shamans of Siberia*. Glastonbury.

HUTTON, Ronald (1999), *The Triumph of the Moon: A History of Modern Pagan Witchcraft*. Oxford.

HUTTON, Ronald (1999a), 'Modern pagan witchcraft.' Willem de Blécourt, Ronald Hutton and Jean La Fontaine, *Wichcraft and Magic in Europe. Volume 6: the Twentieth Century*. London, 1999.

HUTTON, Ronald (2001), *Shamans: Siberian Spirituality and the Western Imagination*. London.

ISAACS, Neil D. (1975), 'Up a Tree: To See *The Fates of Men*.' Lewis E. Nicholson and Dolores Warwick Frese (ed.), *Anglo-Saxon Poetry: Essays in Appreciation*. Notre Dame, Indiana, 1975.

JACOBSON, Esther (2001), 'Shamans, shamanism, and anthropomorphizing imagery in prehistoric rock art of the Mongolian Altay.' Henri-Paul Francfort and Roberte N. Hamayon (ed.), *The Concept of Shamanism: Uses and Abuses*. Budapest, 2001.

JAMES, E.O. (1957), *Prehistoric Religion: A Study in Prehistoric Archaeology*. London.

JOCHELSON, Waldemar (1905), *The Koryak*. New York.

JOCHELSON, Waldemar (1933), *The Yakut*. New York.

KAPELRUD, Arvid S. (1967), 'Shamanistic Features in the Old Testament.' Carl-Martin Edsman (ed.), *Studies in Shamanism*. Stockholm, 1967.

KASAMATSU, Akira, and HIRAI, Tomio (1966), 'An electroencephalographic study on the Zen meditation (Zazen).' Reprinted in Charles T. Tart (ed.), *Altered States of Consciousness*. 3rd ed. San Francisco, 1990.

KEHOE, Alice Beck (2000), *Shamans and Religion: An Anthropological Exploration in Critical Thinking*. Prospect Heights, Illinois.

KEHOE, Alice Beck (2002), 'Emerging trends *versus* the popular paradigm in rock art research.' *Antiquity* 76, 292.

KENSINGER, Kenneth M. (1973), '*Banisteriopsis* usage among the Peruvian Cashinahua.' Michael J. Harner (ed.), *Hallucinogens and Shamanism.* Oxford, 1973.
KIECKHEFER, Richard (1989), *Magic in the Middle Ages.* Cambridge.
KIM, Tae-Gon (1995), 'The symbolic ur-meaning of shamanism and performing arts.' Tae-gon Kim and Mihály Hoppál (ed.), *Shamanism and Performing Arts.* Budapest, 1995.
KJELLSTRÖM, Rolf (1991), 'Traditional Saami hunting in relation to drum motifs of animals and hunting.' Tore Ahlbäck and Jan Bergman (ed.), *The Saami Shaman Drum.* Stockholm, 1991.
KRASHENINNIKOV, Stepan Petrovich (1972), *Explorations of Kamchatka, North Pacific Scimitar.* Portland, Oregon.
KROEBER, Alfred L. (1923), 'American culture and the Northwest Coast.' *American Anthropologist 25.*
KUPER, Adam (1988), *The Invention of Primitive Society: Transformations of an Illusion.* London.
La BARRE, Weston (1970), *The Ghost Dance: Origins of Religion.* New York.
La BARRE, Weston (1972), 'Hallucinogens and the shamanic origins of religion.' Peter T. Furst (ed.), *Flesh of the Gods: The Ritual Use of Hallucinogens.* New York, 1972.
La BARRE, Weston (5th ed. 1989), *The Peyote Cult.* London.
LAKOFF, George and JOHNSON, Mark (1980), *Metaphors We Live By.* Chicago.
LAUFER, Berthold (1917), 'Origin of the word shaman.' *American Anthropologist 19.*
LAYTON, Robert (1997), *An Introduction to Theory in Anthropology.* Cambridge.
LÈVI-STRAUSS, Claude (1963), *Structural Anthropology.* New York.
LEWIS, I.M. (2nd ed. 1989), *Ecstatic Religion: A Study of Shamanism and Spirit Possession.* London.
LEWIS-Williams, J.D. (1997), 'Harnessing the brain: Vision and shamanism in Upper Palaeolithic Western Europe.' Margaret W. Conkey, Olga Soffer, Deborah Stratmann and Nina G. Jablonski (ed.), *Beyond Art: Pleistocene Image and Symbol.* San Francisco, 1997.
LEWIS-WILLIAMS, J.D. (2001), Southern African shamanistic rock art in its social and cognitive contexts.' Neil S. Price (ed.), *The Archaeology of Shamanism.* London, 2001.
LEWIS-WILLIAMS, J.D (2002), *A Cosmos in Stone: Interpreting*

Religion and Society through Rock Art. Walnut Creek, California.
LEWIS-WILLIAMS, J.D. (2002a), *The Mind in the Cave: Consciousness and the Origins of Art.* London.
LEWIS-WILLIAMS, J.D. (2003), 'Putting the record straight: Rock art and shamanism.' *Antiquity* 77, 295.
LEWIS-WILLIAMS, J.D. and DOWSON, Thomas A. (1988), 'The signs of all times: Entoptic phenomena in Upper Palaeolithic art.' *Current Anthropology* 29.2.
LINCOLN, Bruce (1989), *Discourse and the Construction of Society: Comparative Studies of Myth, Ritual, and Classification.* Oxford.
LOMMEL, Andreas (1967), *Shamanism: The Beginnings of Art.* New York.
LUBBOCK, John (1870), *The Origin of Civilisation and the Primitive Condition of Man.* London.
LUNDMARK, Bo (1987), 'Rijkuo-Maja and Silbo-Gåmmoe – towards the question of female shamanism in the Saami area.' Tore Ahlbäck (ed.), *Saami Religion.* Åbo (Turku), 1987.
MacCULLOCH, J.A. (1911), *The Religion of the Ancient Celts.* London.
McCLENON, James (2002), *Wondrous Healing: Shamanism, Human Evolution and the Origin of Religion.* Dekalb, Illinois.
McKENNA, Terence (1992), *Food of the Gods: The Search for the Original Tree of Knowledge. A Radical History of Plants, Drugs and human Evolution.* New York.
MacLELLAN, Gordon (1996), 'Dancing on the edge: shamanism in modern Britain.' Graham Harvey and Charlotte Hardman (ed.), *Paganism Today.* London, 1996. Reprinted in Graham Harvey (ed.), *Shamanism: A Reader.* London, 2003.
MADDOX, John Lee (1929), *The Medicine Man: A Sociological Study of the Character and Evolution of Shamanism.* New York. (Reprinted as *Shamans and Shamanism.* New York, 2003.)
MAKKAY, János (1963), 'An important proof to the prehistory of shamanism: The interpretation of the masked human figure of the cave Les Trois Frères.' *Alba Regia* 2-3. Reprinted in János Makkay, *Two Studies on Early Shamanism.* Budapest, 1999.
MANKER, E. (1996), '*Seite* cult and drum magic of the Lapps.' Vilmos Diószegi and Mihály Hoppál (ed.), *Folk Beliefs and Shamanistic Traditions in Siberia.* Budapest, 1996.
MATTHEWS, John (1991), *Taliesin: Shamanism and the Bardic Mysteries in Britain and Ireland.* London.

MATTHEWS, John (1991a), *The Celtic Shaman: A Handbook*. Shaftesbury.
MERKUR, Daniel (1985), *Becoming Half Hidden: shamanism and Initiation Among the Inuit*. Stockholm.
MIKHAILEV, Tara M., 1987, 'Buryat shamanism.' Marjorie Mandelstam Balzer (ed), *Shamanism: Soviet Studies of Traditional Religion in Siberia and Central Asia*, New York.
MIRONOV, N.D. and SHIROKOGOROFF, S.M. (1924), 'Sramana-Shaman. Etymology of the word "shaman".' *Journal of the Royal Asiatic Society, North-China Branch (Shanghai)* 55.
MONTER, E. William (1976), *Witchcraft in France and Switzerland: The Borderlands during the Reformation*. Ithaca, New York.
MUNN, Henry (1973), 'The mushrooms of language.' Michael J. Harner (ed.), *Hallucinogens and Shamanism*. Oxford, 1973.
MURRAY, Margaret A. (1921), *The Witch-Cult in Western Europe*. Oxford.
MURRAY, Margaret A. (1933), *The God of the Witches*. Oxford.
NEEDHAM, Rodney (1979), *Symbolic Classification*. Santa Monica.
NEWBERG, Andrew, D'AQUILI, Eugene, and RAUSE, Vince (2001), *Why God Won't Go Away*. New York.
NOEL, Daniel C. (1997), *The Soul of Shamanism: Western Fantasies, Imaginal Realities*. New York.
NORDLAND, Odd, 1967, 'Shamanism as an experiencing of " the unreal"'. Carl-Martin Edsman (ed), *Studies in Shamanism*, Stockholm.
O'HAGAN, Sean (2003), 'Making waves.' *The Observer Magazine*, 15 June 2003.
PARK, Willard Z. (1938), *Shamanism in Western North America: A Study in Cultural Relationships*. Evanston and Chicago.
PAVLINSKAYA, Larisa R. (1994), 'The shaman costume: image and myth.' Gary Seaman and Jane S. Day (ed.), *Ancient Traditions: Shamanism in Central Asia and the Americas*. Niwot, Colorado, 1994.
PEARSON, James L. (2002) *Shamanism and the Ancient Mind: A Cognitive Approach to Archaeology*. Walnut Creek, California.
POPOV, A.A. (1996), 'How Sereptie Djaruoskin of the Nganasans (Tavgi Samoyeds) became a shaman.' Vilmos Diószegi and Mihály Hoppál (ed.), *Folk Beliefs and Shamanistic Traditions in Siberia*. Budapest, 1996.
POTAPOV, L.P. (1996), 'The shaman drum as a source of ethnographical history.' Vilmos Diószegi and Mihály Hoppál (ed.), *Shamanism in Siberia*. Budapest, 1996.

Bibliography

PRICE, Neil S. (2001), 'An archaeology of altered states: shamanism and material culture studies.' Neil S. Price (ed.), *The Archaeology of Shamanism*. London, 2001.

PROKOFYEVA, Ye. D, (1963), 'The costume of an Enets shaman.' Henry N. Michael (ed.), *Studies in Siberian Shamanism*. Toronto, 1963.

QUINLAN, Angus R. (2001), 'Smoke and mirrors: Rock art and shamanism in California and the Great Basin.' Henri-Paul Francfort and Roberte N. Hamayon (ed.), *The Concept of Shamanism: Uses and Abuses*. Budapest, 2001.

RÄNK, Gustav (1967), 'Shamanism as a research subject. Some methodological viewpoints.' Carl-Martin Edsman (ed.), *Studies in Shamanism*. Stockholm, 1967.

REICHEL-DOLMATOFF, Gerardo (1972), 'The cultural context of an aboriginal hallucinogen: *Banisteriopsis caapi*.' Peter T. Furst (ed.), *Flesh of the Gods: The Ritual Use of Hallucinogens*. New York, 1972.

REID, Anna (2002), *The Shaman's Coat: A Native History of Siberia*. London.

RIPINSKY-NAXON, Michael (1992), 'Shamanism: religion or rite?' *Journal of Prehistoric Religions* 6.

RIPINSKY-NAXON, Michael (1993), *The Nature of Shamanism: Substance and Function of a Religious Metaphor*. New York.

RIPINSKY-NAXON, Michael (1997), *Sexuality, Shamanism, and Transformation*. Berlin.

ROSE, Elliot (1962), *A Razor for a Goat: A Discussion of Certain Problems in the History of Witchcraft and Diabolism*. Toronto,

ROSS, Anne (2nd ed. 1992), *Pagan Celtic Britain: Studies in Iconography and Tradition*. London.

ROSS, Mairi (2001), 'Emerging trends in rock art research: hunter-gatherer culture, land and landscape.' *Antiquity* 75, 289.

ROUGET, Gilbert (1985), *Music and Trance: A Theory of the Relations Between Music and Possession*. Chicago.

ROZWADOWSKI, Andrzej (2001), 'Sun gods or shamans? Interpreting the 'solar-headed' petroglyphs of Central Asia.' Neil S. Price (ed.), *The Archaeology of Shamanism*. London, 2001.

RUDGLEY, Richard (1993), *The Alchemy of Culture: Intoxicants in Society*. London.

RUSPOLI, Mario (1987). *The Cave of Lascaux: The Final Photographic Record*. London.

RUSSELL, Jeffrey Burton (1972), *Witchcraft in the Middle Ages*. London.

RYDVING, Håkan (1991), 'The Saami drums and the religious encounter of the 17th and 18th centuries.' Tore Ahlbäck and Jan Bergman (ed.), *The Saami Shaman Drum*. Stockholm, 1991.
SHIROKOGOROFF, S.M. (1923), 'General theory of shamanism among the Tungus.' *Journal of the Royal Asiatic Society, North-China Branch (Shanghai)* 54.
SHIROKOGOROFF, S.M. (1935), *Psychomental Complex of the Tungus*. London.
SHUYUN, Guo (1996), 'On the main characteristics of the Manchu shamanic dance.' Vilmos Diószegi and Mihály Hoppál (ed.), *Folk Beliefs and Shamanistic Traditions in Siberia*. Budapest, 1996.
SIIKALA, Anna-Leena (1978), *The Rite Technique of the Siberian Shaman*. Helsinki.
SIIKALA, Anna-Leena (1982), 'The Siberian shaman's technique of ecstasy.' Nils G. Holm (ed.), *Religious Ecstasy*. Stockholm, 1982. Reprinted in Anna-Leena Siikala and Mihály Hoppál, *Studies on Shamanism*. Budapest, 1998.
SIIKALA, Anna-Leena (1984), 'Finnish rock art, animal ceremonialism and shamanic worldview.' Anna-Leena Siikala and Mihály Hoppál, *Studies on Shamanism*. Budapest, 1998.
SIIKALA, Anna-Leena (1987), 'Siberian and Inner Asian shamanism.' Mircea Eliade (ed.), *The Encyclopaedia of Religion*. London, 1987. Reprinted in Anna-Leena Siikala and Mihály Hoppál, *Studies on Shamanism*. Budapest, 1998.
SIIKALA, Anna-Leena (1989), 'The interpretation of Siberian and Central Asian shamanism.' *Serie Orientale Roma* 64. Reprinted in Anna-Leena Siikala and Mihály Hoppál, *Studies on Shamanism*. Budapest, 1998.
SIIKALA, Anna-Leena (2002), *Mythic Images and Shamanism: A perspective on Kalevala Poetry*. Helsinki.
SINCLAIR, Iain (1991), *The Shamanism of Intent: Some Flights of Redemption*. Uppingham.
SISKIND, Janet (1973), 'Visions and cures among the Sharanahua.' Michael J. Harner (ed.), *Hallucinogens and Shamanism*. Oxford, 1973.
SOLOMON, Anne, 1997, 'The myth of ritual origins? Ethnography, mythology and interpretation of San rock art.' *South African Archaeological Bulletin*165
SOMMARSTRÖM, Bo (1987), 'Ethnoastronomical perspectives on Saami religion.' Tore Ahlbäck (ed.), *Saami Religion*. Åbo (Turku), 1987.

Bibliography

SOMMARSTRÖM, Bo (1991), 'The Saami shaman's drum and the star horizons.' Tore Ahlbäck and Jan Bergman (ed.), *The Saami Shaman Drum*. Stockholm, 1991.

SØRENSEN, Preben Meulengracht (1983), *The Unmanly Man: Concepts of Sexual Defamation in Early Northern Society*. Odense.

STEINBRING, Jack (2001), 'The Northern Ojibwa Indians: Testing the Universality of the *Shamanic/Entoptic Theory*.' Henri-Paul Francfort and Roberte N. Hamayon (ed.), *The Concept of Shamanism: Uses and Abuses*. Budapest, 2001.

STONE, Alby (1994), '*Seiðr.*' *Talking Stick* 16.

STONE, Alby (1996), 'The perilous bridge.' *At the Edge* 1.

STONE, Alby (1998), 'Myth before Babel: On the reconstruction of global proto-myths.' *At the Edge* 9.

STRÖM, Folke (1974), Nið, ergi *and Old Norse moral attitudes*. London

STRÖMBÄCK, Dag (1935), *Sejd: Textstudier I Nordisk Religionshistoria*. Stockholm.

STUTLEY, Margaret (2002), *Shamanism: An Introduction*. London.

SZASZ, Thomas (1971), *The Manufacture of Madness: A Comparative Study of the Inquisition and the Mental Health Movement*. London.

TURNER, Victor (1974), *Dramas, Fields, and Metaphors: Symbolic Action in Human Society*. Ithaca, New York.

TURNER, Victor (1987), *The Anthropology of Performance*. New York.

TYLOR, Eward B. (1871), *Primitive Culture: Researches into the Development of Mythology, Philosophy, Religion, Language, Art, and Custom*. London.

ULIN, Robert C. (2nd ed. 2001), *Understanding Cultures: Perspectives in Anthropology and Social Theory*. Oxford.

VAJNSTEIN, S.I. (1996a), 'The Tuvan (Soyot) shaman's drum and the ceremony of its "enlivening".' Vilmos Diószegi and Mihály Hoppál (ed.), *Folk Beliefs and Shamanistic Traditions in Siberia*. Budapest, 1996.

VAJNSTEIN, S.I. (1996b), 'The *erens* in Tuva shamanism.' Vilmos Diószegi and Mihály Hoppál (ed.), *Shamanism in Siberia*. Budapest, 1996.

VASILEVICH, G.M. (1963), 'Early concepts about the Universe among the Evenks (materials).' Henry N. Michael (ed.), *Studies in Siberian Shamanism*. Toronto, 1963.

VASILEVIC, G.M. (1996), 'The acquisition of shamanistic ability among the Evenki (Tungus).' Vilmos Diószegi and Mihály Hoppál (ed.), *Folk Beliefs and Shamanistic Traditions in Siberia.* Budapest, 1996.
VITEBSKY, Piers (2nd ed. 2001), *The Shaman.* London.
VON DITMAR, Karl, 1900, *Reisen und Aufenthalt in Kamtschatka in den Jahren 1851–1855.* St Petersburg.
WALLIS, Robert J. (2003), *Shamans/Neo-Shamans: Ecstasy, Alternative Archaeologies and Contemporary Pagans.* London.
WASSON, R. Gordon (1971), *Soma: Divine Mushroom of Immortality.* New York.
WEISS, Gerald (1973), 'Shamanism and priesthood in the light of the Campa *ayahuasca* ceremony.' Michael J. Harner (ed.), *Hallucinogens and Shamanism.* Oxford, 1973.
ZORNICKAJA, M.Ja. (1996), 'Dances of Yakut shamans.' Vilmos Diószegi and Mihály Hoppál (ed.), *Shamanism in Siberia.* Budapest, 1996.

INDEX

References to illustrations are in **bold**

abagaldai 82
Africa 9, 12, 31, 37, 132–3, **133**
Ahlberg, N. 97
Alaska 68
alcohol 106
Allegro, J.M. 108, 144
Allen, B. 153–4
Alli, A. 156
Altai 8, 111, 113–4, 140
Altai Tatar 113
Altaic languages 54–6, 57–8, 142
altered states of consciousness 132–6; *see also* ecstasy
Amanita muscaria – *see* fly agaric
America, Central 104–5, 108
—, North 5, 8, 9, 10, 23, 26, 30, 31–2, 37, 41, 50, 65, 68, 50, 78, 92, 105–6, 113, 125, 133, 135, 148; *see also* Canada
—, South 10, 23, 30, 31, 32, 50, 104–5, 108, 125
Anand, B.K. 97
animals, locating and charming 48
Anisimov, A.F. 28, 110–11
Arbman, E. 118, 120
Arthurian romances 113
Asia 31
Asia, Central 12, 14, 25, 27–30, 135; *see also* Darkhat; Duar; Mongol
astronomy 77
Australia 8, 12, 68
axis mundi 12, 142; *see also* World Tree
ayahuasca 89, 103, 104; *see also* yagé
Aztec art 106

Bactria 141
Bahn, P.G. 37, 128, 134, 136
Bai Ülgän 113–4
Balázs, J. 103, 107
Baldick, J. 12
Balzer M.M. 30, 56–7, 61
Banisteriopsis 104
Banzarov, D. 124–5
Basehart, H.W. 105
Basilov, V.N. 29, 56, 65, 97, 122
bears 68
Bégouen, H. 125–6
Bell, J. 22
benandanti 9, 39
Biet, A. 23
birds 68, 70, 130–1, **131**
bisons 130, **131**
Björkqvist, K. 97
Black Elk 31
Blain, J. 9, 10, 38, 150–2, 158
Boas, F. 28, 30

177

Bogoras, W. (a.k.a. Bogoraz, V. and Bogoraz-Tan, V.) 27, 28, 33, 54, 56, 59, 103
Boyer, L.B. and R.M 105
Brahmanic 124
Brazil 104
Breuil, H. 126, 128, **129**, 132
bridges 113
Buddhism 13, 29, 81, 137, 139
Burroughs, W. 103, 143
Buryat 54, 79, 80, 82, 124
Butler, J. 60, 64

Campa 105
Campbell, J. 36, 37, 94, 144
Canada 14, 30, 105; see also Inuit
cannabis 107
capi 104
Carroll, P.J. 156
Casanowicz, I.M. 124–5
Cashinahua 104
Castaneda, C. 33, 37, 102–3, 108, 144–5
Castren, M.A. 27
Catherine the Great 27
Catholicism 65
cave paintings – see Paleolithic cave paintings *and* rock art
Cchina, G.S. 97
Celtic myth and religion 8
Celtic shamanism 9, 10, 155–6
Chernetsov, V.N. 112
China 20, 104, 125, 139
Chukcki 27, 54, 56, 59–61, 68, 84, 103, 152
Cinvat bridge 113
Clark, A.J. 39
Clottes, J. 8, 134, 138
cognition 12, 117
Cohn, N. 39, 40
Colombia 104

colonialism 42–5
Comanche 105
Confusicanism 13
consciousness – *see* altered states of consciousness; ecstasy
Cook, C.M. 98, 100
Corradi Musi, C. 90, 101
cosmology 12, 35, 79, 114, 139, 151–2
Coso 133
costume 66–88, 90, 139
Cowan, T. 155
Crawford, L. 147
cross dressing 56, 65
Crowley, A. 103, 143–4
Czaplicka, M.A. 3–4, 15, 27, 33, 34, 56, 58–9, 66, 125

dance 92
d'Aquili, E. 94, 98
Darkhat 80–1
Darwin, C. 42; *see also* evolution
de la Gardie, M.G. 22
de Lesseps, M. 22
de Oviedo, G.F. 23
deer 68, 79
demonstrative shamanism 94
Devereux, P. 100, 109, 145
Devlet, E. 140
Diakanova, V.P. 49, 67, 73, 76, 82, 83, 84
Díaz-Andreu, M. 135
Diderot, D. 21, 24, 26
Diószegi, V. 15, 29, 30, 49, 50–1, 67, 73, 74, 78, 80–2, 86
Ditmar, K. von 103
divination 65, 76
Dixon, R.B. 31
Djaruoskin, S. 51, 53
Dodds, E.R. 9

Index

Dolgihk, B.O. 69, 76
Don Juan 33, 102, 144
Doors, The 144
Douglas, M. 63–4
Dowson, T. 37, 132–6
drugs 8, 32, 41, 89, 92, 94, 97, 102–9, 120, 135, 136, 143, 145
druids 44
drums 75–9, 84, 90, 92, 99, 101, 142
Drury, N. 123
Duar 67
DuBois, T.A. 9, 41
Duerr, H.P. 40
Düngür Centre 153

earth diver bird myths 68
ecstasy and trance 34–5, 89, 92, 94–9, 102, 116, 118, 119, 123, 136, 156
Ecuador 104
Ecuador 32
eeren 81–2
Eliade, M. 1, 4, 7, 8, 11, 12, 14, 34, 35–6, 37, 42, 44, 47, 54, 56, 65, 66, 78, 84, 87, 89, 94, 98, 103, 107, 109, 111, 112, 113, 115, 120, 126, 134, 136, 137, 144, 156
Enets 70–1, 76, 79, 83
entoptic patterns 8, 133
Epic of Gilgamesh 9
epilepsy 98, 100
ergi 65, 152
ergot 135
Eskimo – *see* Inuit
Eurasia 41, 67–8
Europe, Eastern 15
Evenk 2, 14, 16, 29, **72**, 80–4, 104, 106, 109–12, 114, 115, 125, 126, 139
evolution 43–4; 125

Falk, J.P. 26
Findeisen, H. 115
Finland 18, 19, 77, 140
Flaherty, G. 4, 6
fly agaric 103, 106, 109, 135
flying ointments 40, 135
France 125–6, **127**, 142
Francfort, H.-P. 135, 140
Freud, S. 34
Fries, J. 156
Furst, P.T. 105, 108, 145

galloi 65
Gardner, G. 146, 155
gender 54–65
Georgi, J.G. 26–7, 33, 36, **55, 72**, 103, 124
Gheorgiu, D. 80
Ghost Dance 32, 44
Ginsberg, A. 103, 143
Ginzburg, C. 9, 39
Glavatskaya, E. 30
Glosecki, S.O. 9
Gmelin, J.G. 21, 33
Goldi 79, **85**, 111
Goodman, F. 177
Graceva, G.N. 69
Graves, R. 146
Greek theatre 90
Grim, J.A. 32
Guinana 30

Hamayon, R.A. 95, 98–9
Harner, M. 7, 10, 37, 39–40, 45, 89, 94, 108, 145, 147–9
Harrison, M. 40
Harva, U. — *see* Holmberg, U.
Harvey, G. 2, 38–9, 146

179

healing 48, 52
Helvenston, P.A. 135, 136
henbane 135
heredity 48
Hine, P. 155–6
Hirai, T. 97
Hollimon, S.E. 56
Holm, N.G. 199–20
Holmberg, U. (a.k.a. Harva, U.) 29
homosexuality 56–7, 59, 65, 152; see also ergi; gender
Hoppál, M. 34, 44, 51, 86, 87, 140, 154
horse 76, 80–1, 83
Horwitz, J. 91, 121
Høst, A. 150–2
Huautecan 106
Huicjol 105
Huizinga, J. 99
Hultkrantz, A. 12, 14, 31–2, 47–8, 50, 62, 82, 92, 95, 97, 106, 113, 116, 118–9
Humphrey, C. 4, 67
Hunt, N.B. 83
Hutton, R. 4, 14, 15, 20, 30, 146
Huxley, A. 103, 143

Iceland 41
Ides, E.Y. 20
imitative shamanism 94
Indo-European 65
initiation 51, 157
intoxication 94, 117; see also alcohol; drugs
Inuit 30, 41, 65, 78, 82, 84
Iran 113, 142
Isaacs, N.D. 9
Islam 13
Italy 9, 39
Itelmen 54

Jacobsen, E. 140
James, E.O. 126
Japan 54
Jesup, M.K. 28
jimsonweed 106
Jívaro – see Shuar
Jochelson, W. 33, 54, 63, 103, 112
John of Plano Carpini 19–20
Johnson, M. 12
Johnson, R. 20
journeying to other worlds 89–123; see also liminality
Jung, C.G. 36, 37, 144

Kamchadal 103
Kamchatka 21, 24, 103
Kapelrud, A.S. 9
Karagas – see Tofa
Kasamatsu, A. 97
Kehoe, A.B. 7, 12, 37, 43, 135, 138, 149
Kenin-Lopsan, M. 153
Kensinger, K.M. 104
Kerouac, J. 143
Khakas **79**, 140
Khanty 103
Khazak 77, 96, **141**
Kieckhefer, R. 41
Kim, T.-G. 90
Kiowa 105
Kirchner, H. 126, 130, 132
Kjellström, R. 77
Korea 54, 67
Koryak 27, 54, 59, 61, 63, 103–4; 106
Kos 63
Krasheninnikov, S.P. 21, 24, 33, 103
Kroeber, A.L. 31
Kuper, A. 43
Kwakiutl 30

Kyzlasov, Y.M. 50, 53

La Barre, W. 32, 105, 109, 145
Lafitau, J.F. 26
Lakoff, G. 12
lamaism 86, 124, 139
Lamut **xii**
Lapp – see Saami
Lascaux 126, **131**, 130, **131**, 132
Latin (medieval) sources 139
Le Gabillou 126, **127**
Le Jeune, P. 23
Leary, T. 103, 143
legerdemain – see sleight of hand
lekan 81
Les Trois Frères 125–6, 128, **129**, **130**, 132
Lèvi-Strauss, C. 1–2
Leviticus 63–4
Lewis, I.M. 2, 94, 116
Lewis-Williams, D. 8, 37, 132–6, 138
Lilly, J.C. 143
liminality 62–5, 113
Lincoln, B. 64, 65
Lommel, A. 126
Lord of the Rings 151
Lot-Falck, É. 95
Lubbock, J. 42
Lundmark, B. 54
lycanthropy – see werevolves

MacCulloch, J.A. 8
MacLellan, G. 157
Maddox, J.L. 35
magi 19
Makkay, J. 9, 126, 128
Malaysia 113
Manchu 104, 125, 139
Manker, E. 22, 68

Mansi 103, 112
Margiana 141
Martynov, A.L. 140
masks 82
Matthews, J. 155
Mazatec 106
McClenon, J. 52
McKenna, T. 7, 8, 9, 145, 156
mental illness 33, 98
Merkur, D. 83
Mescalero Apache 105
Messerschmidt, D.G. 21
Mexico 105, 106, 108
Michael, H.N. 28
Middle East 65, 141
Mikhailev, T.M. 29
Mikhailowski, V.M. 27, 66, 84
Mongols 19, 67, 80–1, 82, 86, 104, 106, 124, 139, 140; see also Buryat; Daur; Darkhat.
Monter, E.W. 41
Morrison, J. 144
Munn, H. 106
Murray, M. 38–9
mushrooms 137; see also fly agaric; Psilocybe
music 100–1
musical instruments 78, 97; see also drums

Needham, R. 64, 65
Neher, A. 99
Neihardt, J.G. 31
Nenets 20, 103, 122
neo-shamanism 9, 10–11
New Age 35–6, 37
Newberg, A. 94, 98
Ngansan 49, 51, 67, 69, 70, **70**, 76, 78, 83, 84
Nordland, O. 96

Norse literature and myth 18, 68, 113, 139
North America – see America
Óðinn 65, 149–51
O'Hagan, S. 6
Ohlmarks, A. 28, 33
Ojibway 32
Old English poetry 9
Old Testament 9
Onon, U. 67
ordeals 51, 62, 157
Ostyak – see Khanty
other worlds 89–123
'otherness' 9

pain 51, 157; see also ordeals
Palaeolithic cave paintings 8, 37, 39, 52, 86, 125–38
Pallas, P.S. 21
Park, W.Z. 4–5, 31
Paulson, I. 115
Pavlinskaya, L. 67–8, 83, 86
Pearson, J.L. 8
Perason, J.L. 134
performance – see ritual performance
Persinger, M. 98, 100
Peru 104–5
Petrovich, A. 20
peyote 32, 105, 145
Polo, Marco 19
Popov, A.A. 49, 51, 53, **70**
possession 115–9
'prehistoric shamanism' 9, 124–42
priests 65
Prokofyeva, E. 67, 70, 79, 83
prophesy 48; see also divination
prophesy 65

Proto-Indo-European 58
Psilocybe 106
psychopathology – see mental illness
psychopomps 13, 48

queer theory 57, 62
Quinlan, A.R. 135

Rause, V. 94, 98
Reichel-Dolmatoff, G. 104
Reid, A. 30
Rig Veda 104
rites of passage 63–4
ritual performance 89–94, 103, 107–8, 122, 136
rock art 8, 37, 77, 86, 125–42; see also Paleolithic cave paintings
Rose, E. 39
Ross, A. 8
Ross, M. 135
Rouget, R. 95, 97, 101–2
Rozwadowski, A. 134, 141
Rudgley, R. 106, 109
Ruspoli, M. 130
Russell, J.B. 24
Russia ; see also Soviet Union
Russian ethnology 4, 16
Rydving, H. 77

Saami 18, 19, **25**, 41, 50, 68, 76–7, **77**, 82, 84, **93**, 95, 98, 103, 114, 139, 149
sacrifice 48
Sagai 49, 50
Sakha 27, 50, 54, 56, 74, **75**, 79, 83, 95, 103, 140
San 132, **133**, 134
Sarbin, T.R. 116
Scandinavia 9; see also Finland; Óðinn; Saami; seiðr

Scheffer (Schefferus), J. 22, 68
Scythians 65
séance – see ritual performance
seidr 149-52
seiðr 8, 9, 10, 19, 38, 149–52
Selkup 103
sexuality 54–65, 152
shamanic performance – see ritual performance
Sharanahua 104
Shashkov, S. 27
Shinto 13
Shirokogoroff, S.M. 28, 49, 71, 79, 84, 104, 110–11, 115, 125
Shoshone 133
Shuar 32, 89
Shuyun, G. 104
Siberia 9, 10, 12, 14, 15, 16, 25, 26, 27–30, 44, 68, 86, 103, 106, 109, 112, 115, 137–8, 139–40, 152, 153–4; and passim
Sieroshevski, W. 27
Siikala, A.-L. 14, 34, 92, 99–100, 116–8, 140
Sinclair, I. 6
Singh, B. 97
Siskind, J. 105
sky 113
sleight of hand 92, 97
Solomon, A. 134
soma 108
Sommarström, B. 77
Sørensen, P.M. 149
Soviet Union 10; see also Russia; Europe
sowoki 82
Spain 135
staff 79–81, 142
Steinbring, J. 135

Steller, G.W. 26, 103
Stiglmayr, E. 116
Strahlenberg, P.J.T. von 26, 103
Ström, F. 65, 149
Stömbäck, D. 8, 65, 150
Sturluson, S. 149
Stutley, M. 14, 47
Switzerland 40
Szasz, T. 34

Tacitus 80–1
Teleut **79**, 84
Telumni Yokuts 113
temporal lobe seizure 98
therianthropic figures 8, **127**, 128, **129, 130**, 134, 142; see also werewolves
Thévet, A. 23
Thurn, E.F.I. 30
Tibet 81, 86
tobacco 105, 106
Tofa 49, 67, 73–4, 79, 83
trance – see ecstasy
transvestism 63, 65
Troshchanski, V.F. 56
Tukano 104
Tunga; Tungus – see Evenk
Turkic 113
Turner, V. 46, 123
Tuva 49, 67, 73, 76, 79, 80, 81–4, 140, 153–4
Tylor, E.B. 43

Uigurs 73
Uralic languages 54–6, 57–8, 142
Uralic shamanism 8, 113; see also Enets; Khanty; Mansi; Nenets; Nganasan; Saami; Selkup
Uzbek 54, 77, 96, 122

Vajnstein, S.I. 76
van Gennep, A. 30–1, 63–4
Vasilevic, G.M. 49
Vertut, J. 128
Vitebsky, P. 2, 88
völva 41, 150
von Ditmar, K. 103
von Strahlenberg, P.J.T. 26, 103
voudun 118, 150

Wafer, L. 23
Wallis, R.J. 9, 10–11, 38, 121, 150, 156, 158
Wasson, R.G. 104, 107, 108, 144
Weiss, G. 105
werewolves and lycanthropy 9, 40
whips 81
William of Rubruck 19–20

witch crazes 24, 25
witchcraft 9, 38–41, 146, 154–5
Witsen, N. 20, 83, 126
wizards and wizardry 5, 41
World Tree 76–8, 110; *see also* axis mundi

yagé 103, 104, 143; *see also* ayahuasca
Yakut – *see* Sakha
Yaqui 102, 144
Yokuts 113
Yukaghir 103
Yukaghir 54
Yurak 112
Yuruk 103

Zelenin, D. 28
Zornickaja, M.Ja. 95
Zoroastrian myth 113

Also from Heart of Albion Press

BOOKS

The *Explore* series provides accessible introductions to folklore and mythology. Some books provide 'overviews' of quite broad topics, drawing together current academic research with popular beliefs. Future books in the series will deal with more specific topics, but still with the aim of providing a wide-ranging introduction to the topic.

Already published:

Explore Green Men
Mercia MacDermott
with photographs by Ruth Wylie

Explore Folklore
Bob Trubshaw

Explore Mythology
Bob Trubshaw

To be published 2004:

Explore Fairy Traditions
Jeremy Harte

Explore Phantom Black Dogs
edited by Bob Trubshaw

Also from Heart of Albion Press

Also by Alby Stone

YMIR'S FLESH

North European creation mythologies

In isolation the pre-Christian north European creation myths appear fragmented and confused, but a thematic cohesion is apparent when they are taken as a whole and compared to their counterparts in Vedic India, ancient Greece and Rome, medieval Ireland, ancient and medieval Iran, and so on.

Ymir's Flesh gathers together the distorted fragments of this mythology and provides an original and inspiring insight into the complex inter-weaving of mythological themes.

ISBN 1 872883 45 1

A5, 240 pages, illustrated, paperback **£12.95**

Explore Green Men

Mercia MacDermott
with photographs by
Ruth Wylie

Explore Green Men is the first detailed study of the history of this motif for 25 years. Dr MacDermott's research follows the Green Man back from the previous earliest known examples into its hitherto unrecognised origins in India about 2,300 years ago.

The book starts by discussing the 'paganisation' of Green Men in recent decades, then follows backwards through the Victorian Gothic Revival, Baroque, Rococco and Italianate revivals, to their heyday in the Gothic and the supposed origins in the Romanesque. As part of this discussion there is background information on the cultural changes that affected how Green Men were regarded. The author also discusses the comparisons that have been made with Cernunnus, Robin Hood, Jack-in-the-Green, woodwoses, Baphomet, Al Khidr and Bulgarian *peperuda*. She also investigates which pagan god Green Men supposedly represent.

Explore Green Men is illustrated with 110 photographs and drawings, mostly of Green Men who have never before showed their faces in books.

This book will appeal to all with an interest in Green Men and to art historians looking for a reliable study of this fascinating decorative motif.

ISBN 1 872883 66 4

Perfect bound, demi 8vo (215 x 138 mm), 216 pages, 108 b&w photos, 2 line drawings **£9.95**

Also from Heart of Albion Press

Explore Mythology

Bob Trubshaw

Myths are usually thought of as something to do with 'traditional cultures'. The study of such 'traditional' myths emphasises their importance in religion, national identity, hero-figures, understanding the origin of the universe, and predictions of an apocalyptic demise. The academic study of myths has done much to fit these ideas into the preconceived ideas of the relevant academics.

Only in recent years have such long-standing assumptions about myths begun to be questioned, opening up whole new ways of thinking about the way such myths define and structure how a society thinks about itself and the 'real world'.

These new approaches to the study of myth reveal that, to an astonishing extent, modern day thinking is every bit as 'mythological' as the world-views of, say, the Classical Greeks or obscure Polynesian tribes. Politics, religions, science, advertising and the mass media are all deeply implicated in the creation and use of myths.

Explore Mythology provides a lively introduction to the way myths have been studied, together with discussion of some of the most important 'mythic motifs' – such as heroes, national identity, and 'central places' – followed by a discussion of how these ideas permeate modern society. These sometimes contentious and profound ideas are presented in an easily readable style of writing.

ISBN 1 872883 62 1
Perfect bound. Demi 8vo (215 x 138 mm), 220 + xx pages, 17 line drawings. **£9.95**

Also from Heart of Albion Press

Explore Folklore

Bob Trubshaw

'A howling success, which plugs a big and obvious gap'
Professor Ronald Hutton

There have been fascinating developments in the study of folklore in the last twenty-or-so years, but few books about British folklore and folk customs reflect these exciting new approaches. As a result there is a huge gap between scholarly approaches to folklore studies and 'popular beliefs' about the character and history of British folklore. *Explore Folklore* is the first book to bridge that gap, and to show how much 'folklore' there is in modern day Britain.

Explore Folklore shows there is much more to folklore than morris dancing and fifty-something folksingers! The rituals of 'what we do on our holidays', funerals, stag nights and 'lingerie parties' are all full of 'unselfconscious' folk customs. Indeed, folklore is something that is integral to all our lives – it is so intrinsic we do not think of it as being 'folklore'.

The implicit ideas underlying folk lore and customs are also explored. There might appear to be little in common between people who touch wood for luck (a 'tradition' invented in the last 200 years) and legends about people who believe they have been abducted and subjected to intimate body examinations by aliens. Yet, in their varying ways, these and other 'folk beliefs' reflect the wide spectrum of belief and disbelief in what is easily dismissed as 'superstition'..

Explore Folklore provides a lively introduction to the study of most genres of British folklore, presenting the more contentious and profound ideas in a readily accessible manner.

ISBN 1 872883 60 5
Perfect bound, demi 8vo (215x138 mm), 200 pages, **£9.95**

Also from Heart of Albion Press

Masterworks

Arts and Crafts of Traditional Building in Northern Europe

Nigel Pennick

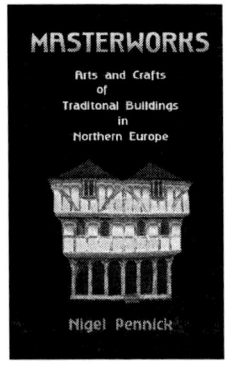

Masterworks is about the traditions of arts and crafts in northern Europe, taking as a starting point the use of timber in building. Timber frame buildings have been constructed over a long period of time over a large territory, mostly northern and north-west Europe. Various regional and local styles have come into being.

Timber buildings display a rich diversity of techniques, forms and patterns developed by generations of master craftsmen working with local materials under similar limitations. The 'arts and crafts' used in the construction of these buildings acknowledge and celebrate the knowledge, traditions, abilities and spiritual understanding of how to work effectively with natural materials. They are living traditions that remain relevant today.

Masterworks is a celebration of this arts and crafts ethos that is present in the traditional buildings of northern Europe.

> "Masterworks ... is written by a man who is not only in tune with his subject matter but is, in fact, a master wordsmith in his own right and deserves credit for this. I personally found this one of his most intriguing and important works to date and cannot recommend it too highly to the discerning reader."
> Ian Read *Runa*

ISBN 1 872883 63 X Perfect bound, Demi 8vo, 163 + viii pages, 23 b&w photos, 15 line drawings **£9.95**

Also from Heart of Albion Press

Snake Fat and Knotted Threads

An introduction to traditional Finnish healing magic

K.M. Koppana

What did the Finnish cunning man carry in his magic pouch? How does one learn the language of the ravens? What is the Origin of the Cat? How do you attract a partner at Midsummer? These and much more are to be found in *Snake Fat and Knotted Threads*.

Snake Fat and Knotted Threads provides a unique resource about traditional Finnish healing magic and spells, folk customs and myths. All this detailed information is based on the author's research and practical experience.

K.M. Koppana has been interested in spells since she was small, being a keen reader of fairy stories. This interest has persisted and she still has an urge to pick up pebbles on walks. She is also a poet and used to edit small magazines, such as the long-gone *Starlight*, which was about the Finnish magical scene. In 2001 she moved from Helsinki to England, settling in the Midlands.

> *Snake Fat and Knotted Threads '*... is a study of the *tietaja* or cunning folk who used such items as human skulls, graveyard dirt and hangmen's nooses in their magical work. They invoked both the old Finnish gods and Christian deities. This is a highly recommended study of a bygone era of magical belief that in modern Finland has been sadly usurped by New Age therapists and neo-pagan Goddess worship.'
> Michael Howard *The Cauldron*

1st UK edition (originally published in Finland).
ISBN 1 872883 65 6 Perfect bound, demi 8vo, 112 pages, 14 b&w photos, 2 line drawings. **£7.95**

Also from Heart of Albion Press

On Sacred Mountains

Martin J. Goodman

'Such narrow, narrow confines we live in. Every so often, one of us primates escapes these dimensions, as Martin Goodman did. All we can do is rattle the bars and look after him as he runs into the hills. We wait for his letters home.'
The Los Angeles Times

Martin J. Goodman's interest in spiritual phenomena goes deeper than most people - he goes out and tests their ability for personal transformation. After his internationally acclaimed books *I Was Carlos Castaneda* and *In Search of the Divine Mother*, astonishing perspectives on the psychedelic shamanism of the Amazon and the guru/devotee relationship, comes this most powerful and daring of adventures.

What is a sacred mountain? Study them all we like, the only way of knowing them is to measure their effects in our own lives. Starting at Mount Ararat, moving to Ireland, passing through the sacred heights of India and Sri Lanka, Martin was then called to the mountain ranges of the American South West. At the highest point of Texas he received a revelation of great promise for the survival of humanity. His journey is a compelling story of intimate encounters, sexual transformation, astounding landscapes, and raw mountain energy. The writing is of a rare quality that turns each experience into our own.

On Sacred Mountains will appeal to those interested in travel, and adds a deep spiritual experience to the travelogue. *On Sacred Mountains* will also interest the 'spiritual searcher', especially those who expect their guides to do more than write from the comfort of their retreats.

ISBN 1 872883 58 3. Perfect bound, demi 8vo (215x138 mm), 138 + ix pages, **£9.95**

Further details of all Heart of Albion titles online at
www.hoap.co.uk

All titles available direct from Heart of Albion Press.
Please add 80p p&p (UK only; email
albion@indigogroup.co.uk for overseas postage).

To order books or request our current catalogue please
contact

Heart of Albion Press

2 Cross Hill Close, Wymeswold

Loughborough, LE12 6UJ

Phone: 01509 880725

Fax: 01509 881715

email: albion@indigogroup.co.uk

Web site: www.hoap.co.uk